Library of Congress
Cataloging-in-Publication Data

On file
ISBN 1-58923-144-9 (softcover)

Portions of The Complete Guide to Finishing Touches for Yards & Gardens
are taken from the Black & Decker® books: Landscape Design & Construction; Building Garden Ornaments; Creating Garden Accents;
Gardens for Birds, Hummingbirds & Butterflies; Fences, Walls & Gates;
Garden Pools; Fountains & Watercourses. Other titles from Creative Publishing international include:

*The New Everyday Home Repairs; Basic Wiring & Electrical Repairs;
Building Decks; Home Masonry Projects & Repairs; Bathroom
Remodeling; Customizing Your Home; Carpentry: Remodeling;
Carpentry: Tools • Shelves • Walls • Doors; Exterior Home Repairs & Im-
provements, Home Plumbing Projects & Repairs; Advanced Home
Wiring; Advanced Deck Building; Built-In Projects for the Home; Refinish-
ing & Finishing Wood; Building Porches & Patios; Advanced Home
Plumbing; Remodeling Kitchens; Finishing Basements & Attics;
Stonework & Masonry Projects; Sheds, Gazebos & Outbuildings; Building
& Finishing Walls & Ceilings; Flooring Projects & Techniques; Complete
Guide to Painting & Decorating; Complete Guide to Home Plumbing;
Complete Guide to Home Wiring; Complete Guide to Building Decks;
Complete Guide to Creative Landscapes; Complete Guide to Home Ma-
sonry; Complete Guide to Home Carpentry; Complete Guide to Home
Storage; Complete Guide to Windows & Doors; Complete Guide to Bath-
rooms; Complete Guide to Ceramic & Stone Tile; Complete Guide to
Flooring; Accessible Home; Open House; Lighting Design & Installation;
Complete Photo Guide to Home Repair; Complete Photo Guide to Home
Improvement; Complete Photo Guide to Outdoor Home Improvement.*

Introduction

Yards and gardens go through ages and stages, just like people. In the beginning, they need everything. Think infants here. But even after the hardscape (structures such as decks, patios, and fences) and the softscape (plant materials such as lawn, shrubs, and trees) are in place, a new or newly renovated yard is like an adolescent: fully formed but still developing.

So, what's missing? Finishing touches. Small structures, furnishings, and accessories that transform *a* yard into *your* yard. That's what this book is all about—adding character and personality to your yard and garden.

Every yard is unique. Of course, the site, soil, terrain, and orientation vary from one area to the next, but the biggest influences are the interests and personalities of the homeowners.

Here's an interesting example: Right after World War II, thousands of identical yards were created in cookie-cutter housing developments across the United States. You know the look—a stark lawn punctuated with one spindly sapling. But within a few years, most of those yards had evolved into reflections of the people who tended them. And by the turn of the century, it was practically impossible to find a single one that had not been redesigned or renovated. People simply love to leave their marks on the landscape.

Think of your landscape as a canvas on which to express yourself. Keep in mind that this process doesn't happen overnight. Instead, it takes place gradually, through a series of choices. Start with your hobbies and interests. Do you love butterflies? What about a butterfly garden by the deck? Is someone in your family a gourmet cook? Maybe a raised-bed herb garden by the kitchen door? If you want to add a water feature, should it be a simple fountain or an elaborate water garden?

Only you and your family can answer questions like these. "Experts" can make suggestions and give you ideas, but the central issue is not what's trendy or what's being shown by designers. Instead, the central issue is what you like and what you have the time and money to build, maintain, and enjoy.

Most of the projects found in this book can be completed in a weekend. It does, however, take a fair amount of time to become familiar with the unique characteristics of your yard, understand what elements it will support, and consider which of those elements will enhance your everyday life. The good news is that this process can be fun. Take stock of what you have and let your imagination wander through a world of possibilities.

If you don't have a lot of experience building projects, start with something simple. Placed to their best advantage, even small projects have major impact on a landscape. Try adding plants to a striking container, installing a birdhouse, or hanging a self-contained fountain on a garden wall. As your confidence builds and your skills expand, you can tackle increasingly larger and more complex projects.

©Jerry Pavia

©Charles Mann

Give careful thought to the materials you choose and how they blend with the rest of the landscape. Repeating the materials used on your house itself or elsewhere in the landscape is always appropriate. For example, if you have wrought iron railings, a wrought iron gate would make a nice focal point in a flower bed.

If you're using stone in the landscape, remember that stone native to the area is well suited to the conditions and usually less expensive than imported or exotic stone. Try edging a planting bed with river rock or fieldstone or coping the edges of a water garden with native limestone.

©Charles Mann

©Saxon Holt

©Coldsnap Photography/Photograph by John Gregor

©Saxon Holt

Whether made from timbers or stone, raised beds add variety to the landscape and often are solutions to problems with poor soil condition or drainage. Trellises and garden walls are interesting additions, as well.

Whatever your landscape dreams may be, with the help of this book, you can make them come true. Starting with the planning stages and moving through to completion, we'll be with you all the way. We'll take a look at the types of tools and materials you'll need and guide you through the process of laying out your project. And when it comes time to start construction, you'll find plenty of informative photos and thorough step-by-step instructions for each project.

This is going to be fun. Let's get started.

Planning

Now that you've decided to embark on a project (or maybe even a couple), you're probably eager to begin digging holes and pounding nails or stacking stone. We don't want to spoil your fun, but it has to be said: Stop. Take a deep breath and take care of some details first. You'll be time and money ahead if you determine exact property lines, have utilities marked, consider the challenges of your site and establish the goals of your project before you gather your tools and head out to the yard.

The first real task is to define the project. Ask yourself these questions:

- What do I want to accomplish with this project?
- What do I want to avoid?
- What challenges do I face?
- What is my budget?
- How much of the work am I realistically able to do myself?
- Do I have additional help available if necessary?
- How much maintenance am I willing to do on this structure over the next 10 years?

The answers to these questions and the information in this chapter will help you develop a plan for the location, type, style, and building materials for your project.

IN THIS CHAPTER

Building Materials

When selecting building materials, consider how the structure should function in addition to how it should look. Your choices affect the style as well as the durability, maintenance requirements, and overall cost of a project. Wood, stone, concrete block, and even copper are traditional favorites, but don't overlook unconventional materials such as hypertufa, a lightweight, durable combination of portland cement, peat moss, and perlite.

Wood remains the most common building material in outdoor construction. Its versatility lends itself to just about any project, from the plain and practical to the elegant and ornate.

The most important consideration in choosing lumber is its suitability for outdoor use. Redwood and cedar are attractive, relatively soft woods with a natural resistance to moisture and insects, ideal qualities for outdoor applications. In some regions, availability may be limited, so check with local building centers before committing yourself to their use.

Pressure-treated pine is stronger and more durable than redwood or cedar, as well as more readily available and less expensive in many areas. Most home centers and lumber yards carry a wide selection of dimensional treated lumber.

Reports about arsenic in treated lumber raised concerns among consumers, and as a result, the lumber industry agreed to stop manufacturing wood treated with chromated copper arsenate (CCA) for residential use as of December 31, 2003. New treatments contain no arsenic or other carcinogenic chemicals. Precautions are still in order, though. Always wear gloves, avoid breathing the sawdust, and do not burn the scraps. Finally, when using treated lumber, be sure to use corrosion-resistant metal fasteners, including nails and screws, approved for use with that product.

Despite its outdoor rating, treated wood should have a fresh coat of stain or sealer applied every two years to maintain its durability and appearance.

Copper pipe is intended for exposure to water and temperature swings, which makes it ideal for outdoor use. The pipe and fittings are inexpensive and can be found at nearly any home center or hardware store.

Natural stone is one of the finest building materials you can use. It offers beautiful color and texture along with unmatched durability and elegance. But these virtues come at a price—natural stone is one of the more expensive building materials you can select, and using it can be a challenge.

Natural fieldstone

Manufactured products offer uniformity and ease of installation. Brick and concrete block are available in a growing variety of sizes and styles, which means you can build distinctive, reasonably priced outdoor structures.

Manufactured brick and block

Natural ashlar

Regulations

First things first. If you're adding a permanent structure to your yard—especially a wall, you need to research local building codes. Building codes will tell you if a building permit and inspection are necessary. Some code requirements are designed to protect public safety, while others help preserve standards of appearance.

Codes may dictate what materials can be used, maximum heights for structures, depths for concrete footings and posts, and setback distances—how far back a wall or structure must be from property lines, streets, or sidewalks. Setback distance is usually 6" to 12" (15.25 to 30.5 cm) and is especially important on a corner lot, since a structure could create a blind corner.

Don't assume that every project meets your local ordinances. Requirements and restrictions vary from one municipality to another, so check the codes for your area. If your plans conflict with local codes, authorities will sometimes grant a variance that allows you to compromise the strict requirements of the code.

Another thing to consider as you plan your project is the placement of any utility lines that cross your property. At no cost, utility companies will mark the exact locations and depths of buried lines so you can avoid costly and potentially life-threatening mistakes. In many areas, the law requires that you have this done before digging any holes. Even if it's not required by law in your area, it's truly necessary.

Depending on how close it is to property lines, a landscape structure can be as much a part of your neighbors' landscapes as your own. As a simple courtesy, notify your neighbors of your plans and even show them sketches; this will help to avoid strained relationships or legal problems. In some cases, you may even decide to share resources or work together on projects that can improve both landscapes.

Wall

2× wall width

Frost line

12" (30.5 cm)

Shown cut away

Set back distance

Property line

©Walter Chandoha

(above) If a structure is more than 2 ft. (61 cm) tall or tied to another permanent structure, it requires footings. Many building codes require that footings be twice as wide as the structure and extend 12" (30.5 cm) below the frost line.

(left) Obey local setback regulations to avoid building any fence too close to property lines or to a street or sidewalk.

Measuring

If you're adding a wall or other permanent landscape structure such as a boulder terrace or planting bed, you'll need to accurately measure your yard and make a detailed scale drawing, called a *site map* (see page 18).

If possible, enlist someone to help you take accurate measurements. If you haven't already done it, now is a good time to ask local utility companies to mark buried utility lines.

If you're working close to the property lines, you also will need to mark them. If you don't have a plot drawing (available from the architect, developer, contractor, or possibly, the previous owner) or a deed map (available from city hall, county courthouse, title company, or mortgage bank) that specifies property lines, hire a surveyor to locate and mark them. File a copy with the county as insurance against possible boundary disputes.

Take careful measurements of your yard and make detailed notes in preparation for creating drawings.

THE SITE PLAN

Accurate yard measurements are critical for estimating quantities and costs of materials. To sketch your survey, follow these steps:

Step A: Sketch your yard and all its main features on a sheet of paper. Assign a key letter to each point. Measure all straight lines and record the measurements on a notepad.

Step C: Plot irregular boundaries and curves, such as shade patterns or low-lying areas that hold moisture after a rainfall. Plot these features by taking a series of perpendicular measurements from a straight reference line, such as the edge of your house or garage.

Step B: Take triangulated measurements to locate other features, such as trees that don't lie along straight lines. Triangulation involves locating a feature by measuring its distance from any two points whose positions are known.

Step D: Sketch elevations to show slopes. Measure the vertical drop of a slope using different sized stakes and string. Connect the string to the stakes so it is perfectly horizontal. Measure the distance between the string and ground at 2 ft. (61 cm) intervals along the string.

Drawing Plans

Good plans make it possible to complete a project efficiently. Plotting locations for walls, gates, and landscape structures makes it much easier to determine realistic budgets, make materials lists, and develop practical work schedules.

From your yard survey (page 17), create a *site map* or scale drawing that establishes the position of all elements in the existing site. An elevation chart also may be helpful for major projects where you have to contend with significant slope.

On a copy of the site map, locate and draw the project layout. Consider how to handle obstacles like large rocks and trees or slopes (page 23); take into account local setback regulations and other pertinent building codes.

When drawing walls with posts, determine proper on-center spacing for those posts: divide the length of the wall into equal intervals—6 ft. to 8 ft. (1.8 m to 2.44 m) spacing is standard.

If your calculations produce a remainder, don't put it into one odd-sized bay. Instead, distribute the remainder equally among all the sections or between the first and last sections.

For structures that have footings, plan enough space for footings that are at least twice as wide as the structure they support. Carefully plot each corner and curve, and allow plenty of space between the footings and obstacles, such as growing trees or low-lying areas where water may collect.

Determining the location for a gate requires a bit of forethought. A gate is intended to provide access, which means size and placement are important to its function. Sidewalks leading into the property are obvious gate locations, but consider the need for side yard and service entrances that allow you to bring large items into and out of your property.

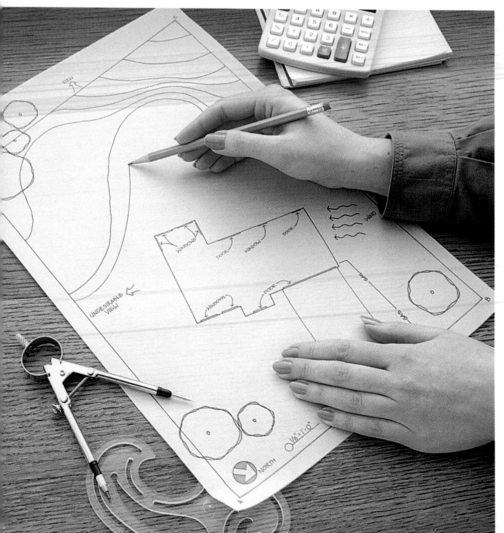

A site map is an overhead view of a fence, wall, or gate setting drawn to scale. It aids in the visualization and planning of a project. From the measurements of your yard survey, convert all actual measurements to scale measurements. (If ⅛" = 1 ft., multiply actual measurements by .125; use the conversion charts on the opposite page. For metric units, let 1 cm = 1 m.) On paper, draw straight boundaries to scale. Scribe arcs with a compass to mark triangulated points, noting the edges and corners of permanent structures, such as your house or garage. Use these points as established references to plot all the elements in the property. To finish the site map, draw contour lines to indicate slope, and mark compass directions, wind patterns, utilities, and any other pertinent information that will influence the location of your fence, wall, or gate.

Determine the size of each gate, including hinge and latch hardware with an extra 4" (10.2 cm) for clearance. Mark the size and location of each to scale on the site map.

When your plans are drawn, test them in your yard. Stake out the structure, run string between the stakes, and drape the string with tarps or landscape fabric. Look at the mock structure from all sides to evaluate its merits; consider how it will obstruct views and access, and how it will blend with other landscape elements.

Once you've worked out the details and decided on a final layout, convert the scale dimensions from the site map to actual measurements. From this information, draw up a materials estimate, adding 10 percent to compensate for errors, oversights, and waste.

Not every project needs extensive plans and maps, but the more steps there are to the construction process, the more important it is to carefully consider all the details. After you begin construction, changes are expensive and time consuming.

Hang tarps or landscape fabric over a stake-and-string frame to get a sense of the size of the structure and its impact on the landscape.

COMMON DECIMAL MULTIPLIERS

Using the following decimal equivalents when converting actual measurements to scale measurements.

Scale	Multiply actual measurements by:
1/16" = 1 ft.	.0625
1/8" = 1 ft.	.125
1/4" = 1 ft.	.25
1/2" = 1 ft.	.5

DECIMAL EQUIVALENTS

Converting actual measurements to scale measurements often produces decimal fractions, which then must be converted to ruler measurements. Use this chart to determine equivalents.

Decimal Fraction	Ruler Fraction	Decimal Fraction	Ruler Fraction
.0625	1/16"	.5	1/2"
.125	1/8"	.5625	9/16"
.1875	3/16"	.625	5/8"
.25	1/4"	.6875	11/16"
.3125	5/16"	.75	3/4"
.375	3/8"	.8125	13/16"
.4375	7/16"	.875	7/8"
		.9375	15/16"

Laying Out a Structure

Once the plans are drawn, the materials delivered, and the tools gathered, it's time to begin the process of construction. Some walls—those built with posts—begin with plotting the line and marking the post locations. Measure the post locations carefully—the more exact those locations, the less likely it is that you'll need to cut pieces to size.

For walls built on footings, determine the outside edges of the footings along the entire site, as for a fence line. Then plot right angles (opposite page) to find the ends and inside edges of the footings.

Laying out a wall with square corners or curves (page 22) involves a little more work than for a straight line. The key in both instances is the same: measure and mark accurately. Proper spacing between the posts and accurate dimensions for footings will provide strength and support for each structure.

TOOLS & MATERIALS

- Stakes & mason's string
- Line level
- Level
- Tape measure
- Framing square
- Plumb bob
- Handsaw
- Reciprocating saw
- Circular saw
- Spring clamps•
  Masking tape
- Pencil
- Spray paint
- Hand maul
- Corrosion-resistant nails or deck screws

HOW TO PLOT A STRAIGHT LINE

Step A: Mark the Line

1. Determine the exact placement of the structure. If it is at the edge of your property lines, plan a setback of at least 6" (15.25 cm) from the legal property lines. (Some regulations may require larger setbacks. Check local building codes.)

2. Draw a site map (page 18). Make sure it is detailed and takes all aspects of your landscape into consideration, with the location of each post accurately marked.

3. Referring to the site map, mark the line with stakes at each end or corner post location, and run mason's string between them.

4. Adjust the string until it is level, using a line level as a guide. TIP: If your wall will include a gate, mark the posts now:

1. To find the on-center spacing for the gate posts, combine the width of the gate and the clearance needed for the hinges and latches, then add the width of one post, typically 4" (10.2 cm).

2. Mark the string with masking tape to indicate where the gate posts will be installed.

Step B: Mark the Posts

Refer to your site map, then measure and mark the post locations on the string, using masking tape. Remember that the tape indicates the center of the post, not the edge.

A. *Mark the line with stakes and mason's string. Using a line level as a guide, adjust the string until it is level.*

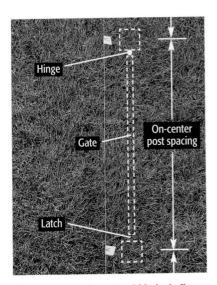

Post spacing for panels installed between posts

8 ft., 4" (2.54 m)

Post spacing for panels attached to faces of posts

8 ft., ½" (2.45 m)

Tip: *Measure the gate width, including hinge and latch hardware, plus the width of one post for the on-center spacing between posts. Mark the locations on the string with masking tape.*

B. *Mark the string at the remaining post locations. Use masking tape to mark the center of the posts.*

Right Angles

If your structure will enclose a square or rectangular area, you probably want the corners to form 90° angles. The most effective method of plotting right angles is the 3-4-5 triangle method. Have someone help you manage the tape measures, if necessary.

HOW TO PLOT A RIGHT ANGLE

Step A: Mark One Side

1. Begin by marking the line with stakes and mason's string.

2. At the location of the outside corner, plant a stake. Connect the corner stake to the previous stake with mason's string.

3. Plant another stake 3 ft. (1.5 m) out from the corner stake along the established line.

Step B: Mark the Adjacent Side

1. Position the end of one tape measure at the outside corner stake, and out along the adjacent, connecting side. Open it past the 4 ft. (2 m) mark and lock it.

A. *Stake out the line, marking the outside corner of the two adjacent sides. Connect the stakes with mason's string, then mark a point 3 ft. out with another stake.*

B. *Position one tape measure at the corner stake and open it past 4 ft. With someone's help, position another tape measure at the 3 ft. stake and open it past the 5 ft. mark. With both tape measures locked, adjust them so they intersect at the 4 ft. and 5 ft. marks.*

NOTE: If using metric measurements, use 1.5, 2, and 2.5 m for this project.

2. Have someone help you position the end of another tape measure at the 3 ft. (1.5 m) stake on the first side. Open it past the 5 ft. (2.5 m) mark and lock.

3. Angle the second tape measure toward the first so the two tapes intersect at the 5 ft. (2.5 m) mark for the diagonal measurement and the 4 ft. (2 m) mark for the perpendicular measurement. Drive a stake at this location.

4. Run mason's string from this stake to the outside corner stake.

The 3 ft. (1.5 m) and 4 ft. (2 m) mason's strings form a right angle. Extend or shorten the mason's string, as needed.

5. Stake out the exact dimensions for the rest of your structure according to your site map.

A. *Plot a right angle. Tie mason's string to a pair of stakes equidistant from the corner stake.*

B. *Plant a stake where the two strings meet, opposite the corner stake, to form a square.*

Curves

A curved wall can add appeal to an otherwise dull landscape. With a few tools, you can make a simple "compass" to plot the curve symmetrically on the ground.

HOW TO PLOT A CURVE

Step A: Form a Square

1. Plot a right angle, using the 3-4-5 triangle method (page 21).

2. Measure and plant stakes equidistant from the outside corner (X) to mark the end points for the curve (Y).

Step B: Create a Compass

1. Tie a mason's string to each end stake, and extend the strings back to the corner stake. Then hold them tight at the point where they meet.

2. Pull this point out, opposite the corner stake, until the strings are taut. Plant a stake (Z) at this point to complete a square.

Step C: Mark the Curve

Tie a mason's string to the stake (Z), just long enough to reach the end points of the curve (Y). Pull the string taut and hold a can of spray paint at the end of it. Moving in an arc between the end points, spray paint the curve on the ground.

This stake equal distance from corners

C. *Tie a string to the final stake—make it just long enough to reach from the final corner stake to the end stakes. Holding the string taut, spray paint the curve on the ground.*

Handling Slope

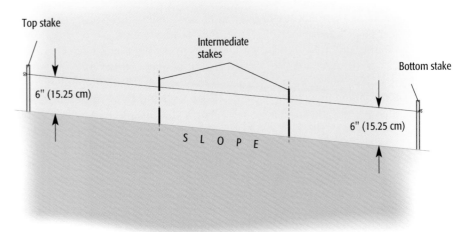

It's considerably easier to build a wall when the ground is flat and level along the entire length of the proposed wall. But few landscapes are entirely flat. Hills, slight valleys, or consistent downward grades are slope issues to resolve while planning your wall. There are two common ways to handle slope: contouring and stepping.

Contouring is the easier of the two solutions. The stringers between the posts run roughly parallel with the ground, so the wall has a consistent height and rolls in unison with the terrain. Contouring works best over large areas of slope.

A stepped wall takes more time and effort, but creates a more structured look. Each section between posts "steps" down in equal increments, creating a uniform line. Stepping works best over gradual slopes. Steep hills or valleys rise too much over short runs and will cause large gaps between the ground and the bottom of the wall.

Whichever method you use, make sure your posts are plumb and properly set in the ground. If they are not, gravity will create structural problems over time.

Refer to this section if you need to adapt any of the designs in this book for a sloped site.

HOW TO CONTOUR A WALL
Step A: Determine Post Locations

1. Outline the location with stakes and string, as shown on page 20. Drive one stake into the ground at the top of the slope and one at the bottom. Make sure the stakes are plumb.

2. Run string between the

A. *Run a string between stakes at the top and bottom of the slope. Mark the post centers on the string, and drop a plumb bob to determine the posthole locations.*

B. *Mark the proper height on each post, and cut it to size with a reciprocating saw or handsaw.*

C. *Clamp the upper stringer at the reference marks on the posts. Scribe the back side of the stringer where it overlaps the post and cut it to size.*

23

stakes, 6" (15.25 cm) above the ground at each stake.

3. Measure and mark equidistant post locations along the string, using pieces of tape.

4. Drop a plumb bob from each piece of tape, and mark the ground with a stake for each post-hole location.

Step B: Set the Posts

1. Dig footings and set the posts in concrete (pages 28 to 29). Allow to cure for 2 days.

2. Measure up from the base of each post and mark cutoff lines for the height, using a framing square.

3. Trim the posts along the cut-off lines, using a reciprocating saw or handsaw. Each post will be the same height, creating a contour line that follows any ground variance.

Step C: Build the Framework & Apply the Siding

1. On each post, measure down from the top, and mark a line for both the upper and lower stringer positions.

2. Clamp a board for the upper stringer between two posts, aligning the top edge with the upper stringer reference marks of each. Scribe each post outline on the back side of the stringer. Remove the stringer and cut it to size, us-ing a circular saw.

3. Position the stringer between the two posts and, at the marks, toenail it into place, using corrosion-resistant nails or deck screws.

4. Repeat #2 and #3 to install the remaining stringers, both upper and lower, in their proper positions.

5. Apply the siding. Mark each board with a reference line, so each will extend evenly above the upper stringer. If necessary, trim the bottoms to maintain 2" (5 cm) of clearance from the ground. Use spacers between the boards to maintain consistent spacing.

HOW TO STEP A FENCE

Step A: Determine the Slope & Post Locations

1. Drive a short stake into the ground at the top of the slope and a longer stake at the bottom. Make sure the top of the longer stake rises above the bottom of the shorter stake. Check the longer stake for plumb with a level.

2. Run string from the bottom of the short stake to the top of the longer one. Using a line level, adjust the string at the longer stake until it is level. Mark the position on the stake.

3. Measure the length of the string from stake to stake. This number is the *run*. Divide the run into equal segments that are between 48" (1.22 m) and 96" (2.45 m). This gives you the number of sections and posts (number of sections + 1). Example: 288" (run) ÷ 72" (section size) = 4 (number of sections).

4. Measure the longer stake from the ground to the string mark for the *rise*. Divide the rise by the number of sections you will have on the slope for the stepping

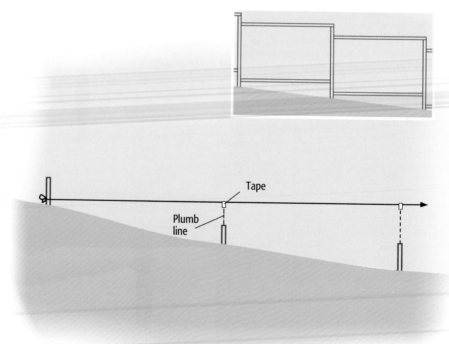

A. *Using stakes and string, determine the run and the rise of the slope, then calculate and mark the post locations.*

measurement. Example: 24" (rise) ÷ 4 (sections between posts) = 6" (step size)

5. Measure and mark the post locations along the level string with pieces of tape.

6. Drop a plumb bob from each post location mark on the string, and mark the ground with a stake.

Step B: Mark & Cut Posts

1. Dig the postholes and set the posts (pages 28 to 29). Allow the

concrete to cure for 2 days.

2. On the post at the bottom of the slope, measure up from the ground and mark the post height. Cut the post at the mark, using a reciprocating saw or handsaw.

3. Use a line level to run a level string from the top of this post to the next post. Mark a reference line on the post.

4. Measure up from this reference line and mark the step size (6" [15.25 cm] in our example). Cut the post to size with a reciprocating saw or handsaw.

5. Measure down from the reference line and mark the lower stringer position.

6. Repeat #3 through #5 for each post, until you reach the top of the slope.

Step C: Attach the Stringers & Siding

1. Measure across the top of the post to the reference line on the next post. Cut the board for the upper stringer to size.

2. Place the stringer with one end on the post top and the other flush against the next post at the reference mark. Make sure the stringer is level, drill pilot holes and attach it, using 3" (7.6 cm) corrosion-resistant deck screws.

3. Measure the distance between the posts, and cut the boards for the lower stringers to size. Continue this process until you reach the top of the slope.

4. Mark each siding board with a reference line so each will extend evenly above the upper stringer. If necessary, trim the bottoms so they're even below the lower stringer. Apply the siding. Use spacers to maintain consistent spacing.

B. *Run a level string from the top of the previous post. Mark the step size on the post, and cut it to height, using a reciprocating saw or hand saw.*

C. *Cut the upper stringers to size. Attach one end to the post top and the other end flush against the next post at the reference mark.*

Footings

Footings provide a stable, level base for brick, block, and poured concrete structures. They distribute the weight of the structure evenly, prevent sinking, and keep the structure from moving during seasonal freeze-thaw cycles.

The required depth of a footing usually is determined by the frost line, which varies from one region to another. The frost line is the point nearest ground level where the soil does not freeze. In colder climates, it is likely to be 48"(122 cm) or deeper. Frost footings (footings designed to keep structures from moving during freezing temperatures) should extend 12" (30.5 cm) below the frost line for the area. Your local building inspector can tell you the frost line depth for your area.

For poured concrete structures, use the earth as a form. Strip sod from around the project area, dig the footings and pour the concrete, then strike off the excess concrete with a screed board resting on the edges of the trench.

For brick, block, and stone projects, build level, recessed wood forms for the footings. Rest the screed on the frames when you strike off the excess concrete to create a flat, even surface.

WHEN PLANNING FOOTINGS:
• Describe the proposed structure to your local building inspector and ask whether it requires a footing and whether the footing needs reinforcement. In some cases, 8"-thick (20.5 cm) slab footings can be used when the subbase provides plenty of drainage.

• Plan to make the footings twice as wide as the wall or structure they will support. They also should extend at least 12" past the ends of the project area.
• Keep footings separate from adjoining structures by installing an isolation board.
• For smaller poured concrete projects, consider pouring the footing and the structure as one unit.

TOOLS & MATERIALS

• Rope or hose	• Wheelbarrow or	• #3 rebar
• Shovel	mixing trough	• 16-gauge wire
• 4-ft. level	• Stakes & string	• Concrete mix
• Reciprocating saw	• 2 × 4s for forms	• Hand maul
• Concrete float	• 3" deck screws	• Drill
• Nails	• Release agent	

HOW TO POUR FOOTINGS
Step A: Mark the Outline & Dig the Trench
1. Using a rope or hose, make a rough outline of the footing; the footing must be twice as wide as the structure it will support and must extend 12" beyond its ends. Outline the project area with stakes and mason's string (page 20).
2. Strip away the sod 6" outside the project area on all sides, then excavate the trench for the footing.
Step B: Build the Forms
1. Cut 2 × 4s to create a frame with inside dimensions equal to the total size of the footing.

A. *Lay out the footing and excavate a trench for it.*

B. *Set 2 × 4 form boards in place, directly under the mason's strings. Drive stakes at 3 ft. intervals to support the form boards.*

2. Use the mason's strings that outline the project as a reference for setting form boards in place. Starting with the long sides, position the boards so the inside edges are directly below the strings.

3. Cut several pieces of 2 × 4 at least 12" long to use as stakes. Trim one end of each stake to a sharp point. Drive the stakes at 3 ft. intervals along the outside edges of the form boards, positioned to support any joints.

Step C: Complete the Forms

1. Drive 3" deck screws through the stakes and into the form board on one side of the trench. Set a level so it spans both sides of the form, then stake the second form board, using the level as a guide. (For large projects, use the mason's strings as the primary guide for setting the height of all form boards.)

2. Add the form boards for the ends of the footing and drive 3" deck screws at the corners.

3. Coat the inside of the forms with vegetable oil or a commercial release agent so the concrete won't bond to them.

4. Tack nails on the outside of the forms to mark locations for control joints at intervals roughly 1½ times the slab's width (but no more than 30 times its thickness).

Step D: Add Rebar Reinforcement

For each grid, cut two pieces of #3 rebar, 8" shorter than the length of the footing; also cut two pieces 4" shorter than the depth of the footing. Bind the pieces together with 16-gauge wire, forming a rectangle. Set the rebar grids upright in the trench, leaving 4" of space between the grids and the walls of the trench.

Step E: Pour the Footing

1. Mix and pour concrete, so it reaches the top of the forms. Screed the surface, using a 2 × 4.

2. If you will be pouring concrete over the footing, press 12" sections of rebar 6" into the concrete. (The tie-rods will anchor the footing to the structure it supports.)

3. Allow the concrete to cure for one week before you build on the footing. Remove the forms and backfill around the edges of the footing.

C. *Attach the form boards to the stakes and secure the joints. Coat the forms with release agent and mark locations for control joints.*

D: *Form a grid with rebar and place it in the trench.*

E. *Fill the forms with concrete, then screed the surface with a 2 × 4.*

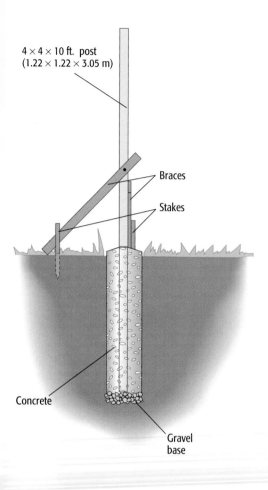

4 × 4 × 10 ft. post
(1.22 × 1.22 × 3.05 m)

Braces

Stakes

Concrete

Gravel
base

Setting Posts

After plotting your line with stakes and string, dig the postholes and set the posts. It is critical that the posts be perfectly aligned and plumb. Dig postholes 6" (15.25 cm) deeper than the post footing depth specified by local building codes, or 12" (30.5 cm) past the winter frost line in cold climates. Good post-setting techniques let you fly through this process.

HOW TO INSTALL POSTS

Step A: Mark Post Locations

1. Transfer the marks from the string to the ground, using a plumb bob to pinpoint the post locations.

2. Mark each post location with a stake, and remove the string.

Step B: Dig Postholes

1. Dig postholes, using a power auger (available at rental centers)

TOOLS & MATERIALS

- Plumb bob
- Stakes & string
- Hand maul
- Power auger or posthole digger
- Shovel
- Coarse gravel
- Carpenter's level
- Concrete
- Mason's trowel
- Pressure-treated, cedar, or redwood 4 × 4 (10 × 10 cm) posts
- Scrap lengths of 2 × 4 (5 × 10 cm)

or posthole digger. Make each hole 6" (15.25 cm) deeper than the post footing depth specified by local building code or 12" (30.5 cm) past the frost line in cold climates. Keep the holes as narrow as possible, usually about twice the width of the post. Corner and gate posts usually require wider footings for extra stability. Check local regulations.

2. Pour a 6" (15.25 cm) layer of gravel into each hole for improved drainage.

A. *Drop a plumb bob from each post reference mark on the string to pinpoint the post centers on the ground.*

B. *Dig postholes 6" (15.25 cm) deeper than specified by local building code. Pour 6" of gravel into each hole to improve drainage.*

C. *Position each post in its hole. Brace the post with scrap pieces of 2 × 4 on adjacent sides, and adjust it until it is plumb.*

Step C: Position the Posts

1. Position each post in its hole. Check posts for plumb with a level. Adjust posts to the correct height by adding or removing gravel until each post is at the same height.

2. Brace each post with scrap 2 × 4s secured to adjacent sides.

3. If you're setting more than one post, make sure they're properly aligned with one another, using mason's string. Adjust if necessary.

Step D: Fill the Postholes

1. Mix concrete and fill each posthole, overfilling them slightly.

2. Check to make sure each post is still plumb, then use a mason's trowel to shape the concrete around the bottom of the post to form a rounded crown that will shed water.

3. Let the concrete cure for 2 days before removing the braces.

D. *Fill the postholes with pre-mixed concrete, overfilling each slightly. Recheck the post for plumb and shape the concrete into a crown to shed water.*

VARIATION: POST SPIKES

An alternative to setting posts in concrete is to use post spikes. Also called post anchors, supports, or mounting spikes, post spikes run between 24" (61 cm) and 30" (76.2 cm) in length, and are designed with a socket head to accommodate 4 × 4 or 6 × 6 posts. Post spikes with swivel heads help make adjustments during installation even easier.

With no holes to dig or concrete to mix, it takes little time or effort to install post spikes. To begin, put an 8" (20.3 cm)-length of post into the socket head, and place the tip of the spike on the post location. Have someone help hold the spike in position as you drive it about 6" (15.25 cm) into the ground, using a sledgehammer. Check the blades of the spike for plumb with a level to make sure you are driving it in straight. Also, make sure the spike remains properly aligned and doesn't twist. Make any necessary adjustments and continue driving the spike into the ground until the base of the socket head is flush with the ground.

Cut a post to the desired height, and insert it into the socket head; check the post for plumb, using a level. Drive 1¼" (3.2 cm) galvanized deck screws (or the hardware screws that came with the post spike) into the pre-routed screw holes, one on each side, of the socket head.

It is best to install the post spikes as you install the fencing. This will allow you to easily maintain the proper spacing between posts and save you from having to cut stringers and siding to special sizes.

Tools & Materials

As a homeowner, you probably already own many of the tools needed for the projects in this book. If there are tools you don't have, you can borrow from friends and neighbors, or rent the specialty tools at your local hardware store or rental center. Make sure you read over the owner's manual and operating instructions for any tools you borrow or rent.

If you decide to buy new tools, invest in high-quality products whenever possible; a few extra dollars up front will cut the expense of replacing worn out or broken tools every few years.

To ensure your safety and prevent damage to your tools, always use a GFCI (ground-fault circuit-interrupter) extension cord when using power tools.

Use corrosion-resistant metal hardware and fasteners for outdoor structures: hinges, latches, fence brackets, deck screws, and nails.

Because these are outdoor structures, connecting hardware, fasteners, and materials need to hold up during extreme weather conditions. The better the materials, the longer the life of the structure.

Metal hardware and fasteners, including nails and screws, should be made from corrosion-resistant metal that is recommended for the wood you are using. Using inappropriate hardware can weaken joints.

For projects involving concrete, estimate your material needs as accurately as possible, then add 10 percent. This will compensate for any oversights and allow for waste. Also, make sure all paints, stains, and sealers are suited for exterior use. Follow the manufacturer's instructions for application.

BASIC TOOLS

Basic tools include:
shovel (1), clamshell digger (2), mason's trowel (3), propane torch (4), flux (5), solder (6), spark lighter (7), jointing tool (8), ratchet wrench (9), pliers (10), 4-ft. level (11), hammer (12), circular saw (13), chalk line (14), mason's string (15), spring clamp (16), drill (17), tape measure (18), jig saw (19), framing square (20), line level (21).

RENTAL TOOLS (not shown)

In addition to these basic tools, you may need to rent tools such as a power auger, cement mixer, and reciprocating saw.

16

21

20

17

19

18

Materials required for building outdoor structures include: paint, stain, sealer, wood glue, duct tape, cement, rebar, and gravel.

Landscape Structures

Beds, borders, and planting areas complete a landscape in much the same way that accessories complete a wardrobe. You can get by without them, but why do it? Terraces, raised planters, and rock-lined beds can be just the right finishing touches for a landscape.

Look at the existing patterns in your yard: Are the paths straight? Do they meet at right angles? This suggests a formal design of rectangular or circular borders. If paths and lawns are casual and curving, informal curves and asymmetrical arrangements will harmonize better.

For major projects, set up simulations to help you visualize the final results. Use a hose or flour to outline each feature. Add cardboard boxes and crumpled newspaper, open umbrellas, and stakes to represent plants, fountains, and trellises. Check your design from all angles (especially from inside the house), adjust it until you're satisfied, and then get to work.

Terraces & Levels

Terraces make slopes easier to manage and may help reduce excess runoff, which can cause erosion. If you have a gentle slope, installing a low terrace can be a great do-it-yourself project.

Check local code and permit requirements if you plan to install any wall higher than 18" (45 cm). If you're contemplating a retaining wall higher than 3 feet (90 cm) or dealing with a very steep incline, unstable soil, drainage, or uneven terrain, consult an engineer.

Start by choosing the location, then decide whether to create one or a series of terraces. Generally, the steeper the slope, the more terraces you need. Measure the change in elevation on your site (see page 23), keeping in mind that a series of measurements may be necessary on long or steep sites.

To tailor your terraces to the slope, decide the height of each terrace, then divide that height into the total rise to find the number of terraces that will be necessary. Alternatively, divide the number of terraces you want into the rise to determine the height of each. Either way, the distance between terraces is found by dividing their number into the run. You can make adjustments as you build the terraces.

Consult your local home improvement store or garden center to determine the amount of stone, sand, and aggregate you'll need. Remove turf grass and other vegetation from the area. This project illustrates the construction of a dry-stacked stone island terrace built from fieldstone on a fairly level site.

TOOLS & MATERIALS

- Stakes and string
- Line level
- Shovel
- Hand tamp
- 4-ft. level
- Sand
- Hand maul
- Fieldstone
- Aggregate

A. *Mark the location of the terrace with stakes and string, then dig an 8 to 12"-deep trench along the run of the terrace.*

B. *Compact the soil at the base of the trench, then add a 4 to 6" layer of sand.*

C. *Working in 4-ft. sections, lay the first course of stone. Add or remove sand beneath the stones to level the course.*

D. *Set and level two stones approximately 4 ft. apart, then fill the space between them. Add courses as necessary.*

HOW TO BUILD TERRACES & LEVELS

Step A: Excavate the Trench

1. Mark the terrace's location with stakes. Fasten a string between stakes to mark its final height. Attach a line level and make sure the string is level; adjust if necessary.

2. Excavate a trench 8 to 12" (20 to 30 cm) deep and slightly wider than the stones, along the run of the terrace. Reserve the excavated soil as fill for the finished terrace.

Step B: Create a Base

1. Compact the base soil of the trench until it is firm, using a tamping tool.

2. Add a 4 to 6" (10 to 15 cm) layer of sand to the base of the trench. (The sand allows you to precisely level the first course of stones.)

Step C: Set the First Course

1. Center the first few stones in the trench. Check them with a 4-ft. level and adjust as necessary. Add sand below the stones in lower areas and remove it in higher areas.

2. Continue laying the first course in approximately 4-ft. sections.

Step D: Stack Additional Courses

1. Still working in approximately 4-ft. sections, set and precisely level two endstones, then fill the space between them. Stack the stones one-over-two to off-set the joints. As you work, cover all joint spaces and step each course back 1 to 2" (25 to 50 mm) from the face.

2. Add remaining courses as necessary.

Step E: Fill the Terrace

1. Add aggregate behind the finished terrace wall to stabilize it and provide drainage.

2. Fill the terrace with topsoil mixed with excavated soil from the trench. Add more topsoil before planting, as the terrace will settle and compact for several weeks after being filled.

E. *Place aggregate behind the wall, then fill the terrace with amended topsoil.*

Planting Bed with Boulders

Using quarry or fieldstone boulders to define the edge of a planting bed is an easy way to dress up your landscape. The boulders provide texture and interest, and additional soil is added to raise the bed above the surrounding lawn. If the underlying soil is compacted, add sand, organic matter, compost, or gypsum to help loosen it before adding topsoil.

Many turf grasses colonize new soil by sending out subsurface roots, or stolons, so dig down at least 6" (15 cm) into the soil before bedding the boulders into sand. Removing roots takes some time during the building process, but it reduces the need for weeding later.

HOW TO BUILD A PLANTING BED
WITH BOULDERS

Step A: Remove the Turf

Mark the bed's outer edges with a hose. Cut away the grass inside the borders with a sod-cutting tool, rolling up sections of the sod for removal. Reserve the sod to finish the site later.

Step B: Dig a Bed

1. With a helper, examine each stone to choose its face side.

2. Move a stone to the edge of the site. Estimate the stone's shape, and dig a bed for it.

Step C: Set the Stone

1. Spread 2 to 4" (50 to 100 mm) of sand in the excavated bed.

2. Place the stone in the bed, rocking it to settle it into the sand.

Step D: Add Remaining Stones

Continue placing other stones, using a mix of low and high stones to define points of interest in the edging.

Step E: Add the Topsoil

With all the stones in place, fill the bed with topsoil. Tamp the soil and water it to settle and fill all the voids.

Step F: Finish the Edges

Patch the grass around the edging with the sod reserved from the bed's center. Plant as desired.

TOOLS & MATERIALS

• Shovel	• Fieldstone boulders	• Topsoil
• Garden hose		• Rake
• Sod-cutting tool	• Sand	• Hand tamp

A. *Mark the borders of the site and cut away the sod within the borders.*

B. *Place a stone at the edge of the site and dig a bed for it.*

C. *Add a 2 to 4" layer of sand to the hole and set the stone in it.*

D. *Place stones around the perimeter of the site.*

E. *Fill the bed with amended topsoil and water it to settle the voids.*

F. *Patch the grass around the boulders and add plants to the bed.*

Butterfly Flower Bed

Butterfly gardens are colorful, pleasantly scented refuges grown within traditional landscape plantings. Setting aside an area for butterflies to gather, feed, and reproduce is easy—simply provide a shallow water source, protection from wind, pets, and foot traffic, and a sunny zone. Add an assortment of trees, shrubs,and flowering plants for fragrance, color, nectar, and food.

A well planned habitat encourages adult butterflies to stay, mate, and lay eggs. That's what butterfly gardening is about—ensuring reproduction, maturity, and another generation. If you're lucky, migrating species that emerge in your garden also may return.

TOOLS & MATERIALS

- Sod-cutting tool
- Shovel
- Flour
- Stakes & string
- Fieldstones
- Sand
- Topsoil
- Shallow water tray

A. *Mark an irregular triangle with about 50 square feet of area. If there is sod within the triangle, remove it.*

HOW TO BUILD A BUTTERFLY FLOWER BED
Step A: Mark the Bed & Remove the Sod

1. Use flour, stakes, and string to define an irregular triangle, about 50 square feet (4.5 m²) in area, within an existing landscape bed or lawn.

2. In grassy areas, use a sod-cutting tool to remove the sod.

Step B: Dig Holes & Set Stones

1. Dig holes about 8" (20 cm) deep at the corners of the triangle and also at points about one third of the length of each side.

2. Fill each hole with a 3" (7.5 cm) layer of sand. Place pairs of fieldstone boulders into each hole, rocking each until it's settled into the sand.

Step C: Add the Soil

Backfill the area with soil about 1 ft. deep (30 cm). Allow the soil to spill around and through the boulders, sloping to the bed beyond the triangle.

Step D: Add Plants & Accessories

1. Set another boulder in one corner of the butterfly bed. Top the stone with a shallow water tray filled with sand. Keeping the sand moist during the season will further attract butterflies.

2. Plant shrubs and flowers as desired. Establish trellises as necessary.

PLANTS THAT ATTRACT BUTTERFLIES

Butterflies generally prefer flat, open-faced flowers that provide a good spot for resting and feeding, or deep-throated flowers that hold abundant nectar.

Flowering shrubs: crape myrtle, wild cherry, honey locust, butterfly bush, and lilacs.

Flowering vines: honeysuckle, mandevilla, morning glory, and wisteria.

Perennial flowers: Shasta daisy and purple coneflowers.

Annual flowers: black-eyed Susan, various daisies, cosmos, and hollyhock. Deep-throated flowers filled with nectar include butterfly weed, monkey flower, nasturtium, and snapdragon.

B. Dig holes at the corners and on the sides of the triangle, then set a pair of stones in each hole.

C. Fill the area with amended topsoil to a depth of 1 ft.

D. Place another stone in one corner and top it with a shallow water tray.

Landscape Planter

Landscape planters are large, permanent fixtures used to create focal points, define walkways, or add interest to a yard. If you have the space and want better control over the soil mix surrounding your trees and shrubs, landscape planters are the perfect hybrid between a container garden and open ground.

Building a landscape planter requires a bit of skill in a variety of construction methods and materials. These include building forms, installing reinforcement rod and pouring the footings (see pages 26 to 27), constructing concrete-block walls, and applying stone veneer. These processes are not particularly difficult, but some of the work is heavy and projects require drying/curing time between steps. Recruit help as necessary and allow plenty of time for planning and construction.

TOOLS & MATERIALS

- Stakes & mason's string
- Line level
- Pencil
- Hand maul
- Circular saw with masonry blade
- ⅜" wood spacers
- 4-ft. level
- Shovel
- Concrete blocks
- Framing square
- Chalk line
- Wheelbarrow or mixing trough
- Mixing hoe
- Concrete mix
- Trowel
- Wire lath
- U-shaped mortar tool
- Mortar bag
- 2 x 4s for forms
- 3" deck screws
- Release agent
- #3 rebar
- 16-gauge wire
- Drill
- Self-tapping masonry anchors
- Stone veneer
- Amended topsoil

HOW TO BUILD A LANDSCAPE PLANTER
Step A: Install the Footings
1. Mark the site with stakes and mason's string. Outline the footings and measure the diagonals to make sure the outline is square. Adjust as necessary.

2. Dig the trenches and set the footings as described on pages 26 to 27.
Step B: Lay Out the First Course
1. Test-fit the blocks for the first course, using ⅜" (9.5 mm) wood spacers to maintain even gaps for mortar. If you need to use less than half a block, trim two blocks instead. For example, if you need 3½ blocks, use four and cut two of them to three-quarters of their length—this produces a stronger, more durable wall. Use a circular saw and masonry-cutting blade to cut the blocks.

2. Use a level to make sure the course is plumb and level and a framing square to make sure the corners are square. Set a mason's string along the outside of the planter, flush with the height of the course.

3. Mark the footing with the positions of the corner blocks.

4. Remove the blocks and snap reference lines that connect the corner marks on the footing.

5. Mix mortar in a wheelbarrow or mixing trough, following the manufacturer's directions. (The mortar should hold its shape when squeezed.)
Step C: Set the First Corner
1. At one corner, dampen the center of the footing, then trowel thick lines of mortar, slightly wider and longer than the base of the first block. Align an end block with the reference lines and set it into the mortar bed. Set a level on top of the block, then tap the block with a trowel handle until it's level.

2. Repeat #2 at the opposite end of one side of the planter.

3. Check that the blocks are flush with the mason's string set up in step B. Adjust the blocks to align with the string. Remove any excess mortar and fill the gaps beneath the blocks.
Step D: Set the First Course
1. Apply mortar to the vertical flanges on the side of a standard block and to the footing. Set the block next to the corner block, leaving a ⅜" layer of mortar

A. *Dig trenches and pour footings twice as wide as the walls of the planter.*

B. *Lay out the first course of block, cutting blocks as necessary. Mark the corners, then remove the blocks and snap reference lines.*

C. *Lay a mortar bed, then set the corner blocks.*

between blocks. Tap the block into position with a trowel handle, using the mason's strings as guides.

2. Install the remaining blocks on this side, working back and forth from each end. Maintain ⅜" joints and keep the course level, plumb, and aligned with the string.

3. When you reach the middle, apply mortar to the flanges on both ends of the block. Slide the block into place and line it up with the string.

4. Repeat Steps C and D to complete the entire first course of the planter.

Step E: Build Up the Corners

1. Trowel a 1" layer of mortar along the top flanges of the corner block of the first course. Scrape off any mortar that falls onto the footing. Begin the second course with a full-sized end block set so that it spans the vertical joint where the two runs meet. Make sure the block is level and plumb.

2. Butter one end of a full-sized block and set it against the end block to form the corner. Use a framing square to make sure the corner is square.

3. Build up the corner three courses high. Keep blocks level and plumb as you go, and check the position with a level laid diagonally across the corner.

4. Repeat with remaining corners.

Step F: Fill in the Subsequent Courses

1. Install the second course of stretcher blocks, using the same method as with the first course. When the second course is completed, use line blocks to set your mason's string for the new course.

2. Scrape off excess mortar and tool the joints with a U-shaped mortar tool.

3. Install each additional course of blocks by repeating this process. Finish the joints as each course is completed. Use a level to make sure the planter walls remain plumb.

Step G: Lay the Top Cap

1. Apply mortar to the top course of block. Ease the corner cap blocks into position—place them gently so their weight doesn't squeeze the mortar out of the joints.

2. Make sure the cap blocks are level and plumb, using a 4-ft. level.

3. Allow the structure to cure thoroughly.

D. *Alternating from one end to the other, set the blocks on one side of the planter. After setting the middle block, repeat the process on the other sides.*

E. *Starting at the first corner, set a full-sized end block so it overlaps the joint at the corner. Build up the corners three courses high.*

Step H: Apply Stone Veneer

1. Attach wire lath to the entire surface of the wall, using self-tapping masonry anchors.

2. Apply a ½" (12.7 mm)-thick layer of mortar over the lath. Scratch grooves into the damp mortar, using the trowel tip. Let the mortar dry overnight.

3. Apply mortar to the back of each veneer piece, then press it onto the planter wall with a twisting motion. Start at the bottom of the wall and maintain a ½" gap between pieces. Let the mortar dry for 24 hours.

4. Fill the joints with fresh mortar, using a mortar bag. Use a U-shaped jointing tool to finish the joints.

5. Let the planter cure for several weeks. Wash it down with water periodically to remove some of the alkalinity from the blocks and mortar.

6. Fill the planter with amended topsoil and add plants as desired.

F. *Fill in the field blocks of the second course, alternating from one end to the other. Tool the joints with a U-shaped jointing tool, then install remaining courses.*

G. *Lay a bed of mortar along the top of the finished walls. Apply mortar to one end of each cap block and set it in place.*

H. *Apply wire lath and then mortar to the surface of the planter, then use mortar to set veneer pieces. Finally, fill and tool the joints.*

43

Raised Shrub Bed

Planting beds for shrubs and small trees can be at ground level or they can be above ground level. Raised beds add interest to a flat site, and in areas with poor soil, they can be filled with good topsoil to provide an excellent base for plants that might otherwise be difficult to grow.

Landscape timbers and galvanized pipe make strong, durable raised beds that are ideal for shrub borders. Pipes pin the timbers together and anchor the planter to the ground. You can lay out the shape of the bed using a flexible garden hose or rope. Move the hose around until it's sized, shaped, and placed exactly the way you want it. Once you're satisfied, mark the outline with flour, marking paint, or stakes.

In most cases, additional topsoil will be needed to fill the bed. If the planting bed will be raised 12" (30 cm) or more off the ground, work the topsoil into the native soil to a depth of about 6" (15 cm). For lower beds, mix the new soil with your native soil to a depth of at least 12".

TOOLS & MATERIALS

- Shovel
- 4-ft. level
- Reciprocating saw
- Drill and spade bit
- Sledgehammer
- Landscape fabric
- Pea gravel
- Landscape timbers
- ½" (12.7 mm) galvanized pipe, 32" long (4)
- Topsoil
- ½" galvanized endcaps (4)
- Flour or marking paint

HOW TO BUILD A RAISED SHRUB BED

Step A: Dig the Trench

Decide on the dimensions and mark the outline of the planter with flour or marking paint. Dig a perimeter trench 10" (25.4 cm) wide and 8" (20 cm) deep.

Step B: Prepare the Base

1. Line the trench with landscape fabric to keep roots from penetrating the structure.

2. Add a 4" (10 cm) layer of pea gravel to the trench.

Step C: Set the First Course of Timbers

1. Lay out the first course of timbers, placing them to create flush corners. Use a reciprocating saw to cut timbers as necessary. Set a 4-ft. level across the timbers and adjust the gravel beneath the timbers until they're level.

2. Using a drill and ⅞" (22 mm) spade bit, drill holes 3" from each end of the timbers.

Step D: Set the Second Course

1. Place the second course of timbers, offsetting the joints log-cabin fashion.

2. Mark and drill holes through the timbers, aligning them with the holes in the first course of timbers.

3. Add the third and final course of timbers, offsetting the joints and drilling holes as before.

Step E: Install the Pipe & Plant the Bed

1. Temporarily install a threaded end cap on a

A. Mark the location of the raised bed, then dig a perimeter trench.

length of galvanized pipe. Using a sledgehammer, drive the pipe through the aligned holes, through the gravel, and into the soil beneath the structure.

2. Remove the end cap and use the sledge hammer to drive the pipe flush with the surface of the timber.

3. Repeat at each corner.

4. Fill the bed with planting soil, working the new soil into the native soil to a depth of about 6" (15 cm).

5. Add shrubs and perennials as desired.

B. *Line the trench with landscape fabric and add an even layer of gravel.*

C. *Place the first course of timbers and drill a ⅞" hole centered 3" from the corner.*

D. *Add two additional courses of timbers, staggering the joints log-cabin fashion.*

E. *Drive galvanized pipe through the holes to pin the timbers together. Fill the bed with soil, then plant shrubs and flowers.*

Wooden Raised-bed Planter

This simple version of a raised bed is as versatile as it is practical. By following the directions as given, you can easily build a planter in a day. For a formal look, use smooth lumber and paint it. For a rustic look, use rough-cut lumber. Either way, be sure to use rot-resistant wood such as cedar, hemlock, redwood, or pressure-treated softwood and corrosion-resistant hardware.

Before beginning this project, measure the site and sketch your design for the planter, using standard lengths of lumber and avoiding compound angles if possible.

TOOLS & MATERIALS

- Sod-cutting tool (optional)
- Shovel
- Topsoil
- Rake
- Clamshell digger
- 4-ft. level
- Reciprocating saw
- Drill with ⅜" bit
- Screwdriver
- 2 × 12" (39 × 286 mm) rot-resistant lumber, as needed for sides & cap
- Circular saw
- Socket wrench
- Stakes and string
- 4 × 4" (72 × 72 mm) rot-resistant post, 8 ft. (2.45 m)
- ⅜ × 5½" (10 × 140 mm) corrosion-resistant carriage bolts (20)
- ⅜" (10 mm) corrosion-resistant nuts & washers (20)
- ⅜ × 3½" (10 × 90 mm) corrosion-resistant deck screws (16)
- Tape measure
- Penetrating sealer or paint
- Pencil

©Saxon Holt

HOW TO BUILD A RAISED-BED PLANTER
Step A: Cut the Lumber

1. Measure, mark, and cut four 2 × 12 sides as indicated by your design; cut the 4 × 4 into four 2-ft (61 cm) lengths.

2. At one end of each section of 4 × 4, drill ⅜" holes for the carriage bolts, three on one side and two on another.

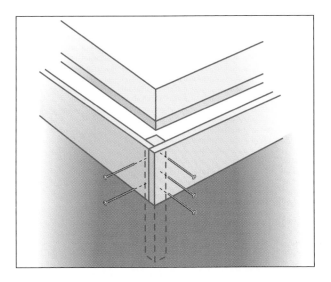

3. Align two side boards with each post. Reach a pencil through the holes in the posts to mark corresponding positions onto the side boards. Drill holes as marked.

Step B: Set the Posts & Attach the Sides

1. Measure the proposed site and determine the dimensions for the raised bed. Clear the site of turf, plants, weeds, and debris.

2. Add soil as necessary and rake to level the site. Mark the corners of the bed with stakes.

3. At each corner stake, dig a 12"-deep (61 cm) posthole. Set the posts in place, replace the soil, and tamp each post into position, checking to make sure each post is square and level.

4. Fasten the side boards to the posts with carriage bolts.

Step C: Add Soil

Fill the bed with fertile, well-textured loam or a complete soil replacement.

Step D: Add the Cap

1. Cut 2 × 12 caps to fit the sides, centered over the boards; miter the ends of each board at 45°.

2. Drill pilot holes, then fasten the cap to the posts and to the side boards, using deck screws.

3. Seal the lumber with clear, penetrating sealer or prime and paint the bed's exterior.

A. *Cut side boards and posts to length, then drill holes for the carriage bolts.*

B. *Set the posts in 12" holes, then attach the side boards, using carriage bolts.*

C. *Fill the bed with high-quality soil.*

D. *Cut 2 × 12 caps and attach them with deck screws.*

Cold Frame

A cold frame allows you to plant seeds 6 to 8 weeks earlier in the season than would otherwise be possible. While a few plants reliably germinate and grow in soil temperatures of 40 to 50°F (4 to 10°C), virtually all do best when soil temperatures are above 60°F (16°C). Planting in warm soil avoids the risk of fungal diseases that can rot seeds or cause seedlings to fail soon after germination.

Install your cold frame over a base of fresh manure covered with a deep layer of topsoil. As the manure decomposes, it will warm the soil above it. The translucent top of the cold frame will capture heat from sunlight and protect the plants within.

TOOLS & MATERIALS

- Circular saw
- Drill
- 4 × 8 ft. (1.2 × 2.4 m) ¾" (20 mm) ACX plywood panel
- 26 × 36" (66 × 90 cm) corrugated fiberglass panel
- 8 ft. 2 × 2" (3.8 × 3.8 cm) treated lumber
- ¼ × 1¼" (6 × 32 mm) corrosion-resistant wood screws
- ½ × ⅛" (12 × 3 mm) corrosion resistant washers (12)
- 2" (50 mm) corrosion-resistant butt hinges and mounting hardware (2)
- Shovel
- Manure or compost
- Plastic liner

Fiberglass Panel Frame Detail

A. *Assemble the box and use wood screws to fasten the pieces.*

Cutting List

Part	Material	Size	Number
Back Panel	¾" plywood	26 × 36" (66 × 90 cm)	1
Front Panel	¾" plywood	22 × 36" (56 × 90 cm)	1
Side Panels	¾" plywood	22 × 26 × 28½" (56 × 66 × 72.4 cm)	2
Vertical Cover Frames	¾" plywood	5½ × 30" (14 × 76 cm)	2
Horizontal Cover Frames	¾" plywood	4 × 36" (10 × 90 cm)	2
Back Corner Braces	2 × 2" (3.8 × 3.8 cm)	26" (66 cm)	2
Front Corner Braces	2 × 2" (3.8 × 3.8 cm)	22" (56 cm)	2

HOW TO BUILD A COLD FRAME

Step A: Assemble the Box

1. Cut the sides, front and back panels, and corner braces as indicated on the cutting list.

2. Assemble the box by fastening the side, front, and back panels to the front and back corner braces.

Step B: Assemble the Cover

1. Cut a ¾"-deep kerf down the center of one long edge of each horizontal cover frame.

2. Drill pilot holes in the cover frame pieces and in the fiberglass panel. Fit the fiberglass into the kerfs and fasten it in place with wood screws.

3. Set the horizontal cover frame pieces and panel on top of the vertical frame pieces. Fasten the frame at the corners, using three wood screws for each.

4. Fasten the fiberglass panel to the vertical frame pieces, using screws and washers.

Step C: Attach the Cover

1. Attach the butt hinges to the inside of the cover, 8" (20 cm) from each back corner.

2. Position the cover and align it with the edges of the box. Fasten the hinges to the back of the box.

Step D: Install the Cold Frame

1. In a sunny, protected spot, dig a rectangular hole, 36 × 42 × 24" (90 × 107 × 61 cm) deep. Add a 10 to 12" layer of fresh manure or nitrogen-rich compost.

2. Line the hole with plastic, then fit the cold frame into it. Backfill soil securely around the frame.

3. Each spring, remove the cold frame, dig down, then add a new layer of manure or compost.

B. *Fasten the fiberglass panel into kerfs cut in the horizontal cover frame, then assemble the cover.*

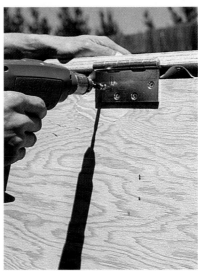

C. *Attach the hinges to the inside of the frame cover and then to the back panel of the box.*

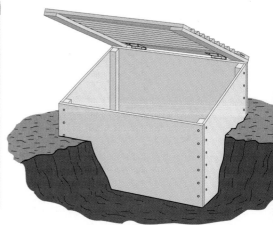

D. *Dig a hole, add a layer of compost, and install the cold frame.*

Masonry Edging

Define your in-ground planting beds with attractive edging—a low line of concrete set along its perimeter. Working with concrete gives you many options for the edging's shape, color, and pattern. To add interest, texture the concrete using split shingle forms or by brushing the concrete as it dries. You also can add color tints or press in stones for surface decoration. Edging simplifies maintenance, too. A crisp band of concrete along the front edge of a planting bed gives it a tidy appearance even when the plants are dormant. Edgings set along walkways discourage people from straying into the beds and divide the beds from the lawn or ground cover. If the edging is set at soil level and wide enough for a mower wheel to traverse, you can edge the lawn as you mow rather than trimming it later.

TOOLS & MATERIALS

- Garden hose, string, or flour
- Sod-cutting tool
- Hand maul
- Sledgehammer
- Shovel
- Hammer
- 1 × 2" (19 × 38 mm) stakes
- Form boards
- 16d nails
- 4-ft. level
- Mixing trough
- Concrete mix
- Concrete float
- Concrete edging tool
- Hoe
- Striker board

A. *Dig a 6"-deep trench along the edge of the planting bed.*

B. *Install the form boards and nail them into the stakes for support.*

C. *Mix concrete and fill the forms.*

D. *Use a striker board to remove the excess concrete and smooth the surface.*

HOW TO CREATE MASONRY EDGING

Step A: Mark & Dig the Trench

1. Mark the path of the trench, using a garden hose, string, or flour. Remove the sod from the marked path.

2. Drive stakes approximately 2 feet (60 cm) apart along the trench location.

3. Dig a trench 6" (15 cm) deep.

Step B: Install the Forms

1. Position the form boards on each side of the trench, 1" (25 mm) from the bottom and sides of the trench. Square the tops of the forms and make sure they are level.

2. Brace the first stake by placing a sledgehammer behind it; nail diagonally through the form boards and into the stake. Repeat with remaining stakes.

Step C: Pour the Concrete

1. Using a mixing trough or wheelbarrow and hoe, mix concrete according to manufacturer's instructions.

2. Fill the forms to the top with concrete. Use a shovel to vibrate the concrete and settle it against the sides and bottom of the forms.

Step D: Shape the Concrete

Using a scrap 1 × 4 as a striker board, smooth the concrete. Move the striker board across the top of the form, filling hollows, removing excess concrete, and making the surface roughly level.

Step E: Tool the Edges & Cut Control Joints

1. After the water of formation is absorbed and while the concrete is still workable, use a steel edging tool to finish the edges of the concrete.

2. At 4 ft. (1.3 m) intervals, crease the concrete to provide control joints. If desired, add surface textures. Let the concrete cure overnight.

3. Remove the forms and fill soil around the edging as desired.

E. *Tool the edges of the concrete, cut control joints, and allow concrete to cure.*

Walls

Wall. The word itself evokes visions of a barrier—tall, solid, and imposing. But in your yard, walls can't be defined in such a limited way. Landscape walls serve many purposes: They can define the property boundaries, separate living areas within the yard, and screen off unpleasant views or utility spaces.

With a temporary wall, you can create privacy and intimacy without building a permanent structure. On the other hand, if you want permanence, few things could be more durable than masonry walls. Masonry walls, such as glass block, concrete block, stone, or stone veneer, can introduce new textures and patterns into your landscape.

Living walls are another striking option. In some spots, a hedge might be just the thing to create a dense visual screen, diffuse wind, or absorb noise. Trellis walls, such as the post and wire trellis or the framed trellis wall, provide beautiful backdrops for your favorite vines or lush border gardens.

Using simple building techniques, the projects in this chapter offer a wide variety of choices for practical, visually appealing walls. Properly constructed, the walls you build should last decades with little maintenance.

©Charles Mann

Types of Walls

Before deciding what style of wall you want to build, take a close look at what purpose you want the wall to serve. Walls, in contrast to fences, do not necessarily enclose an area. But like fences, they can partially or completely block a view, define your property lines, or provide privacy. They also can prevent or direct movement between two areas.

And in smaller lengths, some structures you may not think of as walls, such as trellises and arbors, can serve as backdrops to your landscape.

If you'd like to define your yard but retain a natural-looking landscape, a tall, dense hedge may be the best choice. On the other hand, if you need to provide privacy and security, mortared block may be the most effective solution.

Generally, the purpose for your wall will dictate its size, but consider its setting and the size of your lot when you're deciding on dimensions. Local codes often set regulations regarding size, as well as acceptable materials, footings and other reinforcements, and bulding permits. Always check local building codes before beginning any building or landscaping project.

Living Walls

Whether spaced closely in a hedge or trained to grow over a trellis, plants create living walls that soften the texture of a landscape.

- Post & Wire Trellis
- Wall of Arbors
- Framed Trellis Wall
- Hedges

Block Walls

Concrete or glass, blocks produce sturdy, durable walls that are surprisingly easy to build. Low block walls are used mostly for effect, but full-size mortared block walls also provide excellent security.

- Mortarless Block Wall
- Mortared Block Wall

Stone Walls

With or without mortar, stone walls lend a sense of permanence to a landscape. Though more expensive and time-consuming to build than other types of walls, stone walls stand for decades as testimony to the builder's patience and craftmanship.

- Dry Stone Wall
- Mortared Stone Wall

Post & Wire Trellis

Successful gardens often seem to be studies in contrast. Great gardeners blend and contrast plant forms, colors, and textures, using each to its greatest advantage. Texture is an important element of this design equation.

To create the illusion of depth in a shallow planting bed, designers recommend using a vertical display of fine-textured foliage as a backdrop for several plants with large, coarse leaves.

Although many trellises are designed to support a riot of flowers or a rambunctious layer of foliage, few provide an adequate showcase for the type of delicate texture required in this situation.

It may sound like a big challenge to build a trellis that accomplishes this mission, matches the average person's construction abilities, and falls within a reasonable budget, but this project is remarkably simple. By topping cedar posts with decorative finials and stringing a lattice of plastic-coated wire between them, you can create a trellis that would be ideal for many garden settings.

The best plants for this trellis are twining climbers with small leaves. Among annual vines you can try sweet pea or cardinal climber. Good perennial vines include trumpet creeper, English ivy, and winter creeper. You can put your climbers in the ground or select a variety that thrives in planters or pots. Be sure, however, that the plants you choose are well suited to the light exposure they'll receive.

TOOLS & MATERIALS

- Tape measure
- Posthole digger or power auger
- Carpenter's level
- Drill
- Stakes & mason's string
- Reciprocating saw
- Wheelbarrow
- Trowel
- Hammer
- Wood sealer
- Compactible gravel
- Quick-setting concrete mix
- 8 ft. (2.44 m) cedar 4 × 4s (10 × 10 cm) (2)
- Scrap 2 × 4s (5 × 10 cm)
- Deck post finials (2)
- 2 × 3 corrosion-resistant fence brackets (4)
- 8 ft. (2.44 m) cedar 2 × 4s (5 × 10 cm) (2)
- 1" (2.54 cm), 1½" (3.8 cm) pan-head sheet metal screws
- 1½" (3.8 cm) screw eyes
- Plastic-coated wire or clothesline
- Small corrosion-resistant finish nails

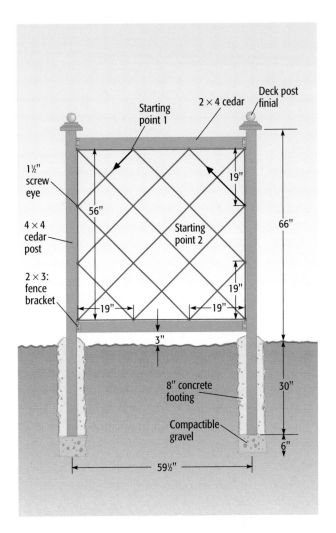

HOW TO BUILD A POST & WIRE TRELLIS
Step A: Prepare & Set the Posts

1. Apply wood sealer to the bottom 2½ ft. (76 cm) of each post and let dry. For extra protection, let the bottom of the post soak in wood sealer overnight.

2. At the chosen site, mark the posthole locations by setting two wooden stakes in the ground, 59½" (151 cm) apart.

3. Dig the postholes 36" (91 cm) deep. Doing this job properly requires a posthole digger or power

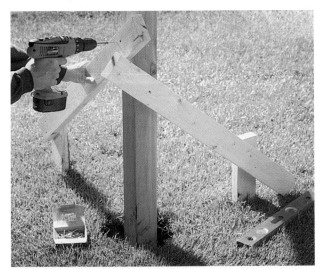

A. *Dig two 36" (91 cm)-deep postholes, then add a 6" (15 cm) layer of gravel to each. Set a post into each hole, and align it. When it's plumb, use 2 × 4s to brace the post in position.*

B. *Pour quick-setting concrete into the postholes, adding concrete until it's slightly above ground level. Form the wet concrete into a gentle mound around the base of the post.*

auger. Put a 6" (15 cm) layer of compactible gravel in the bottom of each posthole.

4. Set the first post into a hole. Take a carpenter's level and make sure the post is plumb on two adjacent sides.

5. When the post is plumb, use stakes and scrap pieces of 2 × 4 to brace it in position. Repeat the

process for the other post.

6. When both posts are plumb and braced, use a mason's string to make certain the tops and sides are aligned. Adjust as necessary.

Step B: Pour the Footings

1. Following the manufacturer's instructions, mix quick-setting concrete in a wheelbarrow. Mix only enough for one post—quick-setting concrete sets in about 15 minutes.

2. Pour the concrete into one posthole, until the concrete is slightly above ground level.

3. Check the post one more time to make sure it's plumb and properly aligned.

4. With a trowel, form the wet concrete into a gentle mound around the base of the post.

5. Repeat the process for the other post, taking care that it's plumb and aligned with the first post.

6. Let the concrete set for one to two hours.

Step C: Install the Finials

1. Check the tops of the posts to make sure they're level. If not, use a reciprocating saw to trim one post until it's level with the other.

2. Set a decorative deck post finial on top of each post. Drill two pilot holes on each side and secure the finials with small corrosion-resistant finish nails.

Step D: Install the Stringers

1. Attach the bottom 2 × 3 fence brackets with 1½" pan-head sheet metal screws, 3" (7.6 cm) above the bottom of each post.

C. *On top of each post, set a decorative deck finial. Drill pilot holes and secure the finials with small corrosion-resistant finish nails.*

D. *Attach the fence brackets 3" (7.6 cm) from the bottom of the posts, using sheet metal screws.*

E. *Run wire diagonally between the screw eyes on the posts and stringers.*

2. To make the stringers, measure the distance between brackets and cut two cedar 2 × 4s to length. Insert one 2 × 4 in the bottom set of brackets and attach it with 1" pan-head sheet metal screws.

3. Measure 56" (1.4 m) up from the top of the first stringer. Install top brackets and fasten the second 2 × 4 to the top set of brackets.

Step E: Install the Screw Eyes & String the Wire

1. Starting in one corner where a stringer meets a post, make a mark on the inside edge of the stringer, 19" (48 cm) from the corner. Next, mark the inside face of the post, 19" (48 cm) from the corner. Repeat the process for the remaining three corners.

2. Drill pilot holes and attach screw eyes at each of the marked points. At the corners, angle the pilot holes at 45° toward the center of the trellis frame.

3. Using plastic-coated wire or clothesline, begin putting the trellis together by knotting the wire on the screw eye at the marked starting point. Feed it through the closest screw eye on the post and down through the screw eye below that. Following the diagram on page 57, continue stringing the wire in a diagonal, back and forth pattern, finishing at the lower screw eye on the opposite post.

4. Beginning at the second starting point (as indicated on the diagram on page 57), string a second wire. Thread it as described above to complete the opposing diagonal runs.

VARIATION: SIMPLE TRELLIS PLAN

1. You can build an easier, less decorative version of the Post & Wire Trellis without the stringers and the crosshatch wire layout. Start by following the directions for Steps A to C.

2. Measuring 1" (2.54 cm) from the inside tops of the posts, mark the location of the first screw eye. Then continue marking screw eye locations every 8" (20 cm) down the post, putting the last mark a few inches off the ground. Repeat the process for the other post.

3. Drill pilot holes and install the screw eyes, twisting them so the "eyes" are parallel to the ground, not at right angles to it.

4. Attach the plastic-coated wire with a secure knot to one of the top screw eyes. Feed the wire through the screw eye on the opposite side, then down through the screw eye directly below.

5. Pull the wire across to the second screw eye down on the opposite side, feeding it through and down to the screw eye directly below. Keep the wire as taut as possible at every run.

6. Continue this process until you reach the final screw eye, then knot the wire securely.

HANGING BASKETS ADDITION

1. To make use of the outside or front edge of the posts, install decorative brackets for hanging plants. Position brackets along the side or front of the post as desired, centered across the post. Mark the screw holes and drill pilot holes. Each post should accommodate at least two brackets.

2. Attach brackets with the screws supplied, and hang planter baskets.

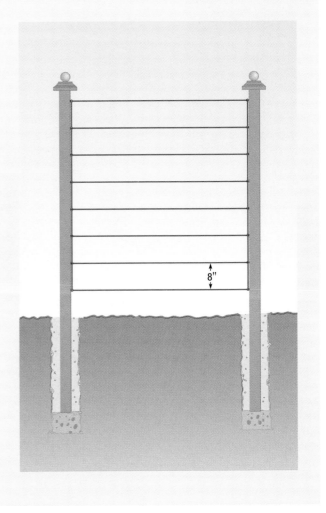

8"

Wall of Arbors

Rather than acting as a barrier, this wall of arbors welcomes visitors with open arms. Planted with roses or flowering vines, it creates a luxurious, ornamental accent to your yard or garden. Gracefully connected side-by-side, these arched arbors could, in addition to providing an accent to your yard, mark a property line or define an outdoor living space. And with well chosen plantings, they can either partially screen out or enhance a view, depending on your preferences. Copper plumbing materials go together much like children's construction toys, so these arbors are fun to build. If you're new to soldering, this is a good project to learn on—the size is manageable and the joints don't have to be absolutely watertight. Just work carefully and remember that if you don't get the joints right the first time, the materials aren't wasted. You can reheat the solder, pop off and clean the fittings, and start again. You do, however, have to be precise about the alignment of certain pieces (page 61) so the arbors fit together well when you connect them to one another.

TOOLS & MATERIALS

- Tape measure
- Tubing cutter
- Drill
- Round file (optional)
- Propane torch
- Hand maul
- Plywood scraps, at least 10 × 40" (25 × 100 cm) (2)
- 6 to 8" (15 to 20 cm) pieces of ⅜" (8 mm) dowel (4)
- 1 × 2s (2.5 × 5 cm), at least 46" (117 cm) long (2)
- 1" (2.5 cm) deck screws (8)
- ½" (1 cm) copper pipe (5 10-ft. [3.05 m] sticks per arbor)

- Wood glue
- ½" (1 cm) copper tees (20 per arbor)
- ½" (1 cm) copper 45° elbows (4 per arbor)
- ½" (1 cm) copper 90° elbows (2 per arbor)
- Emery cloth or nylon scouring pad
- Wire brush
- Flux & flux brush
- Solder
- #3 rebar, 36" (91 cm) sections (2 per arbor)
- Stakes & string

HOW TO BUILD A WALL OF ARBORS

Step A: Cut the Pipe & Build a Support Jig

1. Measure, mark, and cut the copper pipe, following the cutting list shown below. Clean and flux the pipes.

2. To build a support jig, start with two scraps of plywood at least 10" (25 cm) wide and 35 to 40" (89 to 102 cm) long. Draw a line down the center of each piece of plywood, then drill two ⅜" (8 mm) holes, 20" (51 cm) apart along the line. Glue a 6 to 8" (15.25 to 20 cm) piece of dowel into each hole.

3. On each of two 1 × 2s, draw a pair of marks 42½" (108 cm) apart. Lay the 1 × 2s across the pieces of plywood, aligning the marks on the 1 × 2s with the lines on the plywood to set the exact spacing for the sides of the arch. Secure the 1 × 2s to the plywood, using 1" screws.

Cutting List

For each arbor, you need ½" (1 cm) copper pipe in these lengths:

Length	Quantity
15" (38 cm)	4
14¾" (37.5 cm)	4
2" (5 cm)	4
20" (51 cm)	4*
19½" (49.5 cm)	12
9¾" (25 cm)	12 or 20**

* For first and last arbor

** 12 for first and last arbor,
   20 for each intermediate arbor

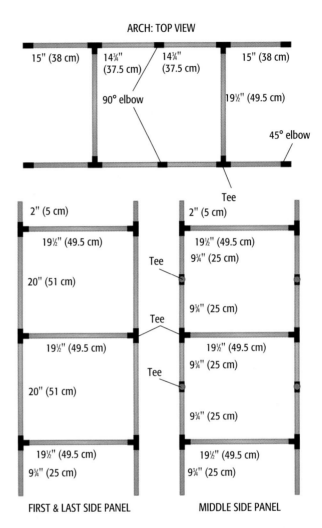

ARCH: TOP VIEW

15" (38 cm) 14¾" (37.5 cm) 14¾" (37.5 cm) 15" (38 cm)

90° elbow   19½" (49.5 cm)

45° elbow

Tee

FIRST & LAST SIDE PANEL

2" (5 cm)
19½" (49.5 cm)
20" (51 cm)
19½" (49.5 cm)
20" (51 cm)
19½" (49.5 cm)
9¾" (25 cm)

MIDDLE SIDE PANEL

2" (5 cm)
19½" (49.5 cm)
9¾" (25 cm)
Tee
9¾" (25 cm)
Tee
19½" (49.5 cm)
9¾" (25 cm)
Tee
9¾" (25 cm)
19½" (49.5 cm)
9¾" (25 cm)

A. *Make a support jig: attach pieces of dowel to scraps of plywood, then use 1 × 2s as spacers to set the distance between the sides of the jig.*

Step B: Construct the Leg Assemblies

1. Slide a 9¾" (25 cm) length of pipe over the first dowel, add a tee, then alternate pipe and tees as indicated on the drawing on page 61.

2. Slide a 9¾" (25 cm) length of pipe over the second dowel, then alternate tees and pipe as indicated.

3. Fit 19½" (49.5 cm) lengths of pipe between pairs of tees to form horizontal supports.

4. Repeat #1 through #3 to construct a leg assembly for the other side of the arbor.

Step C: Solder the Leg Assemblies

Disassemble the pieces and solder the joints in each leg assembly, working from the ground up. When the joints are cool, set the assemblies aside. NOTE: In order to connect the arbors, it's very important that you solder the open tees so they're exactly perpendicular to the plane of the leg assemblies.

Step D: Construct the Arch

1. Working on a flat surface, connect two 14¾" (37.5 cm) lengths of pipe, using a 90° elbow. Add a tee, then a 15" (38 cm) length of pipe to each side. Repeat to form a second, identical arch.

2. Slide a 45° elbow onto each dowel of the support jig, then slide the legs of the arches onto those elbows.

B. *Dry fit the leg assemblies: alternate pipe and tees to form the legs, then add horizontal supports.*

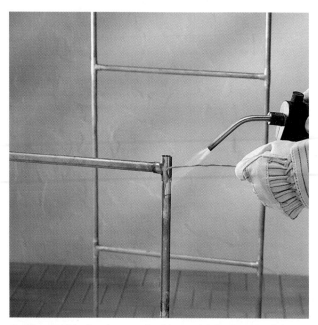

C. *Disassemble the pieces and solder each joint, working from the ground up.*

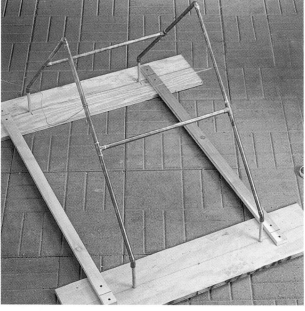

D. *Using 90° elbows, pipe, and tees, build the arch assemblies. Connect the arches with horizontal braces and tees.*

3. Add 19½" (49.5 cm) lengths of pipes between sets of tees, forming horizontal supports as indicated on page 61.

4. Disassemble the pieces and build the arch assembly, soldering as you go (see pages 246 to 247). When the joints are cool, set the assembly aside.

5. Put the leg assemblies back onto the support jig and fit the arch assembly into place; solder the joints.

6. Repeat Steps B, C, and D to build as many arbors as necessary.

Step E: Install the First Arbor

1. Use stakes and string to create a straight line for the position of the arbors. Set the arbors in place, 19½" (49.5 cm) apart and aligned with the string.

2. Push down on the sides of the first arbor to mark the position of the legs on the ground; remove the arbor. At two opposite corners, drive a 3-ft. (91 cm) piece of rebar about 18" (46 cm) into the ground. (Caution: buried utility lines are dangerous. Have your provider mark the utilities before digging any holes or driving anything deep into the soil.)

3. Fit two legs of the arbor over the buried rebar, firmly anchoring it in place.

Step F: Connect the Remaining Arbors

1. Flux the ends of a 19½" (49.5 cm) piece of pipe as well as the tees on the inside faces of the first two arbors. Set the second arbor into place, aligned with the strings and 19½" (49.5 cm) from the inside face of the first arbor. Add the horizontal braces that connect the arbors.

2. Mark the leg positions and anchor two legs on the second arbor.

3. Solder the joints on the horizontal braces.

4. Repeat this process to install the remaining arbors.

E. *Position the first arbor, and press its legs into the ground to mark their positions. At two opposite corners, drive 36" (91 cm) pieces of rebar 18" (46 cm) into the ground. Settle the arbor over the rebar.*

F. *Position and anchor the second arbor. Add horizontal braces, then solder them into position.*

Framed Trellis Wall

This simple design creates a sophisticated trellis wall that would work in many settings. Part of its appeal is that the materials are inexpensive and the construction remarkably simple.

It can be used as an accent wall, a backdrop to a shallow garden bed, or a screen to block a particular view. As a vertical showcase for foliage or flowers, it can support a wide display of colorful choices. Try perennial vines such as golden clematis (Clematis tangutica) or trumpet creeper (Campsis radicans). Or, for spectacular autumn color, plant Boston ivy (Parthenocissus tricuspidata). If you prefer annual vines, you might choose morning glories (Ipomoea tricolor) or a black-eyed Susan vine (Thunbergia alata). The possibilities go on and on—just make sure that the plants you select are well suited to the amount of sunlight they'll receive.

Depending on the overall look you want to achieve, you can paint, stain, or seal the wall to contrast with or complement your house or other established structures. Well-chosen deck post finials also can help tie the wall into the look of your landscape.

This project creates three panels. If you adapt it to use a different number of panels, you'll need to revise the materials list.

TOOLS & MATERIALS

- Tools & materials for setting posts (page 28)
- Tape measure
- Framing square
- Hammer
- Chalk line
- Line level
- Reciprocating saw or handsaw
- Paintbrush & roller
- Circular saw

- Drill
- Caulk gun
- Nail set
- Pressure-treated, cedar, or redwood lumber: 4 × 4 posts, 10 ft. (4)
  2 × 4s, 10 ft. (3)
  1 × 4s, 10 ft. (12)
  1 × 1s, 10 ft. (12)
  4 × 8-ft. lattice panels (3)
- 1 × 6 post caps

- Paint, stain, or sealer
- 10d corrosion-resistant casing nails
- 6d corrosion-resistant finish nails
- 4d corrosion-resistant finish nails
- Construction adhesive
- Deck post finials (4)

A. *Set posts and let the concrete dry thoroughly. Snap level chalk lines to indicate the positions for the stringers. At the line for the top stringer, measure up 10" and draw a cutting line on each post.*

HOW TO BUILD A FRAMED TRELLIS WALL

Step A: Set the Posts

1. Mark the post positions 4 ft. apart, as indicated in the diagram at right. Dig holes and set the posts (pages 28 to 29). NOTE: The distance between the faces of the posts should be 4 ft.—*not* 4 ft. on center. It's important to maintain the 4 ft. spacing between posts as accurately as possible.

2. On the first post, measure and mark a point 77" from the ground. Using a framing square, draw a level line across the post at the mark. Tack a nail in place along the line, and tie a chalk line to it. Stretch the chalk line to the opposite post, then use a line level to level it. Remove the line level and snap a line across all 4 posts.

3. On each post, measure down 75" (1.9 m) from the chalk line and draw a line across the

Cutting List

Part	Lumber	Size	Number
Posts	4 × 4 (10 × 10 cm)	10 ft. (3.05 m)	4
Stringers	2 × 4 (5 × 10 cm)	48" (1.22 m)	6
Back frame			
Top & bottom	1 × 4 (2.54 × 10 cm)	41" (1.04 m)	6
Sides	1 × 4 (2.54 × 10 cm)	72" (1.83 m)	6
Front frame			
Top & bottom	1 × 4 (2.54 × 10 cm)	48" (1.22 m)	6
Sides	1 × 4 (2.54 × 10 cm)	65" (1.65 m)	6
Stops			
Top & bottom	1 × 1 (2.54 × 2.54 cm)	48" (1.22 m)	12
Sides	1 × 1 (2.54 × 2.54 cm)	70½" (1.79 m)	12
Lattice panels	4 × 8 (10 × 20 cm)	48 × 72" (1.22 × 1.83 m)	3
Post caps	1 × 6 (2.54 × 15 cm)	4½ × 4½" (11.4 × 11.4 cm)	4

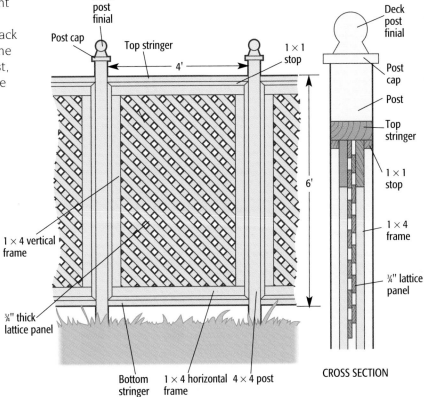

Deck post finial

Post cap

Top stringer

4'

1 × 1 stop

1 × 4 vertical frame

¾" thick lattice panel

Bottom stringer

1 × 4 horizontal frame

4 × 4 post

Deck post finial

Post cap

Post

Top stringer

1 × 1 stop

1 × 4 frame

¾" lattice panel

6'

CROSS SECTION

post, using a framing square.

4. Mark a line 10" (25.4 cm) above the chalk line. Trim off the posts along these lines, using a reciprocating saw or handsaw. Paint, stain, or seal the posts, including the cut ends.

Step B: Prepare Pieces & Position Stringers

1. Cut the stringers, back and front frame pieces, stops, lattice panels, and post caps as indicated on the cutting list on page 65. Paint, stain, or seal these pieces.

2. Transfer the level lines to the inside face of the posts, using a framing square.

3. Working between the two center posts, position the top stringer; make sure the top of the stringer is even with the marked line. Attach the stringer, toe-nailing it with 10d corrosion-resistant casing nails. Align the bottom of the stringer with the marked line and secure it in the same way.

Step C: Add Stops to the Back of the Fence Frame

Position a 1 × 1 stop flush with the back edge of the stringer and post, as indicated on the cross section on page 65. Drill pilot holes approximately every 8" (20 cm), then drive 6d corrosion-resistant finish nails through the stop and into the fence frame.

Step D: Set Up the Back Frame

1. On a level work surface, position the pieces of the back frame to form a 4 × 6-ft. (1.22 m × 1.83 m) rectangle with butted joints. Measure the opposite diagonals. Adjust the frame until these measurements are equal, ensuring that the frame is square.

2. Run a bead of construction adhesive around the center of the back frame. Set the lattice panel in place, making sure it's square within the frame.

Step E: Attach the Front Frame

Set the front frame into place, with the joints butted in the opposite direction of those on the back frame. Square the frame as described in Step D, then secure the frame with 4d corrosion-resistant finish nails driven every 6" (15.25 cm). Sink the nails, using a nail set. Let the adhesive cure, according to manufacturer's directions.

Step F: Install the Framed Lattice Panel

1. Set the panel in place between the center posts, positioned firmly against the stops.

2. Position 1 × 1 stops around the front edges of the frame. Push the stops in until they hold the panel snugly in place. Drill pilot holes approximately every

B. *Transfer the level lines to the inside of the posts, using a framing square. Install the first set of stringers between the center posts, even with the marked lines.*

C. *Add the stops to the back side of the fence frame. Drill pilot holes and nail the stops in place with 6d corrosion-resistant finish nails.*

6" (15.25 cm) and drive 6d corrosion-resistant finish nails through the stops and into the fence frame.

Step G: Complete the Wall

1. Repeat Steps B through F to install the left and right panels.

2. Set a post cap over each post, positioned so that the overhang is equal on all sides. Nail the trim in place, using 6d corrosion-resistant finish nails.

3. On top of each post cap, draw diagonal lines from corner to corner, forming an X. Drill a pilot hole through the center of each X, then install a deck post finial in each hole.

D. *Set up the pieces of the back frame, butting the joints. Square the frame, then apply a bead of construction adhesive along the center of the frame. Carefully set the lattice panel in place.*

E. *Set the front frame in place, butting the pieces in the opposite direction of the back frame. Drive 4d corrosion-resistant finish nails every 6" (15.25 cm) to secure the front frame to the lattice panel and back frame.*

F. *Set the panel in place between the center pair of posts. Add stops on the front side, then drill pilot holes and nail the stops in place, using 6d corrosion-resistant nails.*

G. *Install the remaining panels and add post caps to the posts. Add a deck finial to each post.*

Mortarless Block Wall

Far from an ordinary concrete block wall, this tile-topped, mortarless block wall offers the advantages of block—affordability and durability—as well as a flair for the dramatic. Color is the magic ingredient that changes everything. We added tint to the surface bonding cement to produce a buttery yellow that contrasts beautifully with the cobalt blue tile. However, you can use any combination that matches or complements your wall's surroundings.

Mortarless block walls are simple to build. You set the first course in mortar on a footing that's twice as wide as the planned wall and extends 12" beyond each end. You stack the subsequent courses in a running bond pattern.

The wall gets its strength from a coating of surface bonding cement that's applied to every exposed surface. Tests have shown that the bond created between the blocks is just as strong as traditional block-and-mortar walls.

The wall we have built is 24" (61 cm) tall, using three courses of standard 8 × 8 × 16" (20 × 20 × 41 cm) concrete blocks and decorative 8 × 12" (20 × 30.5 cm) ceramic tiles for the top cap.

Choose a durable, exterior ceramic tile and use a thinset exterior tile mortar. Be sure to select an exterior grout as well.

TOOLS & MATERIALS

- Stakes and mason's string
- Hammer
- 4-ft. level
- Line level
- Tape measure
- Framing square
- Shovel
- Wheelbarrow or mixing box
- Hand maul
- Hand tamp
- 4-ft. level
- Chalk line
- Circular saw with masonry-cutting blade
- Masonry chisel
- Line blocks
- Mason's trowel
- Notched trowel
- Square-end trowel
- Groover
- Tile cutter
- Caulk gun
- Rubber grout float
- Sponge
- Hoe

- Compactible gravel
- 2 × 4s (5 × 10 cm) for footings
- #3 rebar
- 16-gauge wire
- Vegetable oil or release agent
- Cement mix
- Sheet plastic
- Concrete blocks (end, half, & stretcher)
- Type N mortar
- Corrugated metal ties
- Wire mesh
- Surface-bonding cement
- Fortified exterior thinset mortar
- 8 × 12" (20 × 30 cm) ceramic tile rated for exterior use
- Matching bullnose tile
- Tile spacers
- Sand-mix exterior grout
- Silicone caulk
- Grout sealer

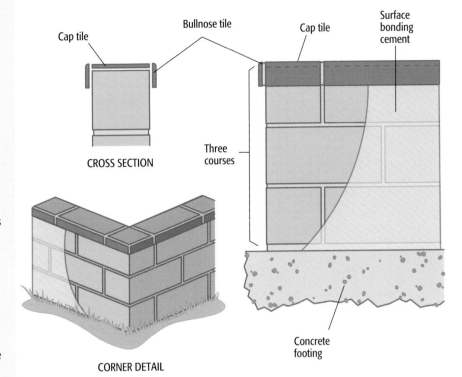

CROSS SECTION

CORNER DETAIL

HOW TO BUILD A MORTARLESS BLOCK WALL
Step A: Dig Trenches for the Footings

1. Lay out the location of the wall (pages 22 to 23), then use stakes and mason's string to outline a footing that is twice as wide as the proposed wall. Measure the diagonals to make sure the staked outline is square, then use a framing square to make sure the corners are square. Adjust if necessary.

2. Strip away the sod 6" (15 cm) beyond the outline on all sides, then dig a trench for the footing. The bottom of the trench should be 12" (30 cm) below the frost line and roughly level.

3. Lay a 6" (15 cm) layer of compactible gravel subbase into the trench. Tamp the subbase thoroughly.

Step B: Build Forms & Add Reinforcement

1. Build and install 2 × 4 forms to outline the footing (pages 26 to 27), aligning the forms with the mason's strings. Drive stakes along the outside of the forms to anchor them in position, then adjust the forms to level.

A. *Mark the wall and footings with stakes and string, then dig a trench for the footings.*

2. Make two #3 rebar grids to reinforce the footing: For each grid, cut two pieces of #3 rebar 8" (20 cm) shorter than the length of the footing and two pieces 4" (10 cm) shorter than the depth of the footing. Bind the pieces together with 16-gauge wire, forming a rectangle. Set the rebar grids upright in the trench, leaving 4" (10 cm) of space between the grids and the walls of the trench. Coat the inside edges of the forms with vegetable oil or commercial release agent.

Step C: Pour the Footing

1. Mix and pour concrete so it reaches the top of the forms. Work the concrete with a shovel to remove any air pockets.

2. Drag a short 2 × 4 as a screed along the top of the forms. Add concrete to low areas, then level again with the screed.

3. When concrete is hard to the touch, cover the footings with plastic and let the concrete cure for 2 to 3 days. Remove the forms and backfill around the edges of the footings. Add compactible gravel to bring the surrounding areas level with the surface of the footings.

4. Let the footing cure for a week.

Step D: Lay Out the First Course of Block

1. Lay out the blocks for the entire first course. If you need to use less than half a block, trim two blocks instead. For example, if you need 3½ blocks, use four and cut two of them to ¾ their length—this produces a stronger, more durable wall.

2. Use a level to make sure the course is plumb and a framing square to make sure the corners are square. Set a mason's string flush with the height of the course, along the outside of the wall.

3. Mark the position of the end and corner blocks on the footing, using a pencil.

4. Remove the blocks. Snap chalk lines to connect the end and corner marks for reference lines.

Step E: Set the First Course

1. Mix a batch of mortar, then mist the footing with water, roughly three or four block lengths from the end of the wall. Lay a ⅜" (1 cm)-thick bed of mortar on the misted area, covering only the area inside the reference lines.

2. Set an end block into the mortar bed at the corner. Place a stretcher block into the mortar bed directly against the end block with no spacing between the blocks. Place the next stretcher block in

TIP: MAKING ISOLATION JOINTS

If your wall abuts another structure, such as the foundation of your house, slip a piece of ½" (1.25 cm)-thick asphalt-impregnated fiberboard into the end of the trench to create an isolation joint between the footing and the structure. Use a few dabs of construction adhesive to hold the fiberboard in place.

The fiberboard keeps the concrete from bonding with the structure, which allows each to move independently. This minimizes the risk of damage during freeze and thaw cycles.

B. *Build 2 × 4 forms and stake them in place. Make rebar grids and put them upright in the trench. Coat the inside edges of the forms with release agent.*

C. *Fill the forms with concrete, screed the concrete level, then float the surface.*

D. *Lay out the first course of block, cutting blocks as necessary. Mark the ends and corners, then remove the blocks and snap reference lines.*

E. *Mist the footing with water, then lay a ⅜" (1 cm)-thick bed of mortar inside the reference lines.*

exactly the same manner. Use the mason's string as a guide to keep the blocks level and properly aligned.

3. Repeat this process, working on 3 to 4 ft. (1 to 1.5 m) at a time, until the first course is complete. Periodically check to make sure the wall is plumb and level and the corners are square.

Step F: Build Up the Corners & Ends

1. At a corner, begin the second course with a full-sized end block stacked so that it spans the vertical

F. *Starting at the corner, stack a full-sized end block so it overlaps the vertical joint at the corner. Build the corners and then the ends three courses high.*

joint where the two runs meet. Make sure the block is level and plumb. If a block requires leveling, cut a piece of corrugated metal tie and slip it underneath. If a block is off by more than ⅛" (3 mm), remove the block, trowel a dab of mortar underneath, and reposition the block.

2. Butt a full-sized stretcher block against the end block to form the corner. Use a framing square to make sure the corner is square.

3. Build the corner up three courses high. Keep blocks level and plumb as you go, and check the position with a level laid diagonally across the corners of the blocks.

4. Build up the ends of the wall three courses high; use half-sized end blocks to offset the joints on the ends of the wall.

Step G: Fill in the Subsequent Courses

1. Set your mason's string level with the corner and end blocks of the second course.

2. Fill the second course with stretcher blocks, alternating from the end to the corner until the blocks meet in the middle. Maintain a standard running bond with each block overlapping half of the one beneath it. Trim the last block if necessary, using a circular saw and masonry-cutting blade or a hammer and chisel.

3. Use a level to check for plumb, and line blocks and a line level to check for level. Lay wire mesh on top of the blocks.

4. Install the top course, then fill block hollows

G. *Fill in the subsequent courses. On the next to the last course, lay wire mesh over the block, then install the final course. Fill the block hollows with mortar.*

H. *Apply the surface-bonding cement to damp blocks, using a square-end trowel. Smooth the cement and cut grooves as necessary.*

with mortar and trowel the surface smooth.

Step H: Apply Surface-bonding Cement

1. Starting near the top of the wall, mist a 2 × 5-ft. (61 × 150 cm) section on one side of the wall with water. (The water keeps the blocks from absorbing all the moisture from the cement once the coating is applied.)

2. Mix the cement in small batches, according to the manufacturer's instructions, and apply a ¹⁄₁₆" to ¹⁄₈" (2 to 3 mm)-thick layer to the damp blocks, using a square-end trowel. Spread the cement evenly by angling the trowel slightly and making broad upward strokes.

3. Use a wet trowel to smooth the surface and to create the texture of your choice. Rinse the trowel frequently to keep it clean and wet.

4. To prevent random cracking, use a groover to cut control joints from top to bottom, every 48" (122 cm). Seal the hardened joints with silicone caulk.

Step I: Set the Tiles

1. Lay out the 8 × 12" ceramic tiles along the top of the wall, starting at a corner. If any tiles need to be cut, adjust the layout so the tiles on the ends of the wall will be the same size.

2. Apply latex-fortified exterior thinset mortar to the top of the wall, using a notched trowel. Spread the mortar with the straight edge, then create clean ridges with the notched edge. Work in small sections at a time.

3. Place the corner tile, twist it slightly, and press down firmly to embed it in the mortar. Place each tile in this same manner, using tile spacers to keep the tiles separated.

4. Lay out the bullnose tile on each side of the wall. Again, start in a corner and make sure the tiles at the ends of the wall will be the same size. Cut tile as necessary.

5. Apply mortar to the sides of the wall. Set the bullnose tile in the same way that you set the top tile. Tape the tile in place until the mortar dries.

6. Remove the spacers and let the mortar cure for at least 24 hours.

Step J: Grout the Tile

1. Mix a batch of sanded grout. NOTE: adding latex-fortified grout additive makes it easier to remove excess grout.

2. Spread a layer of grout onto a 4- to 5-ft. (1- to 1.5-m) area of tile. Use a rubber grout float to spread the grout and pack it into the joints between tiles. Use the grout float to scrape off excess grout from the surface of the tile. Scrape diagonally across the joints, holding the float in a near-vertical position.

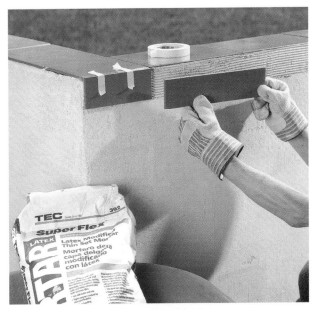

I. *Lay out the tile along the wall, then set it, using exterior thinset mortar.*

J. *Grout the joints, using a rubber grout float. Wipe the film from the tile and let it dry. Polish the tile with a soft, dry rag.*

3. Use a damp sponge to wipe the grout film from the surface of the tile. Rinse the sponge out frequently with cool water, and be careful not to press down so hard that you disturb the grout.

4. Continue working along the wall until you've grouted and wiped down all the tile. Let the grout dry several hours, then use a cloth to buff the surface until any remaining grout film is gone.

5. Apply grout sealer to the grout lines.

Gates

Although gates are uncomplicated, we ask a lot of them. These simple structures need to welcome family and invited guests at the same time that they turn away intruders. Successful gates need to operate smoothly and keep their attractive appearance for many years with little maintenance.

A gate's allure and interest depend on its materials, color, and pattern, but its strength and durability depend on its structural design and how well it's built. No book can describe gates for every situation, but once you understand the fundamental elements of building a gate, a world of possibilities opens up. The style of your fence and existing landscape will strongly influence your decisions, but after reading through this chapter, you should be able to build a range of gates—from a dramatic trellis gate combination to a security-conscious arched gate.

Building a gate offers you the opportunity to stretch your imagination and make use of unexpected materials. For example, salvaged metal and stained glass make quite a splash when recycled into gates.

As these projects show, gates give you a chance to make a statement. We hope they also show you that gates are about connection—not just to a fence or wall, but to the lives of the people on the other side.

IN THIS CHAPTER

Types of Gates

©Charles Mann

The type of gate you build will depend on the purpose you want it to serve. Security gates should be tall, sturdy, and difficult to climb—which generally rules out horizontal siding. Gates in privacy fences typically need tall, closely spaced, solid siding.

As you plan your gate, pay particular attention to the width of the opening. If a gate is too wide, it will sag from the sheer load of its own weight. Typically, 48" is the limit for a hinged, unsupported gate. If your opening is wider than that, use a pair of gates.

Another important issue to consider is which way you want the gate to swing. Spend some time thinking about how the gate will be used, and make sure there will be enough space to maneuver the gate as well as an adequate place to stand while opening and closing it. This is especially important if the gate will be positioned at the top or bottom of a slope or steps.

The next step is to choose hardware for the gate, including hinges and latches. The clearance necessary between the gate and the posts will vary, depending on the hardware you select—check hardware packages for specific requirements. If you're building a gate to fit an existing opening, adjust the gate's dimensions to allow the required amount of clearance. If you're planning a gate for a proposed fence, plan the placement of the gate posts so there is adequate clearance.

The best frame style for a gate depends on its size and weight. Z-frames are perfect for lightweight gate styles. Perimeter-frames provide support for larger or heavier gates. Both frame styles typically need cross braces to keep the gate square and to prevent sagging.

Basic Gates

The basic gate frame styles—perimeter and Z-frame—can be adapted to a wide variety of gate styles. By varying the shape, size, and spacing of the siding, you can create gates to suit almost any style of fence.

Gate with Stained Glass

This gate's eye-catching stained glass display allows light to filter through without sacrificing privacy. Thanks to the frame design, it's easy to adapt this gate to the dimensions of any stained glass window or other display piece.

Arched Gate

Designed to complement a tall fence, this striking gate combines ornamental metal with cedar. Positioned at eye level, the salvaged metal accent actually enhances the security function of the gate by allowing you to see who's approaching.

Trellis Gate Combination

Designed to support a lush bower, this trellis gate combination provides a dramatic and welcoming entry. While it's certainly more time-consuming to construct than a basic gate, the design is deceptively simple, and its beauty makes it well worth the effort.

Basic Gates

If you understand the basic elements of gate construction, you can build a sturdy gate to suit almost any situation. The gates shown here illustrate the fundamental elements of a well-built gate.

To begin with, adequate distribution of the gate's weight is critical to its operation. Because the posts bear most of a gate's weight, they're set at least 12" (30 cm) deeper than fence posts. Or, depending on building codes in your area, they may need to be set below the frost line in substantial concrete footings.

However they're set, the posts must be plumb. A sagging post can be reinforced by attaching a sag rod at the top of the post and running it diagonally to the lower end of the next post. Tighten the knuckle in the middle until the post is properly aligned. A caster can be used with heavy gates over smooth surfaces to assist with the weight load.

The frame also plays an important part in properly distributing the gate's weight. The two basic gate frames featured here are the foundation for many gate designs. A Z-frame gate is ideal for a light, simple gate. This frame consists of a pair of horizontal braces with a diagonal brace running between them. A perimeter-frame gate is necessary for a heavier or more elaborate gate. It employs a solid, four-cornered frame with a diagonal brace attached at opposite corners.

In both styles, the diagonal brace must run from the bottom of the hinge side to the top of the latch side, to provide support and keep the gate square.

There are a multitude of hinge, latch, and handle styles available. Whichever you choose, purchase the largest hinges available that are in proportion with your gate, and a latch or handle appropriate for the gate's purpose.

Z-frame

Perimeter frame

©Jerry Pavia

TOOLS & MATERIALS

- Tape measure
- Level
- Framing square
- Circular saw
- Paintbrush
- Drill
- Spring clamps
- Combination square

- Jig saw
- Pressure-treated, cedar, or redwood lumber as needed:
  - 1 × 2s (2.5 × 5 cm)
  - 2 × 4s (5 × 10 cm)
- Paint, stain, or sealer
- Gate handle or latch

- Hinge hardware
- 2" (5 cm) corrosion-resistant deck screws
- 2½" (6.3 cm) corrosion-resistant deck screws

HOW TO BUILD A Z-FRAME GATE

Step A: Calculate the Width & Cut the Braces

1. Check both gate posts on adjacent sides for plumb, using a level. If a post is not plumb, reinforce it with a sag rod. When both posts are plumb, measure the opening between them.

2. Consult the packaging on your hinge and latch hardware for the clearance necessary between the frame and gate posts. Subtract this figure from the measurement of the opening. The result will be the finished width of the gate. Cut two 2 × 4s to this length for the frame's horizontal braces.

Step B: Attach the Diagonal Brace

1. On the fence, measure the distance from the bottom of the upper stringer to the top of the lower stringer. Cut two pieces of scrap 2 × 4 to this length to use as temporary supports.

2. On a flat work surface, lay out the frame, placing the temporary supports between the braces. Square the corners of the frame, using a framing square.

3. Place a 2 × 4 diagonally from one end of the lower brace across to the opposite end of the upper brace. Mark and cut the brace, using a circular saw.

4. Paint, stain, or seal all the lumber for the gate, and let it dry completely.

5. Remove the temporary supports, and toenail the brace into position, using 2½" corrosion-resistant deck screws.

Step C: Apply the Siding

1. Position the frame so the diagonal brace runs from the bottom of the hinge side to the top of the latch side, then plan the layout of the siding to match the position and spacing of the fence siding. If the final board needs to be trimmed, divide the difference and trim two boards instead. Use these equally trimmed boards as the first and last pieces of siding.

2. Clamp a scrap 2 × 4 flush against the bottom brace as a placement guide. Align the first and last

A. *Make sure the gate posts are plumb, then measure the distance between them and calculate the dimensions of the gate.*

B. *Place a 2 × 4 diagonally across the temporary frame, from the lower corner of the hinge side, to the upper latch-side corner, and mark the cutting lines.*

C. *Align the end boards of the siding flush with the edge of the frame and attach with screws. Using spacers, position and attach the remaining siding to the frame.*

D. *Shim the gate into place. Mark the position of the hardware on the gate and gate posts, drill pilot holes and attach the hardware.*

boards, flush with the ends of the braces. Attach these two boards to the horizontal braces, using pairs of 2½" corrosion-resistant deck screws.

3. Attach the rest of the siding, using spacers as necessary.

Step D: Hang the Gate

1. Shim the gate into position and make sure it will swing freely. Remove the gate.

2. Measure and mark the hinge positions on the gate. Drill pilot holes, and secure the hinges to the gate using the screws provided with the hardware.

3. If your latch hardware doesn't include a catch, add a stop on the latch-side post. Clamp a 1 × 2 in place, then shim the gate back into position, centered within the opening. Use a level to make sure the gate is level and plumb, and the stop is properly positioned. Drill pilot holes and secure the stop to the post, using 2" corrosion-resistant deck screws.

4. With the gate shimmed into position, mark the hinge-side post to indicate the hinge screw locations, then drill pilot holes. Fasten the hinges to the post, using the screws provided with the hardware.

5. Install the latch hardware to the opposite gate post and the catch to the gate, according to the manufacturer's instructions.

HOW TO BUILD A PERIMETER-FRAME GATE

Step A: Build the Gate Frame

1. Determine the gate width and cut the horizontal braces, as for a Z-frame gate (page 79, Step A).

2. On the fence line, measure the distance from the bottom of the upper stringer to the top of the lower stringer. Cut two pieces of 2 × 4 to this length for the vertical braces.

3. Paint, stain, or seal the lumber for the gate and siding, then let it dry thoroughly.

4. Position the pieces of the frame and measure from one corner to the diagonally opposite corner. Repeat at the opposite corners. Adjust the pieces until these measurements are equal, which indicates that the frame is square. Secure each joint, using 2½" corrosion-resistant deck screws.

Step B: Attach the Diagonal Brace

1. Position the frame on a 2 × 4 set on edge, running diagonally from the lower corner of the hinge side to the opposite latch-side corner. Support the frame with 2 × 4 scraps underneath the opposing corners, if necessary.

2. Make sure the frame is square, and scribe the corners of the frame on the board. Transfer the cut marks to the face of the 2 × 4, using a combination

A. *Determine the lengths of the horizontal and vertical braces of the frame. Lay out the frame, check it for square, and secure the joints with 2½" corrosion-resistant deck screws.*

B. *Scribe the opposite corners of the frame on the 2 × 4 diagonal brace. Cut the brace, using a circular saw with the blade adjusted for the appropriate bevel angle. Toenail the brace in place.*

square. Cut with a circular saw, making sure to set the saw blade to the appropriate bevel angle.

3. Toenail the brace into position, using 2½" corrosion-resistant deck screws.

Step C: Attach the Siding

1. Lay out the siding on the frame, making sure that the diagonal brace runs up from the bottom hinge-side corner to the opposite top latch-side corner. Use wood scraps the same width as the gaps between the pickets in the fence line for spacing. If a board must be ripped to fit, rip the first and last boards to the same width.

2. Clamp a scrap 2 × 4 flush against the bottom brace as a placement guide. Align the first and last boards, flush with the ends of the braces. Attach these two boards to the horizontal braces, using pairs of 2½" corrosion-resistant deck screws.

3. Attach the rest of the siding, using spacers as necessary.

4. Paint, stain, or seal the gate and allow it to dry thoroughly. Mount the hardware and hang the gate as you would a Z-frame gate (opposite page).

C. *Secure the first and last siding boards to the frame, aligning them flush with the edges. Using scrap wood as spacers, attach the remaining siding.*

Gate with Stained Glass

This gate design started with a stained glass piece we wanted to showcase and grew from there. We know it's unlikely that you'll find a piece with the same dimensions, so we designed a structure that's easy to adapt. Basically, you need to build the frame, cut an opening, and use angle iron to hold your stained glass in place.

The beauty of this gate lies not only in the particular stain glass you choose to display, but also in the opportunity to make it uniquely your own creation. We've chosen a picket shape that reflects the diamond design in our stained glass piece, but any

combination that appeals to you can be made to work.

Although this design includes a catch on the latch side post to keep the gate from swinging through the posts, a stained glass inset may not be a great choice for a gate that will be frequently used by young children. In that case, you could use an acrylic panel that mimics stained glass or showcase a completely different type of accent piece.

TOOLS & MATERIALS

- Tape measure
- Circular saw
- Paintbrush
- Hammer
- Chisel
- Drill
- Screwdriver
- Framing square
- Level
- 1½" (3 cm) corrosion-resistant deck screws
- 2½" (6.3 cm) corrosion-resistant deck screws

- Paint. stain, or sealer
- Pressure-treated, cedar, or redwood lumber:
  ¾" (19 mm) trim 8 ft. (2.44 m)
  1 × 4s (2.5 × 10 cm),
  6 ft. (2 m) (10)
  2 × 4s (5 × 10 cm),
  10 ft. (3 m) (3)
- Angle irons (8)
- Corrosion-resistant 4d finish nails
- Hinge & latch hardware
- Stained glass window

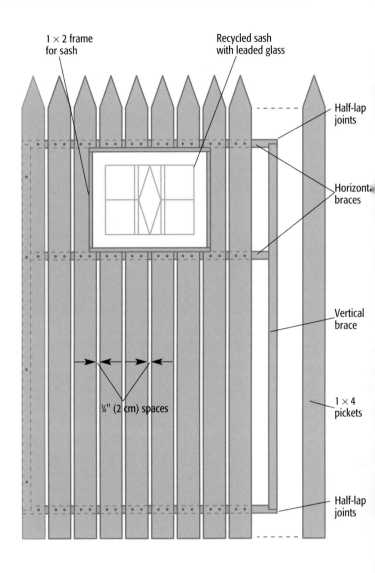

HOW TO BUILD A GATE WITH STAINED GLASS
Step A: Prepare the Lumber & Build the Frame

1. Measure the opening between the gate posts and determine the finished size of your gate. Compare your actual dimensions to those in the cutting list at right and make any necessary adjustments. Cut the lumber for the gate.

2. Paint, stain, or seal the pieces on all sides and edges. Let them dry thoroughly.

3. Lay out the parts of the frame and mark the cutting lines for the half-lap joints (see diagram at right). To make a half-lap joint, set the depth of a circular saw to ¾" and cut along the marked line; make a cut approximately every ⅛ to ¼" (3 to 6 mm), working from the end of the board or joint area back toward that

A. *Lay out the frame, then mark and cut the lap joints. Assemble the frame, check it for square, and secure the joints with screws.*

Cutting List

Part	Type	Length	Number
Frame			
Horizontal braces	2 × 4 (5 × 10 cm)	41¾" (1.06 m)	2
	2 × 4 (5 × 10 cm)	38¾" (1 m)	1
Vertical braces	2 × 4 (5 × 10 cm)	62½" (1.6 m)	2
Trim			
Horizontal	¾" (19 mm)	22" (56 cm)	2
Vertical	¾" (19 mm)	15¾" (40 cm)	2
Siding Slats	1 × 4 (2.5 × 10 cm)	72" (1.83 m)	10

B. *Mark the position for the middle brace, then screw it in place, working through the face of the frame and into the brace.*

C. *Secure the first piece of siding to the frame, aligning it flush with the right edge of the frame. Using a 1 × 4 as a spacer, add the remaining siding.*

first cut. Remove the waste material and smooth the cut surface, using a hammer and chisel. Repeat with each of the marked joints.

4. Position the pieces of the outer frame and measure from one corner to the diagonally opposite corner. Repeat at the opposite corners. Adjust the pieces until these measurements are equal, which indicates that the frame is square. Secure each joint, using 1½" corrosion-resistant deck screws.

Step B: Add the Middle Brace

Measure the stained glass window you have chosen; add 1½" to this measurement. Measure down from the bottom edge of the top brace, and mark this distance on the inside face of each side of the frame. Carefully align the top of the middle brace with these marks. Drive three 2½" corrosion-resistant deck screws through the face of each side of the frame and into the brace.

Step C: Attach the Siding

1. Shape the top of the pickets as desired. Draw a reference mark 6" (15.25 cm) down from the top of each picket.

2. Place a picket on top of the frame, the right edge of the picket flush with the right edge of the frame. Adjust the picket so the reference line is even with the top edge of the frame's first horizontal brace. Drill pilot holes and attach the picket to the frame, using two 1½" corrosion-resistant deck screws.

3. Set a scrap 1 × 4 on edge and hold it flush against the attached picket. Position a new picket

flush against the spacer and screw it in place; drive two screws into each of the frame's horizontal braces. Reposition the spacer and continue until all the pickets are in place.

Step D: Cut Out the Display Area

1. From the back of the gate, set the stained glass piece in place within the frame. Measure to make sure the piece is centered within the frame, then mark the four corners. Remove the stained glass and drill a hole at each mark.

2. Turn the gate over and draw lines to connect the holes. Use a framing square and tape measure to make sure the lines create an opening that is square and centered within the frame.

3. Set the depth on a circular saw to ¾" (2 cm) (the thickness of the pickets), and cut along the marked lines. Remove the siding in the cut-out area.

Step E: Install the Display Piece

1. Attach two pieces of angle iron to each corner of the frame of the stained glass, using 1½" galvanized deck screws. Make sure the top of each angle iron is flush with the top of the frame.

2. Position the stained glass piece within the opening, aligning the front edge of the frame with the front edge of the pickets. Secure the stained glass piece by driving screws through the angle iron and into the frame.

Step F: Add Decorative Trim

Set the decorative trim in place, concealing the joints between the pickets and the frame of the stained glass piece. Drill pilot holes and carefully

D. Position the stained glass piece within the frame and drill holes to mark the corners. Connect the corners and use a circular saw to cut out the opening.

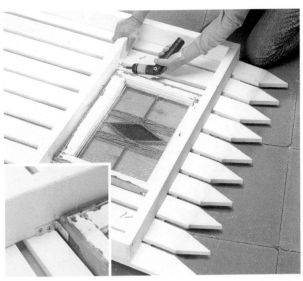

E. Attach angle irons to the display piece; drive screws through the angle iron and into the frame to secure the display piece.

F. Cut trim boards to fit and nail them into position to cover the gaps between the pickets and the display piece.

G. Install the latch hardware on the gate post, then mark the catch positions on the gate; install the catch on the gate siding.

nail the trim in place, using corrosion-resistant finish nails.

Step G: Hang the Gate

1. Measure and mark the hinge positions on the gate. Drill pilot holes and drive screws to secure the hinges to the gate.

2. Shim the gate into position, centered within the opening. Use a level to make sure the gate is level and plumb. Mark the post to indicate the hinge screw positions, then drill pilot holes. Fasten the hinges to the post, using the screws provided with the hinge hardware.

3. Position the catch hardware on the opposite post. Mark the screw positions and drill pilot holes; drive screws to secure the latch in place.

4. Mark the latch positions on the gate. Drill pilot holes and secure the catch, using the screws provided with the hardware.

Arched Gate

With its height and strategically placed opening, this gate is a great choice for maintaining privacy and enhancing security with style. No ordinary "peephole," the decorative cast iron provides a stunning accent and gives you the opportunity to see who's heading your way or passing by. The arch of the gate also adds contrast to the fence line and draws attention to the entryway.

This gate is best suited to a situation where you can position it over a hard surface, such as a sidewalk or driveway. The combined weight of the lumber and the cast iron makes for a heavy gate. To avoid sagging and to ease the gate's swing, you'll need to include a wheel on the latch side of the gate. Over a solid surface such as concrete or asphalt, the wheel will help you open and close the gate easily.

Shaping the top of the arch is a simple matter: Just enlarge the pattern provided on page 250 and trace it onto the siding. Then cut the shape, using a jig saw.

This piece of cast iron came from a banister we found at a salvage yard. We used a reciprocating saw with a metal-cutting blade to cut it to a usable size.

TOOLS & MATERIALS

- Tape measure
- Circular saw
- Paintbrushes & roller
- Hammer
- Chisel
- Drill
- Jig saw
- Level
- Framing square
- Spring clamps
- Caulk gun
- Salvaged piece of ornamental metal
- Paint, stain, or sealer

- Pressure-treated, cedar, or redwood lumber:
  2×4s (5×10 cm), 10 ft. (3 m) (3)
  1×4s (2.5×10 cm), 8 ft. (2.5 m) (13)
- Posterboard or cardboard
- Construction adhesive
- 16d nails

- 1¼" (3 cm) corrosion-resistant deck screws
- 2" (5 cm) corrosion-resistant deck screws
- 1½" (4 cm) mending plates (6)
- 2½" (6.5 cm) bolts and nuts (6)
- Gate wheel
- Hinge & latch hardware
- Gate handle
- Finish nails

HOW TO BUILD AN ARCHED GATE

Step A: Prepare the Lumber

1. Measure the opening between the gate posts and determine the finished size of your gate. (Check the packaging of your hinge and latch hardware for clearance allowances.) Compare your actual dimensions to those in the diagram below, then check the cutting list and make any necessary adjustments. Cut the lumber for the gate.

2. Paint, stain, or seal the pieces on all sides and edges. Let them dry thoroughly.

Step B: Build the Frame

1. Lay out the parts of the frame and mark the

A. *Measure the gate opening and finalize the dimensions of the gate. Cut the pieces, and then paint, stain, or seal the lumber.*

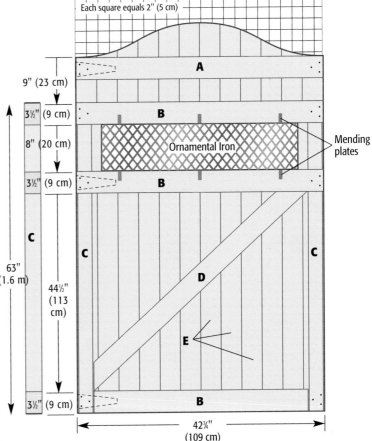

B. *Set the blade depth on a circular saw to ¾" (2 cm). Mark the joint, then make a cut every ⅛ to ¼" (3 to 6 mm) in the joint area. Remove the waste material, using a hammer and chisel.*

		Cutting List		
Key	**Part**	**Type**	**Size**	**Number**
A	Siding brace	1×4 (2.5×10 cm)	42¾" (1.09 m)	1
B	Horizontal braces	2×4 (5×10 cm)	42¾" (1.09 m)	3
C	Vertical braces	2×4 (5×10 cm)	63" (1.6 m)	2
D	Diagonal brace	2×4 (5×10 cm)	6 ft. (1.83 m)	1
E	Siding	1×4 (2.5×10 cm)	8 ft. (2.44 m)	12

cutting lines for the half-lap joints (see diagram, page 87). To make a half-lap joint, set the depth of a circular saw to ¾" (2 cm) and cut along the marked line; make a cut approximately every ⅛ to ¼" (3 to 6 mm), working from the end of the board or joint area back toward that first cut. Remove the waste material and smooth the cut surface, using a hammer and chisel. Repeat with each of the marked joints.

2. Position the pieces of the frame and measure from one corner to the diagonally opposite corner. Repeat at the opposite corners. Adjust the pieces until these measurements are equal, which indicates the frame is square. Secure each joint, using 1¼" corrosion-resistant deck screws.

Step C: Add the Diagonal Brace & Wheel

1. Position a 2 × 4 so it runs from the bottom of the hinge side of the frame to the first horizontal brace on the latch side. Mark the angle of the cutting lines, then cut the brace to fit, using a circular saw.

2. Toenail the brace into position, using 1¼" corrosion-resistant deck screws.

3. Screw a gate wheel into the vertical support on the latch side of the frame.

Step D: Add Siding & Cut the Display Opening

1. Clamp a 2 × 4 across the bottom of the frame to act as a reference for the length of the siding. Position the 1 × 4s even with the lower edge of the clamped 2 × 4; use 16d nails as spacers between boards. For each 1 × 4, drive three 2" corrosion-resistant deck screws at each horizontal brace.

2. Working from the back side, mark a line across the siding, 9" from the top of the gate. Run a bead of construction adhesive on the siding; position the brace along the line and clamp it in place. When the adhesive is dry, drive two screws through each piece of siding and into the brace.

3. Starting 15" down from the top of the gate, mark an opening to fit the display piece (the opening shown here is 9¼ × 35"). Use a framing square to make sure the opening is square and centered on the front of the gate.

4. Set the depth on a circular saw to ¾" (the thickness of the siding), and cut along the marked lines. Remove the siding in the cut-out area.

Step E: Shape the Top of the Gate

1. Using the grid method or a photocopier, enlarge the pattern on page 250 and transfer it to a large piece of posterboard or cardboard.

2. Cut out the shape, then trace it onto the top of the gate. Cut the siding to shape, using a jig saw.

Step F: Install the Display Piece

1. Drill three equally spaced holes across the top and bottom of the cast iron piece. To drill into cast iron, start with a small bit and move through increasingly larger bits, drilling slowly and wearing safety goggles.

C. *Position a diagonal brace from the bottom of the hinge side to the top of the first horizontal brace of the frame. Mark and cut the brace, then fasten it in place, using 1¼" corrosion-resistant deck screws.*

D. *Add the siding—use 16d nails as spacers and 2" corrosion-resistant deck screws to secure the boards to the frame. Add the siding brace, then cut out the siding in the display area (inset).*

2. Set the cast iron into place and mark corresponding holes onto the horizontal braces at the top and bottom of the cutout. Remove the cast iron and drill a hole at each mark, drilling all the way through the frame.

3. Set the cast iron back into position and line up the holes. For each hole, insert a bolt through a 1½" mending plate, the cast iron, and then the frame. On the back side of the gate, secure the bolts with nuts. Adjust the mending plates so they are square, then mark and drill through the siding and the frame. Install a bolt in each hole, again using nuts to secure the bolts on the back of the gate.

Step G: Hang the Gate

1. Mount the hinges on the gate. Measure and mark the hinge positions. Drill pilot holes and drive screws to secure the hinges to the gate.

2. Shim the gate into position, centered within the opening. Use a level to make sure the gate is level and plumb; test to be sure the wheel can roll freely. Mark the post to indicate the hinge screw positions, then drill pilot holes. Fasten the hinges to the post, using the screws provided with the hinge hardware.

3. Position the latch hardware on the opposite post. Mark the screw positions and drill pilot holes; drive screws to secure the latch in place.

4. Mark the catch positions on the gate. Drill pilot holes and secure the catch, using the screws provided with the hardware.

5. Install a gate handle, according to manufacturer's instructions.

F. *Drill holes through the cast iron and the lumber, then bolt the cast iron into place.*

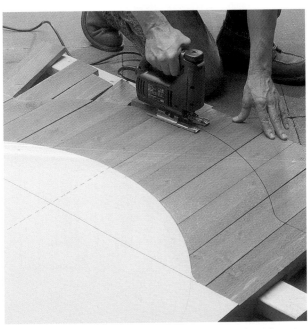

E. *Make a template and transfer the arch shape to the siding. Cut along the marked lines, using a jig saw.*

G. *Mount the hinges on the gate and shim it into position. Fasten the hinges to the post, then install the latch hardware on the gate and post.*

Trellis Gate Combination

This trellis gate combination is a grand welcome to any yard. But don't let its ornate appearance fool you—the simple components create an impression far beyond the skills and materials involved in its construction.

This gate is best suited to a location where it will receive plenty of sunlight to ensure an abundant canopy of foliage. It's best to choose perennials rather than annuals, since they will produce more luxurious growth over

time. Heirloom roses are a good choice, providing a charming complement to the gate's old-fashioned look and air of elegance.

Larger, traditional styles of hardware that show-case well against the painted wood also will enhance the gate's impressive presentation. The hardware and the millwork that we used are available at most building centers, but you might want to check architectural salvage shops. They may have unique pieces that add another touch of character to the piece.

As with most of our projects, you can alter the dimensions of this project to fit an existing opening. Just recalculate the materials and cutting lists, and make sure you have enough lumber to accommodate the changes.

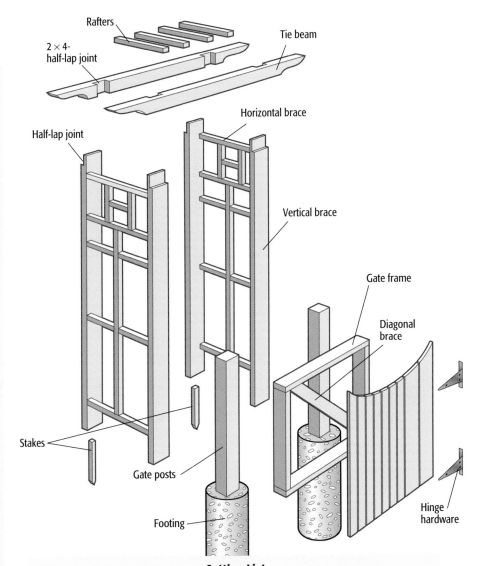

Rafters

2 × 4-half-lap joint

Tie beam

Half-lap joint

Horizontal brace

Vertical brace

Gate frame

Diagonal brace

Stakes

Gate posts

Footing

Hinge hardware

TOOLS & MATERIALS

- Tape measure
- Circular saw
- Paintbrush
- Bar clamps
- Drill
- Carpenter's level
- Framing square
- Jig saw
- Hammer
- Chisel
- Hand maul
- Spring clamps
- Pressure-treated, cedar, or redwood lumber:
  - 2 × 2s (5 × 5 cm), 8 ft. (2.5 m) (8)
  - 2 × 4s (5 × 10 cm), 8 ft. (2.5 m) (9)
  - 1 × 4s (2.5 × 10 cm), 8 ft. (2.5 m) (4)
  - 1 × 6 (2.5 × 15 cm), 8 ft. (2.5 m) (1)
  - 1 × 2 (2.5 × 5 cm), 4 ft. (1.25 m) (1)
- Paint, stain, or sealer
- Stakes & string
- 24" (60 cm) pressure-treated stakes (2)
- 3" (7.5 cm) corrosion-resistant lag screws
- Cardboard or posterboard
- Sandpaper
- 2½" corrosion-resistant deck screws
- Victorian millwork brackets (2)
- Corrosion-resistant 6d finish nails
- 1½" (6.5 cm) corrosion-resistant deck screws
- Hinge hardware
- Gate handle
- Flexible PVC pipe

Cutting List			
Part	**Type**	**Length**	**Number**
Frames			
Horizontal braces	2 × 2 (5 × 5 cm)	12" (30.5 cm)	2
	2 × 2	15¾" (40 cm)	8
	2 × 2	33" (83.8 cm)	6
Vertical braces	2 × 2	17" (43.2 cm)	4
	2 × 2	54½" (1.38 m)	2
	2 × 4 (5 × 10 cm)	87½" (2.22 m)	4
Stop	1 × 2 (2.5 × 5 cm)	46½" (1.18 m)	1
Top			
Tie beams	2 × 4	72¾" (1.85 m)	2
Rafters	2 × 2	33" (83.8 cm)	4
Gate			
Horizontal braces	2 × 4	40½" (1.03 m)	2
Vertical braces	2 × 4	32¾" (83.2 cm)	2
Diagonal brace	2 × 4	49½" (1.26 m)	1
Siding	1 × 4 (2.5 × 10 cm)	45¼" (1.15 m)	7
	1 × 6 (2.5 × 15 cm)	45¼" (1.15 m)	2

©Saxon Holt

A. *Cut and lay out the pieces for each side of the trellis frame, then secure each joint with 2½" corrosion-resistant deck screws.*

HOW TO BUILD A TRELLIS GATE
Step A: Assemble the Trellis Frames

1. Measure the opening between the gate posts and determine the finished size of your gate and trellis. Compare your dimensions to the ones in the diagram on page 91, then check the cutting list and make any necessary adjustments. (The tie beams for the trellis should be about 32" (82 cm) longer than the width of the gate.) Cut the lumber for the trellis and gate.

2. Paint, stain, or seal the pieces on all sides and edges. Let them dry thoroughly.

3. Lay out one side of the trellis, following the diagram on page 91. Mark the cutting lines and cut the joints (for more information on lap joints, see pages 87 and 88), then set the frame back together. When you're satisfied with the layout and sure the frame is square, secure the joints, using two 2½" galvanized deck screws in each joint.

4. Repeat #3 to build the remaining trellis frame.

Step B: Anchor the Frame to the Gate Posts

1. Referring to the diagram and to your own gate measurements, mark the positions of the trellis frame on the ground, using stakes and string. Make

B. *Position the trellis frames, clamping them against the gate posts. Attach the frame to the posts with 3" lag screws.*

C. *Square the trellis frames, then secure the free end of each frame to stakes, using 3" lag screws.*

sure the layout is square by measuring from corner to corner and adjusting the stakes until these diagonal measurements are equal.

2. Set one trellis frame into position, with the inside face of the frame flush with the inside face of the gate post. Drive a 24" pressure-treated stake behind the opposite side of the frame to hold the trellis in position. Drill three evenly spaced pilot holes through the frame and into the gate post. Attach the frame to the post, using 3" lag screws.

3. Repeat #1 and #2 to attach the other trellis frame to the opposite post.

Step C: Secure the Free Sides of the Frames

1. Check the position of the free sides of the frames and measure the diagonals to ensure the layout is square.

2. Clamp each frame to its stake and check the frame for level. Adjust as necessary. When the trellis frame is level, drill pilot holes and attach the frames to the stakes, using 3" lag screws.

Step D: Install the Tie Beams

1. Using the grid method or a photocopier, enlarge the pattern at right, and transfer it to a large piece of cardboard. Cut out the pattern, then trace the shape

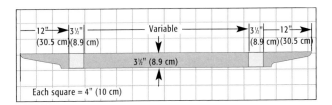

onto the ends of each 2 × 4 tie beam.

2. Cut the beams to shape, using a jig saw. Mark and cut the lap joints as described in Step A. Sand the cut surfaces, then touch them up with paint, stain, or sealer and let them dry thoroughly.

3. Position a tie beam flush with the top of the posts. Clamp the beam into place and drill pilot holes through it and into each post. Drive five 1½" corrosion-resistant deck screws into each joint to attach the tie beam to the posts.

4. Repeat #3 to install the remaining tie beam.

Step E: Attach the Rafters

Hold a 2 × 2 in position between the tie beams, flush with the top of the beams. Drill pilot holes through the tie beams, one into each end of the rafter; secure the rafter with 2½" corrosion-resistant

D. *Cut 2 × 4s, using the grid pattern, for tie beams. Dado each to accommodate the trellis frame post tops, then clamp into position and attach with five 1½" corrosion-resistant deck screws at each joint.*

E. *Attach four evenly spaced 2 × 2s between the tie beams for rafters, using 2½" corrosion-resistant deck screws.*

deck screws. Repeat, placing a total of four evenly spaced rafters across the span of the tie beams.

Step F: Add the Trim

Set a millwork bracket into place at each of the corners between the tie beams and the trellis frame posts. Drill pilot holes and secure the brackets, using finish nails.

Step G: Build the Gate Frame

1. Lay out the parts of the gate frame and measure from one corner to the diagonally opposite corner. Repeat at the opposite corners. Adjust the pieces until these measurements are equal and the frame is square. Secure each joint, using 2½" corrosion-resistant deck screws.

2. Position a 2 × 4 so it runs from the bottom of the hinge side of the frame to the first horizontal brace on the latch side. Mark the angle of the cutting lines, then cut the brace to fit, using a circular saw. Use 2½" corrosion-resistant deck screws to secure the brace into position.

Step H: Add the Siding

1. Clamp a 2 × 4 across the bottom of the frame to act as a reference for the length of the pickets.

F. *Add millwork brackets at each corner where the tie beams and the trellis frame posts meet. Secure with finish nails.*

G. *Lay out the gate frame pieces, check for square, and secure the joints with 2½" corrosion-resistant deck screws. Mark and cut the brace, then screw it in place, using 2½" corrosion-resistant deck screws.*

H. *Clamp a 2 × 4 across the bottom of the gate frame as a guide, then attach the siding. Begin with two 1 × 6s on the hinge side, then finish with 1 × 4s. Use scraps of ⅜" plywood as spacers.*

Position the siding flush with the lower edge of the clamped 2 × 4.

2. Align the right edge of a 1 × 6 flush with the right edge of the frame. Drill pilot holes and attach the siding to the frame, using 1½" corrosion-resistant deck screws.

3. Set scraps of ⅜" plywood in place as spacers, then add a second 1 × 6. Continuing to use the ⅜" plywood as spacers, cover the remainder of the frame with 1 × 4 siding.

Step I: Hang the Gate

1. Measure and mark the hinge positions on the gate. Drill pilot holes and drive screws to secure the hinges to the gate.

2. On the handle-side post, clamp a 1 × 2 in place to act as a stop for the gate. Shim the gate into position, centered within the opening. Use a carpenter's level to make sure the gate is level and plumb and the stop is properly positioned. Mark the position of the stop and set the gate aside. Drill pilot holes and secure the stop to the post, using 2½" corrosion-resistant deck screws.

3. With the gate shimmed back into position, mark the hinge-side post to indicate the hinge screw locations, then drill pilot holes. Fasten the hinges to the post, using the screws provided with the hinge hardware.

Step J: Shape the Siding & Add the Gate Handle

1. Cut a piece of flexible PVC pipe 52½" (133 cm) long (or 12" [30.5 cm] longer than the width of your gate). Clamp the PVC at the top of the outside edges of the last piece of siding on each side of the gate.

2. Tack a nail just above the first horizontal brace of the frame at the center of the gate. If this happens to be between two pieces of siding, set a scrap behind the siding to hold the nail. Adjust the PVC until it fits just below the nail and creates a pleasing curve.

3. Trace the curve of the PVC onto the face of the siding. Remove the pipe and cut along the marked line, using a jig saw. Sand the tops of the siding and repair the finish as necessary.

4. Mark the handle location on the gate. Drill pilot holes and secure the handle, using the screws provided by the manufacturer.

I. *Clamp a 1 × 2 to the latch-side gate post and secure with 1½" corrosion-resistant deck screws.*

J. *Clamp the ends of a length of PVC pipe at each end of the gate top. Deflect the pipe down to create the curve, and trace. Cut to shape, using a jig saw.*

Water Features

Every living thing responds to the presence of water. Children and adults will reach out to touch a waterfall or pause to catch the reflections in a peaceful garden pond. Wildlife, given the right circumstances, will make homes nearby. Adding a garden pool is a wonderful way to bring the sights, sounds, and feel of water to a yard or garden.

The style of a garden pool should complement its location as well as your personal style. Some pools lend themselves to the symmetry of formal landsapes, others mimic nature in their spontaneity and fit well with more casual landscapes. Spend some time dreaming and imagining before settling down to plan your project. And remember to factor in your commitment to on-going maintenance, lest your dreams be bigger than time and tolerance realistically allow.

A quick note: All of the design and building techniques described in this chapter will help you establish an environment appropriate for freshwater fish, but we don't specifically address water quality, plants for a fish pond, or the on-going care of fish. For advice and expertise on those matters, talk with your fish supplier or check sources such as the Internet and other books.

Designing & Planning a Water Feature

Like many activities, success in water gardening is rooted in good preparation. Good planning is essential to reaping the full rewards of a water feature and adequately nurturing aquatic plants. While it may be motivating to pick up a shovel and start digging out a streambed, knowing how that step fits into the overall project makes the process easier and more successful.

At first glance, it may be obvious where a water garden fits into your landscape. It's a good idea, however, to confirm a proper location using the following criteria:

Grade: Place ponds or pools on level ground near the highest point in the yard, a place high above the water table and safe from any runoff. Streams or watercourses are best on gentle slopes.

Climate: Water gardens need 5 to 6 hours of sun daily.

Soil: Sample soil at your proposed site to determine its type. Clay soil provides a stable base for pond and pool liners. Plan to stabilize sandy soil before installing a liner.

Utilities: Have utility lines marked by your utility providers. Move or adjust the dimensions or even the site of the water garden so it doesn't interfere with the utility lines.

Concept to Design

Create a garden plan on graph paper or using a computer software program developed for landscape design. Good design mixes common sense with a few universal rules while recognizing past successes learned through experience: If the concept and vision feel right, they probably are; if you're going with conventional wisdom, the probability of your success increases.

Begin with a base plan to indicate everything that exists on your site now. Start with a copy of your property's survey for an accurate rendering—they're usually available from the local building department—or measure your property and carefully transfer the distances to scaled graph paper. Mark the placement of your home, other permanent structures, and features you plan to retain on the site: existing trees, planting beds, paths, and decks or patios. Mark the location of all underground utility lines. Accurately record the dimensions and locations of these components. Add to this the information you've discovered

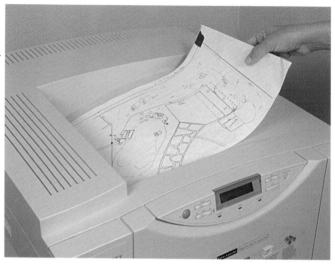

Use a photocopier's enlarging and reducing function to increase the scale of your plans and make details clear. Use computer software design programs to draw clean, clear site plans and detail construction plans.

about your garden: the sun and shade pattern, the wind direction, and any changes of elevation on your site.

Place an overlay of tissue paper on your base plan, or make several photocopies of it for experimentation. Try different shapes and placements for your water garden. Consider different configurations, sizes, and styles. Once you're satisfied it meets your needs for use and purpose, transfer the shape, scale, and placement of the feature to a fresh tissue overlay. This will be the master plan for your water feature—use it to prepare details and elevation drawings.

Working on your master plan, use different colored pencils to indicate existing features and structures and those that will be newly built. Show existing and new plants by indicating their planting location with a point, then drawing a colored circle around the point to indicate their spread when they grow to their mature size.

Date your plan. Record later adjustments in another color. Date the addendum for a clear record of your decisions. Once you're satisfied with your design, make photocopies, using the machine's enlarging function to make detailed drawings at larger scales.

If your project is complex, make separate detail drawings for each construction element. Show elevations—a cutaway profile—of the site, material specifications for utility runs, and construction details.

Remember that most locales require you to comply with regulations, codes, and covenants. Use your plan when applying for building permits and approvals, and when inspectors come to call.

Try out your ideas on paper before you proceed to the garden. Photocopies of your base plan make exploring ideas easy. Use tracing paper overlays to sketch your ideas in colored pencil. After you have decided on a shape, layout, and design, copy your working diagram onto the base plan.

Planning & Designing a Water Garden

The purpose of an accurate, scaled bird's-eye view plan for your water garden is to specify every necessary component. It's your single reference for site placement of elements, choice of building materials and plants, and construction details. It also may be required for permits and inspections. The plan serves as an archive record of your project's specifications after completion. To create your plan on paper, follow these steps:

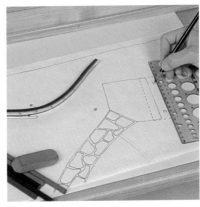

A. *On scaled graph paper, draw the site and its measurements in the general area of the feature. Include existing structures, trees, and all utility lines, plus changes of elevation. This is your base plan.*

B. *On a tissue paper overlay or photocopy, experiment with different options for your feature's location, style, and structure until you're satisfied.*

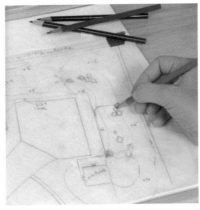

C. *Transfer your final measurements to a clean overlay. Draw electrical supplies and water sources, the path of your recirculating pipe, and the position of the skimmer intake and water discharge.*

D. *Use colored pencils to mark edge materials and landscape plant choices around the pond. Remember that the pond requires full sun and access. Next, choose aquatic plants and indicate their planting points.*

E. *Transfer your plant selections to a list for easy reference and for use when you visit your aquatic nursery. Note your plant requirements, including bloom color, season of bloom, variety, selection, and care needs.*

Waterproof Liners

(right) Liners—whether rigid and preformed or flexible—underlay nearly all water features. They retain water, of course, but also prevent soil from entering the feature. Lined features usually are bordered by rock and should be layered with gravel, both to disguise the liner and to protect it from sunlight.

(bottom) Waterproof flexible liners underlay most natural-appearing water gardens. The liners are made of EPDM, a flexible butyl rubber material similar to tire inner tubes. It is easy to lay and trim. With proper installation and protection from sunlight, it usually will last 20 years or more.

The primary purpose of a waterproof liner is to enclose and retain water. It also helps maintain the water's quality. There are two types of liners, flexible and rigid.

Flexible liners are sheets that conform to any water garden's size, shape, or depth. They fold or crease to accommodate curves, marginal shelves, and other contours. They are ideal for large, asymmetrical garden ponds and pools, and especially are well suited for streams and watercourses. The best flexible liners are made from butyl or EPDM rubber. Thinner PVC and polyethylene liners are unsuitable for pond or stream water features. Rigid liners are best for small projects and raised pools.

Liners are available in dark and light colors; darker colors tend to appear more natural, enhance reflection, and allude to greater depth. Protect all liners from the sun to keep them from aging. Water, rock, plants, and edging materials help shield the liner. A liner's topmost section can become exposed if the water level drops from evaporation. The toughest liner materials—rigid fiberglass and flexible butyl rubber—usually can withstand short-term UV exposure without incurring cracks, leaks, or other damage.

Selecting Pool Liners

Pool liners are available in three common forms: rigid plastic, EPDM flexible rubber, and PVC flexible plastic. Rigid liners, also called molded and preformed liners, are created in a mold with a set shape and have limited flexibility. The best flexible liners are those made of rugged, durable, EPDM rubber—a tire inner-tubelike material. They will last many years and allow you to create complex shapes. PVC liners are inexpensive, easy to puncture, and require replacement before either other type. Bring your garden plan and site measurements, and consider these details when choosing a liner for your water feature:

A. *Rigid pools are made from plastic and more durable fiberglass. Available in a limited number of sizes and shapes, they generally have modest water capacities and appear larger out of the ground than when installed.*

B. *The best flexible liners are made of EPDM. Choose liners that will span your feature's length and width, after adding double its maximum depth to each measurement. Avoid joining two liners, if possible, because such points are prone to leaks.*

C. *Select dark colors that create an illusion of depth and enhance reflection. You will cover the entire liner with gravel and boulders to protect it from UV exposure that could cause premature aging.*

D. *Consider combining smaller pools to create larger features, as you would to construct the header and reservoir pools of a stream. Flexible liners appear most natural for home applications; the preformed liners are quick and easy to install.*

Recirculating Pumps

Pumps circulate the water in your feature. They are reliable and easy to install, adjust, and maintain. Besides powering fountains or streams, pumps circulate water through pipes to submerged filters and skimmers, where the water is cleaned and recirculated. A pump also comes in handy when it's time to clean the pool or pond. Attach a hose to the pump's cleanout outlet, and it pumps out the water.

Most residential water gardens use a submersible, underwater pump. It sits on raised legs or a platform above the bottom to reduce the hazard of sediment and debris clogs. The pump draws water through an intake pipe and a filter screen, which catches debris that could clog and damage motor parts, and pushes it to another location through a pressurized delivery pipe. Surface-mounted pumps, located in concealed enclosures above ground and away from the feature, are more common in water gardens with large streams and multiple elements, or those that cover a large area.

Select a pump based on its capacity, which is measured in gallons per hour (gph) (liters per hour [lph]). Some pumps' flow rates may be listed in gallons per minute [gpm] (liters per minute [lpm]). If your pump will lift water a considerable height, also consider its pressure of flow rate, or head height. Generally, a pump should be able to circulate half of the water volume contained in your feature in an hour's time. Moving water uphill, some distance, or to deliver a broad fountain pattern typically requires pumps with higher gph (lph) and pressure ratings.

Pumps move water from the reservoir pool to the header pool, lifting it in the process. Most pumps run continuously and are maintenance-free and durable. Choose one based on the volume of water in your feature.

Selecting Pumps for Water Features

A. *Calculate the volume of water in your pond or stream by multiplying its average length, width, and depth. The pump's flow rate in gph (lph) should equal or exceed the total pond volume. Even large-volume pumps are of modest size. The pump shown is an above-ground model rated at 1,000 gph (3,875 lph).*

Know its purpose before you choose a pump. Some units deliver a high volume at low pressure, best suited for streams; others a low volume at high pressure, better suited for fountains. Understand the purpose and you will be able to pinpoint the correct unit. Pump makers have simplified the process by offering compatible piping and related components. Use only components designed and rated for outdoor and underground use. To choose a pump, follow these steps:

B. *The best choice for most water features is a submersible pump. High-efficiency models are designed to use less power and are most reliable. Choose a pump with raised feet around its intake to reduce the potential for sediment clogs. Plan to install it in a skimmer intake box or mounted on a raised platform.*

C. *For complex features, or for sites where maintenance access is restricted, choose an above-ground pump. Locate it near a power supply, close to the intake. If needed, enclose it in a weatherproof housing.*

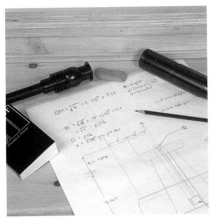

D. *For fountains, calculate the height and diameter of your desired spray pattern. Check information contained with the spray head assembly, as most fountain packages provide general pump guidelines.*

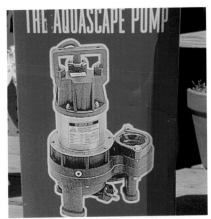

E. *Check the information on the housing and package for the pump's electrical requirements, the necessary size and type of piping, and compatibility with accessories.*

Fountains & Waterspouts

Basically, all fountains operate identically: a concealed recirculating pump designed to deliver a low volume of water at a high pressure is attached to one of the various styles of nozzles or fountainheads, creating the desired effect. Waterspouts—also called bubblers, simple sprays, and splash boxes—have a water reservoir buried underground. The reservoir contains the pump that pushes water through tubing to the waterspout, replicating a natural, bubbling spring.

Fountains either have an integral, dedicated pump or are connected by a delivery pipe to a remote pump fitted with other components. The size of the pump dictates the height and intensity of the spray, so it's important to select the proper-sized pump for your desired pattern. Even so, the flow rate on many pumps can be adjusted within a range, allowing you some control over the fountain's pattern. Generally, keep the height of the spray less than one-half the width of the pool or pond.

Your choice of the fountain or waterspout itself is governed by your imagination and compatibility within your design. Fountains generally are best suited for

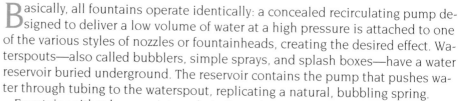

formal water features, such as the center of a pool. Waterspouts do well in more casual settings. These easily created features are great for close up contemplative viewing in such locations as a deck, patio, or balcony. They add the sensual qualities of moving water and its burbling, magic music to small-space gardens.

Fountains exist in a host of patterns, from dramatic rotating jets and geysers to tiered domes, rings, bell and tulip shapes, and arching streams; fountains contained within statues or other decorative ornaments add new design elements to your garden. Match the scale of your fountain and its water display to the site you have selected and to the surrounding plants and structures.

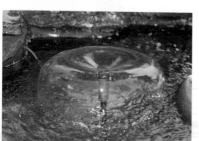

Keep other considerations in mind as you choose your fountain or waterspout. If you plan to include fish or plants, avoid fountains constructed with lead fixtures; lead leaches toxins into the water that are a hazard to plants and animals alike. Remember also that while fish can tolerate moving water, some deep-water plants, surface floaters, and oxygenating plants prefer still water with little current. Choose fountains with deep reservoirs if you plan to plant them with aquatic plants; the greater water volume will help keep the quality of the water pure and healthy.

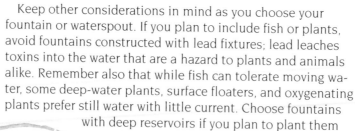

A wide choice of spray patterns are available from many garden centers, water garden nurseries, and home improvement stores: (left, top to bottom) A spray bubbler, bell, and a two-tier spray.
(right, top to bottom) Two-level Tiffany, and a square pattern.

A. *Choose a fountainhead style, diameter, and spray pattern. For pumps acquired separately, choose a pump rated to deliver water at a flow rate and pressure matching the head fixture. The power cord length should match your site.*

Selecting a Fountain

The width of your fountain's pool should be more than twice the height of the fountainhead to avoid water overspray and wind carried mist. The exposed portions of most fountains are made from reconstituted stone, precast concrete, plastic, or fiberglass, allowing you many options for design, durability, and weight. The hidden, operational components often are included or available separately in kits. Look for these elements as you select a fountain for your water feature:

B. *Pick your fountain basin with the scale of your site in mind. It should include still water areas where aquatic plants may be positioned away from falling water and currents.*

C. *If you plan to use lighting to provide drama at nighttime, choose a fountain made of a material that will permit drilling holes for wiring.*

D. *For in-pond fountains, choose a pump-fountainhead unit with a spray pattern that fits your pond and design.*

E. *To install a fountain on a deck or other raised surface, choose a model light enough to be supported when filled with water or construct a masonry base.*

Planning Power for the Site

The size of the pump and the demands of other electrical features determine your overall power needs and whether you need to add a dedicated GFCI-protected circuit or can transform power to 12-volt DC form. Confirm specific requirements with your local building department regarding distance between the outlet and the water feature, whether conduit with insulated wire or cable is to be used, and permit requirements. Within the requirements imposed by local codes, follow these steps:

WHAT'S YOUR LOAD?

Add the electrical demands of all the components to determine your total load demand. If your load exceeds 15 amps, you'll need a dedicated, 120-volt alternating current (AC) circuit drawn from the main electrical service panel; higher loads may require a 240-volt circuit. Very small demands, however, may be supplied by a low-voltage direct current (DC) transformer, which changes alternating current to direct. Install all outdoor outlets with a required ground-fault circuit interrupter (GFCI) and insulating ground, which automatically shut off electricity to the entire circuit when the power is interrupted, surges, or short-circuits. Before adding a circuit, always note the overall load demands of your home, which are indicated on the electric service panel.

A. *Add the requirements for wattage, voltage, and amperage listed on the label of each device in the system. Reserve 25% extra for future needs.*

B. *If you need a new circuit, check the service panel for an available breaker slot to service your feature.*

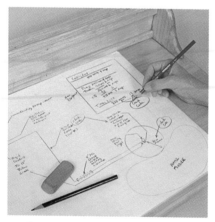

C. *If an existing circuit has sufficient capacity, plan the wiring run on paper as an extension and obtain permits before proceeding, or consult with an electrician.*

D. *Note the distance between the source and the feature's outlet, and itemize needed materials: junction boxes, outlets, conduit and wire or cable, stripping tools, and a multimeter tester.*

Accents

Properly finishing a water garden is an important aspect of its construction and is essential to its overall appearance and enjoyment. Plan all your finishes and garden additions in advance, including edging materials and accessories, so their needs can be accommodated during construction. All additions should serve your garden's purpose and be selected to suit your garden style.

How the water feature is edged affects its function and beauty. Your selection of edging materials is an opportunity to showcase your personal creativity. As a practical matter, edging materials cover the edge of the liner, mask the line around the feature's perimeter and the surrounding soil, and protect the liner from exposure to the sun. Aesthetically, the material choice can make edges clear and distinct—usually best suited for a formal garden—or help blend and obscure the line to create a more natural appearance. Edging materials include coping stones, boulders, ceramic tile, sandy beaches, turf grass borders, and pebble shorelines. Consider combining several different materials and textures, providing both visual interest and a range of surfaces for plants and wildlife, extending the enjoyment of the garden and providing access to the water.

Accessories include large and small touches that make your garden fit your needs. Large construction projects such as decks and patios often are combined with water gardens, but many water feature accessories are smaller projects. To gain access to your garden and pond, consider a bridge or a series of boulders that double as stepping stones peeking out from the water. If your garden is to be a place of quiet reflection, install benches or other seating nearby. Artwork—from fountains, statues, and viewing balls to original sculptures—adds personality to your water garden. Carefully placed urns, containers, planters, and other elements add both visual interest to the feature and increase the variety of landscape plants that you can use.

Surface lighting (below left) and submerged fixtures (below right) both are wired to a low-voltage DC transformer. Using low voltage avoids hazard of shock and allows easy installation using simple tools.

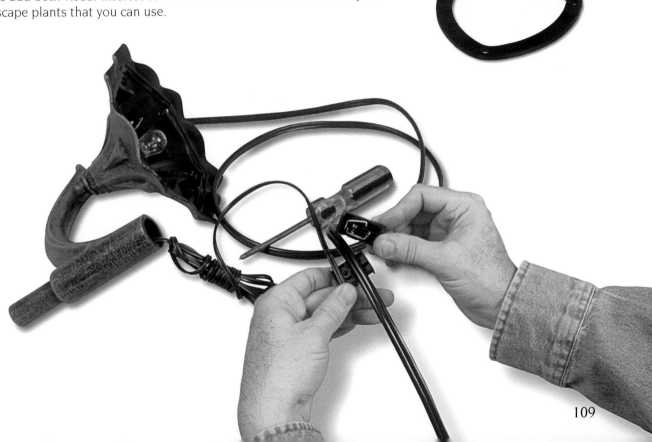

Installation & Construction

This section presents hands-on instruction for building the structural features of your water garden, from simple, freestanding, self-contained gardens to sophisticated waterfalls with lights, from installing a watertight streambed to staging a fountain, and each step in between. It includes easy to follow, step-by-step instructions for bringing utilities to the site and installing both rigid and flexible liners. Information on assembling pumps and fountains is included, along with methods for finishing the edge of the feature so it provides safe, secure access while blending nicely into the garden.

Depending on your skills and comfort with such activities as excavation, basic carpentry, plumbing, and electrical systems, you may pick and choose which segments of your water garden construction you'll do yourself. If you decide to seek expert help or a tradesperson for some aspects of your instal-lation, you'll still find this chapter helpful as a guide to what occurs and why. Understanding the entire construction process allows you to properly articulate your plans and expectations, and inspect the work as it is completed.

For the most part, the tasks outlined here apply to all water gardens, regardless of size or style: bring utilities to the site, lay out the feature and excavate, install pumps and liners, and add finishing touches and accents. Depending on the complexity of your design, you might establish streambeds and install waterfalls, fountains, and lights. To gain an understanding of all the tasks involved and to establish your construction schedule, review the appropriate list on pages 112 and 113. Check the instructions for each step to determine the skills, tools, and equipment needed. For a basic understanding of these tasks, consider creating a self-contained water garden—it's an excellent first project.

IN THIS SECTION

Water Feature Project Planner

Conceptually, there are few limits to the types and styles of water features you may conjure, create, and enjoy. There are a few basic types of projects, however, that you can alter to fit your scale, scope, climate conditions, and personal taste. If your goal is to create a dramatic water garden with many elements, pick and choose from the steps listed for each project when planning its components. To help you plan the most common water feature construction projects, listed here are the specific steps for each of four projects:

GARDEN POND WITH PREFORMED LINER

GARDEN POND WITH FLEXIBLE LINER

SIMPLE STREAM
OR WATERCOURSE

STREAM WITH WATERFALL

Water & Electrical Supplies

Most water features need a dedicated water supply and an electrical supply nearby. Bringing a water line to the site makes maintaining water levels automatic and makes it easy to refill the pool after you clean it. To power the pump and other electrical equipment, you'll need power at the site.

Your first priority when bringing water or electricity to your site is to verify the code requirements with your local building department. The scope of your project may require a permit before you begin, as well as periodic inspections during the process. You also must locate all underground utilities before digging.

You'll make underground connections from the source—a water main or manifold—to a dedicated hose bib or water supply connection near the pool; you also may want to install an automatic refill float valve that replaces the water whenever the level drops. To prevent overfilling due to precipitation or a stuck valve, consider installing an overflow valve and a drain pipe bypass extension from the pool.

Confirm your power requirements and create a plan for running wire from your electric panel or a previously existing outlet to the site. Bury wires in an underground trench. If the trench is less than 18" (46 cm) deep, run separate conductor and grounding wires inside rigid metal or PVC conduit. For deeper trenches, run direct burial cable using conduit protection only where the cable descends into or emerges from the ground. Connect the run to an above-grade junction box near the pool. The GFCI-protected outlet should be housed in a weatherproof box at least 12" (30 cm) above grade and 30" (76 cm) or more from the pool. Before filling the trench, place flat stones to protect the buried conduit or cable against subsequent excavation or garden digging. Use only materials rated for outdoor, underground use.

To make it easier and safer to maintain your water garden, consider installing options such as above-ground shut-off or flow-controlling valves; a switch or automatic timer that controls low-voltage lighting or fountains; and a three-way switch box rather than a single outlet to accommodate future expansion.

Installing a Water Supply

Adding one or two spigots in your yard brings water right to the areas where you typically water plants or clean up garden equipment.

Your local plumbing code may have requirements for the types of pipe you can use, so check before you begin. Also, if local plumbing codes require it, apply for required permits and arrange for necessary inspections.

A. *Cut into the main water supply line and attach a compression tee, a gate valve, and a backflow preventer.*

B. *Dig a trench from the water supply to the site of the pool.*

WARNING

Electrical shock can cause fatal injury. Contact your local utility companies before digging in your yard.

TOOLS & MATERIALS

- Drill & spade bit
- Tubing cutter
- Trenching machine
- Shovel
- Soldering materials
- Copper tee fittings
- ¼" copper pipe
- 1" schedule 40 PVC pipe
- 2-part PVC primer
- Antisiphon backflow preventer
- Risers (2)
- Hose bib
- Gate valve
- Compression tee

HOW TO INSTALL A WATER SUPPLY

Step A: Tap into the Water Supply

1. Turn off the water at the household main.

2. Cut the water line and attach a compression tee, a gate valve, and an antisiphon backflow preventer to keep pond water from siphoning into your drinking supply.

NOTE: If a nearby irrigation supply line already exists, cut it and add a lateral extension to lead to the site of your pool.

Step B: Cut the Trench

Using a trenching machine (available at rental centers), dig a trench from the water supply to the site.

Step C: Run Pipe to the Site

Lay 1" (25 mm) schedule 40 PVC pipe in the trench. Join sections with 2-part PVC primer, and cement ell and tee fittings.

Step D: Bring the Pipe to Ground Level

1. Install two risers at the extension line's end.

2. Attach a hose bib to one of the risers.

3. Attach a gate valve to the other riser. (The gate valve will be connected to the pool's float valve assembly later.)

4. Turn on the water and flush any debris out of the line.

Step E: Refill the Trench

1. Carefully check the entire length of the line for leaks.

2. Backfill the trench with soil from the excavation. Tamp and settle the soil, then replant with grass or groundcover to blend in with the surrounding landscape.

C. *Cut and fit PVC pipe from the water supply to the site of the pool.*

D. *Install two risers at the end of the pipe run. Attach a hose bib to one riser and a gate valve to the other.*

E. *Check the line for leaks, then refill the trench and replace the groundcover.*

115

Installing an Electrical Supply

In most cases, you can add this outlet to an existing circuit as shown here. If that's not advisable, have an electrician add a dedicated circuit to your service panel and tap into that.

HOW TO INSTALL AN ELECTRICAL SUPPLY

Step A: Plan the Route & Dig the Trench

1. Plan a convenient route from an accessible indoor junction to the proposed site. Drill a 1" (2.54 cm)-diameter hole through an exterior wall, near the junction box.

2. Mark the underground cable run from the hole in the wall to the location for the receptacle.

3. Dig an 8 to 12" (20 to 30 cm)-wide trench along the marked route. Make the trench at least 12" deep, or as deep as required by local code.

Step B: Install the LB Connector & Conduit

1. Install the LB connector over the hole in the wall.

2. Measure and cut a length of conduit about 4" (10 cm) shorter than the distance from the LB connector to the bottom of the trench. Attach the conduit to a sweep fitting, using a compression fitting. Attach a plastic bushing to the open end of the sweep to keep the sweep's metal edges from damaging the cable.

3. Attach the conduit assembly to the bottom of the LB connector, then anchor the conduit to the wall, using pipe straps.

4. Cut a short length of conduit to extend from the LB connector, through the wall, to the inside of the house. Attach the conduit to the LB connector from the inside of the house, then attach a plastic bushing to the open end of the conduit.

Step C: Assemble & Install the Receptacle Post

1. Drill or cut a 1½" (3.8 cm) hole through the side of a 2-gallon plastic bucket, near the bottom.

2. Mount the receptacle box to the post with corrosion-resistant screws screws. Position the post in the bucket.

3. Measure and cut a length of conduit to run from the receptacle box to a point 4" (10 cm) above the base of the bucket. Attach the conduit to the receptacle box and mount it to the post with pipe straps.

4. Insert a conduit sweep through the hole in the bucket and attach it to the end of the conduit, using a compression fitting. Thread a plastic bushing onto the open end of the sweep.

5. Dig a hole at the end of the trench. Place the bucket with the post into the hole, then fill the bucket with concrete and let it dry completely.

Step D: Lay the UF Cable

1. Measure the distance from the junction box in the house out to the receptacle box. Cut a length of UF cable 2 ft. (61 cm) longer than this measurement. Strip 8" of the outer sheathing at each end of the cable.

2. Lay the cable along the bottom of the trench between the house and the site.

3. Open the cover on the LB connector and feed a fish tape down through the conduit and out of the sweep. Feed the wires through the loop in the fish tape, then wrap electrical tape around the wires up to the sheathing.

A. *Plan and mark the route from the junction box to the site. Dig a trench along the marked path.*

B. *Mount the LB connector over the hole in the wall. Assemble a length of conduit and sweep fitting.*

C. *Assemble and attach the receptacle box and conduit to the post, then position the assembly at the end of the trench and fill the bucket with concrete.*

D. *Measure and cut UF cable and lay it in the trench. Use a fish tape to pull the cable up into the LB connector.*

TOOLS & MATERIALS

- Drill with 1" bit
- Shovel
- Tape measure
- Trenching machine
- Tube cutter
- Multi-meter tester
- Wire cutters
- Utility knife
- Fish tape
- Wire strippers
- Screwdriver

- Electrical tape
- LB connector
- Metal sweeps
- 1" metal conduit (6 ft.)
- Compression fittings
- Plastic bushings
- Pipe straps
- 2-gallon bucket
- 4-ft. 4 × 4 post

- Corrosion-resistant screws
- Metal outdoor receptacle box
- Concrete mix
- UF cable
- GFCI receptacle
- Wire connectors
- Cable staples
- Grounding pigtail

4. Using the fish tape, carefully pull the end of the cable up through the conduit to the LB connector.

Step E: Fish the Cable into the Receptacle Box

1. At the other end of the trench, feed the fish tape down through the conduit and out of the sweep.

2. Attach the exposed wires to the loop in the fish tape, and secure them with electrical tape.

3. Pull the cable through the conduit up into the receptacle box. About ½" (13 mm) of cable sheathing should extend into the box.

Step F: Connect the GFCI Receptacle

1. Using wire strippers, remove ¾" (19 mm) of the wire insulation around the two insulated wires extended into the receptacle box.

2. Attach a bare copper pigtail to the grounding terminal on the back of the receptacle box. Join the two bare copper wires to the green grounding lead attached to the GFCI, using a wire connector.

3. Connect the black circuit wire to the brass

screw terminal marked LINE on the GFCI. Connect the white wire to the silver terminal marked LINE.

4. Carefully tuck all the wires into the receptacle box, then mount the receptacle. Install the cover plate.

Step G: Connect the Cable at the Junction Box

1. From inside the house, extend the fish tape through the conduit and LB connector. Attach the cable wires to the fish tape, then pull the cable into the house.

2. Anchor the cable along framing members to the junction box, using wire staples.

3. Turn off the power to the circuit serving the junction box. Remove the junction box cover.

4. Use a screwdriver to open a knockout in the side of the junction box. Pull the end of the UF cable into the box through the knockout, and secure it with a cable clamp. About ½" of the outer sheathing should extend into the box, and the individual wires should be about 8" long. (Cut away excess wire.)

5. Using a wire stripper, remove ¾" of the wire insulation from the insulated wires.

6. Unscrew the wire connector attached to the bare copper grounding wires inside the box. Position the new grounding wire alongside the existing wires and replace the wire connector.

7. Using the same technique, connect the new black wire to the existing black wires and connect the new white wire to the existing white wires. Replace the junction box cover.

Step H: Test the Current

Restore the power to the circuit, then use a multi-meter tester to measure the strength, consistency, and voltage of the current. When the installation is successful and approved, refill the trench.

E. *Using the fish tape, pull the cable through the conduit and up into the receptacle box.*

F. *Connect the GFCI by joining the grounding wires with a wire connector and connecting the black wire to the brass LINE terminals, the white wire to the silver LINE terminal.*

G. *Extend the UF cable into the junction box. Connect the new wires to the existing wires, using wire connectors.*

H. *Restore power and test the power at the receptacle.*

Pond Layout & Excavation

Mark the dimensions of your pond or stream from your garden plan, including its overall depth and the placement and size of marginal shelves. For rigid liners, trace the outline of the liner and its interior shelves onto the soil. Use a length of hose, flour, or spray paint to mark the outline.

HOW TO LAYOUT & EXCAVATE A POND

Step A: Mark the Outline

Outline the shape of the pond or stream. If you're using a symmetrical rigid liner, place it upside down on the site and mark its shape. For an irregular shaped liner, place stakes to create an outline, including any interior shelves. For flexible liners, follow the design dimensions from your garden plan.

Step B: Excavate the Site

1. Establish a level line above the excavation, using stakes, string, and a line level.

2. Excavate the entire site. If you're creating shelves, dig the entire site to the level of the shallowest shelf, then mark and dig the next deepest section. Continue excavating, creating progressively deeper sections as you move to the middle.

3. Use a straightedge and level to check the edges, shelves, and bottom for level.

Step C: Add Landscape Fabric & Sand

1. Line the base, sides, and shelves of the hole with landscape root-barrier fabric.

2. Backfill the excavation with a 4" (10 cm) layer of builder's sand. Rake the sand smooth, using the string as a level reference. Make sure the correct depth has been met at every point.

TOOLS & MATERIALS

- Stakes & string
- Tape measure
- Line level
- Shovel
- Hose, flour, or spray paint
- 4-ft. level
- Straightedge
- Rake
- Landscape fabric
- Sand

A. *Mark the outline of the liner or pool at the site.*

B. *Dig out the site and check the excavation for level.*

C. *Add a 4" (10 cm) layer of sand to the hole and rake it smooth.*

Installing a Recirculating Pump System

Locate submersible pumps in a skimmer box or within the feature, near the intake point. Place above-ground pumps within 5 ft. (1.5 m) of their intake. Bury a recirculating pipe, keeping it easily accessible, and attach a check valve to prevent siphoning.

HOW TO INSTALL A RECIRCULATING PUMP SYSTEM

Step A: Position the Skimmer

1. At the pool's edge and opposite the point of the water's entry into the pool, locate a skimmer or intake box.

2. Dig a shallow trench for the recirculating pipe, extending it from the skimmer to the pump, then to the discharge.

Step B: Lay the Pipe

1. Cut and fit PVC pipe to run from the skimmer to the pump, then to the discharge.

2. Use a two-part PVC primer and solvent to cement all junctions of pipe in the recirculating loop.

Step C: Add Fittings

Install an O-ring compression fitting to the skimmer or intake box and to the outflow box or discharge pipe. Use the adhesives, fastening materials and fittings recommended by the equipment manufacturer.

Step D: Position the Skimmer & Connect the Pump

1. Position, mark, and excavate a hole for the skimmer or intake box so the top edge of the intake will be positioned 1 to 3" (25 to 75 mm) above the future water level.

2. Set the unit in position and check it with a level. Add or remove soil as necessary to level the unit.

3. Attach the check valve to the pump, place the pump into the box, and connect the outflow hose to the recirculating pipe leading to the discharge at the header pool or waterfall.

TOOLS & MATERIALS

- Shovel
- 4-ft. level
- Skimmer or intake box
- PVC pipe as necessary
- Tape measure
- Two-part PVC primer and solvent
- O-ring compression fittings (2)
- Check valve

A. *Position a skimmer at the edge of the pool, opposite the water supply. Dig a trench between the skimmer and the pump, then on to the discharge.*

B. *Connect PVC pipe and fittings, using two-part PVC primer and solvent.*

C. *Install compression fittings on the skimmer and discharge pipe, following manufacturer's directions.*

D. *Attach the check valve and connect the outflow hose to the recirculating pipe.*

Pumps & Liners

Lasting pump operation depends on protecting the pump and its accessories from harm while keeping them accessible for routine maintenance and adjustment. Whether you're using a rigid or flexible liner, the excavated area must be properly prepared to receive, house, and protect it.

Pumps: Place submersible pumps and other accessories above the liner to keep the unit free of debris and protect the liner; padded concrete blocks make an excellent, stable, elevated pump base. House above-ground pumps in a weatherproof box to protect them from the elements. Bury delivery pipes from the pump to the header pool or outlet to hide as well as protect them. In cold winter climates, install a drain valve at the system's lowest point.

Accessories: Choose accessories compatible with pumps and pipes to ease installation and ensure proper operation. Pump accessories include its filters, both those integral to the pump and any stand-alone filters; an automatic refill float valve to maintain water level; a check valve, which prevents backflow of water flow through the pump; and a skimmer to act as a supplemental filter and remove floating debris.

Rigid liners: Excavate a hole that's level and matches the liner's contours. Level it so the water will be uniform and equipment will operate properly. Support all contours of the rigid liner—the rim, bottom, and any marginal shelves—to keep the weight of the water from cracking the liner and causing leaks. Install stable underlayment, then use the topsoil removed during excavation to backfill under the liner. If your soil is loose, mix three parts soil with one part cement to stabilize the liner at the rim.

Flexible liners: Sheets of flexible liner material mold to most excavated area's contours. Remove rocks or debris that might puncture the liner under the water's weight. Underlayment further protects and cushions the liner. As the liner first fills with water, smooth out wrinkles and folds; if sections must be joined, overlap them at least 18" (46 cm), using compatible self-sealing tape to secure the joints.

Installing a Rigid Preformed Liner

The secret of installing a preformed liner is excavating to the correct shape, depths, and slope to match its exact dimensions. Finish the excavation and place the underlayment of sand, then install the liner.

HOW TO INSTALL A RIGID PREFORMED LINER

Step A: Position the Liner

1. Gently set the liner in place, making sure its bottom and shelves are set evenly and the liner's lip is flush with the level excavated area.

TOOLS & MATERIALS

- Shovel
- 4-ft. level
- Hand tamp
- Preformed liner
- Compactible gravel
- Cement mix (optional)
- Sump pump
- Submersible recirculating pump
- Coping stones

---

2. Check level across the length and breadth of the liner. To adjust, press down firmly in slightly high points or add and remove sand as required.

Step B: Backfill the Site

1. Fill around the liner's sides and rim, using compactible gravel. Avoid disturbing the liner's position and level. If the feature is large, use a long straight-edge to span its sides. If your soil is loose, mix one part cement into three parts soils; use as backfill.

2. Compact the margins around the liner, using a tamping tool. Maintain an even level along the perimeter.

Step C: Add Water

1. Fill the liner with water. Use a sump pump to remove any sediment.

2. Install a submersible recirculating pump. If desired, add a fountainhead.

Step D: Place Coping Stones

Trial fit your coping stones or other edging materials to cover the edges of the liner.

A. *Set the liner into the excavated site and make sure it's level within the site.*

B. *Backfill around the liner, then compact the surrounding area.*

C. *Add water, then install a submersible recirculating pump.*

D. *Test-fit the coping stones, arranging them to cover the edges of the liner.*

Installing a Flexible Liner

Installing a flexible liner is simple once the excavation is completed (see page 118). Flexible liners mold to the exact shape of the hole. You'll need helpers to hold the edges of the liner while you position and anchor it.

Step A: Position the Underlayment Fabric

In the prepared excavation site filled with a layer of sand, spread the landscape fabric. Overlap seams by at least 12" (30 cm). Smooth any folds or wrinkles.

Step B: Add the Liner Material

1. Stretch the flexible liner over the underlayment, covering the entire area. Smooth any wrinkles and avoid making seams. If seams are absolutely necessary, overlap the pieces by 18" (46 cm) and seal the seams with compatible double-sided EDPM joint tape.

2. Weight the edges of the liner with stones to hold it in position as you smooth and fit the liner into the excavated shelves and bottom.

3. Trim the liner, leaving a 2-ft. (60 cm) wide margin.

Step C: Connect the Liner to the Skimmer & Header Boxes

1. Fit the liner to the skimmer and header boxes, trimming as necessary.

2. Use aquarium-grade silicon sealant on all joints and fasten parts with corrosion-resistant fasteners to avoid leaks.

Step D: Cover the Liner with Stones

Fill the fitted liner with washed gravel, cobble, and boulders to protect it from punctures and exposure to sunlight.

TOOLS & MATERIALS

- Heavy-duty scissors
- Flexible liner
- Double-sided EDPM joint tape
- Landscape fabric
- Aquarium-grade sealant
- Washed gravel, cobble, or boulders
- Corrosion-resistant fasteners

A. *Line the excavated site with underlayment fabric.*

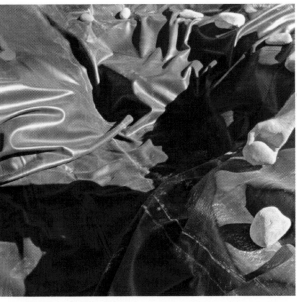

B. *Stretch the liner over the underlayment, fit it to the contours of the pool, and trim it.*

C. *Fit the liner around the skimmer and header boxes, and seal all the joints.*

D. *Cover the liner with a layer of washed gravel and river rock.*

Advanced Watercourses

Anyone who's hiked in the wilderness most likely has had the pleasant experience of coming across a natural spring welling up from the ground. You can achieve a similar natural effect by building a stream in your garden, or you can create a point of architectural interest in a more formal landscape by installing a watercourse. If you choose to expand the stream or watercourse to include changes in elevation, you also can add the sound and sight of falling water.

All streams and watercourses should be appropriately scaled to the rest of your garden. They are most effective when their design is in keeping with the overall style of the surrounding landscape and your home. Generally, traditional settings are best suited to streams, while modern settings are compatible with watercourses. While stylistically different, the basic components of streams and watercourses are the same. Both have a header pool at their top that begins the water feature and a reservoir pool or basin at their bottom end that also contains the pump.

Ideas for more complex designs to create a unique water feature include intermediate pools placed along the course, changes in elevation and direction, and bubbling fountains. There's also ample opportunity to add shoreline rocks and plants.

Seamlessly blending your entire garden landscape into the water feature may take a season or more. Choose perennial plants well adapted to your climate and suitable for carefree maintenance. Allow them freedom the first season to grow into the site.

The slope of the stream from the header to the reservoir—top to bottom—should be about a 3 percent grade, determined by dividing the rise—height difference—by the run—distance between the header and reservoir pools. Avoid stagnating the flow with a too-shallow grade or creating uncontrollable torrents with one that is too steep. Rely on the pump's capacity to control the volume of water flow. Remember that abrupt changes of elevation—cascades and waterfalls—are planned independently from the stream's grade (page 127). Line the header and reservoir pools with either rigid or flexible liners, and the watercourse channel itself with a flexible liner. If your goal is a natural appearance, remember that creeks in nature flow into deep pools that gradually shallow above the next riffle or cascade.

Streams and watercourses require a steady, full flow of water facilitated by a recirculating pump. The required size, or capacity, of the pump is determined more by the water volume of the reservoir and header pools than by how fast you want the water to flow.

Lining a Stream

Line streams in the same manner as pools and ponds. Excavate and line the header and reservoir pools, and excavate for the stream (page 118). Set any waterfalls (see page 127).

For long watercourses, overlap liner segments and seal the seams with double-sided EPDM adhesive joint tape.

HOW TO LINE A STREAM

Step A: Dry Fit the Spill & Foundation Stones

Dry fit all the waterfall spill and foundation stones before finalizing your excavation. Check the relative elevation of all spill stones, allowing an extra 4¼" (11 cm) for the thickness of the sand base and the stream liner.

Step B: Fasten the Liner to the Header

1. Stretch the liner into position and recheck the elevations of the spill stones.

2. Fasten the liner to the header or filter, using aquarium-grade silicon sealant and corrosion-proof fasteners.

Step C: Position Liner in Stream

1. Position any seams in the liner beneath spill stones. Lay the lower-stream liner under the upper-stream section, overlapping the joint by 18" (45 cm). The top end should be positioned above the final water level of the lower-stream section.

2. Seal all of the joints with EPDM joint tape, then secure the spill stones on top of the liner, using concrete mortar or waterproof expanding urethane foam (see page 129).

Step D: Line the Stream with Stones & Flush It with Water

1. Fill the stream liner with washed gravel, river rock, and boulders to protect the liner from punctures and UV rays.

2. Flush the stream with water, using a sump pump to remove water and sediment until the water is clear. Cleaning the stream keeps sediment and debris from reaching the reservoir pool and clogging the pump and filter.

TOOLS & MATERIALS

- Flexible liner
- Aquarium-grade sealant
- Double-sided EPDM joint tape
- Corrosion-proof fasteners
- Spill & foundation stones
- Concrete mortar or waterproof expanding urethane foam
- Washed gravel, river rock, and boulders
- Sump pump

A. *Place and check the elevation of the stones for the spill and foundation.*

B. *Use aquarium-grade silicon sealant and corrosion-proof fasteners to fasten the liner to the header or filter.*

C. *Line the stream bed, overlapping all joints by 18" (45 cm). Seal the joints with EPDM joint tape.*

D. *Fill the stream with stones and add water. Use a sump pump to remove water and sediment until the water runs clear.*

Cascades & Waterfalls

Cascades and waterfalls require abrupt changes in elevation that interrupt the flowing stream or watercourse. Generally, a fall of about 6" (15 cm) will deliver the optimum look and sound. Plan on a deep receiving pool beneath each waterfall, then a slowly rising streambed as the flow approaches the next waterfall.

(top right) Plan planting sites within the margin of the water feature, as was used here as the location for a fern. (bottom) Protect still-water plants from fast-moving currents by constructing a deep pool beneath waterfalls, then filtering the water through rock before it enters the main pool.

A foundation stone sits at the point of the elevation change with a spill stone on top of it. The placement of the spill stone is very important, both vertically and in orientation to level. It should extend over the edge of the foundation stone so the water can fall freely into the stream or pool below. It should be placed to partially dam or slow the stream, building a head of water behind.

The spill stone's design regulates the way the water falls. Gate stones set to each side channel water toward the stone's center and block flow around its edges. In a cascade, the water runs in a smooth curtain over a flat sill from one level to another. In a waterfall, the water splashes down over a rugged rock formation. The width of the spill stone—and how water is channeled to it—affects the appearance and intensity of the falls.

A stream with a cascade or waterfalls requires a recirculating pump and delivery pipe specifically designed to deliver a high volume of water. The greater the elevation change from the header pool to the reservoir pool, the stronger the pump required. If you want a stream or watercourse with rushing water, choose a pump with excess capacity.

Creating Waterfalls

When natural streams change elevation, they flow from deep pools to gradual shallows, then spill over into a lower pool. In a water feature, install foundation and spill stones to mimic this effect. The stones form a shallow basin behind the waterfall, retaining water in the stream even if the pump is turned off. The spill stone's width, contour, and placement determine how the water will fall.

HOW TO CREATE A WATERFALL

Step A: Line the Stream

1. Dig a Z-shaped shelf at the site of the waterfall.
2. Line the stream (page 125). If seams are necessary, position them under the future waterfall and overlap the liner sections by 18" (45 cm), with the upstream section on top of the lower stream section. Apply double-sided EPDM joint tape between the liner sections to create a waterproof seal.

Step B: Set the Foundation Stones

1. Spread mortar or waterproof expanding urethane foam on the liner, within the Z-shaped shelf. Position the foundation stones and adjust until they are exactly level.
2. Apply mortar or foam to the top of the foundation stones, then bed the spill stone in place. Make sure it is level and it sits below the edge of the stream's liner.

Step C: Add Gate Stones

1. Place a gate stone on each side of the spill stone. These stones should rise above the liner edge and direct water to the center of the stream.
2. Bed cobblestones in the mortar or foam beneath the spill stone to disguise the gap.

Step D: Fill the Streambed

Fill the streambed with gravel and cobblestones above and below the waterfall to hold and protect the liner.

TOOLS & MATERIALS

- Shovel
- 4 ft. level
- Flexible liner
- Double-sided EPDM joint tape
- Concrete mortar or expanding urethane foam
- Spill stone
- Gate stones
- Washed gravel and cobblestones
- Foundation stones

A. *Line the stream with a flexible liner. If seams are necessary, position them under the waterfall and seal them with EPDM tape.*

B. *Set the foundation stones and then the spill stone, using mortar or expanding foam to secure them.*

C. *Install gate stones, then place cobblestones strategically to disguise the mortar or foam beneath the spill and gate stones.*

D. *Cover the liner along the streambed with washed gravel and cobblestones.*

Coping Stones

The most prominent finishing touch for a water feature is its edging material. The edging material must be installed correctly to ensure safety while enhancing the entire water garden.

Although edging materials primarily serve aesthetic functions, they also conceal the edges of the liner, hide pump cables, camouflage light fixtures, keep surrounding soil and water from entering the feature, and protect the liner from damaging UV rays. Edging materials also serve a valuable safety function, clearly marking the edge and perhaps even barring access to hazardous areas of a water feature. This is an especially important consideration for those with young children or visitors.

The term coping refers to any material on top of a vertical structure, such as the walls of the water feature. Coping stones are a common edging around pools and also are appropriate for traditional ponds and streams. Set the stones to slope away from the water slightly. Position them to overhang the water's edge, concealing the liner and providing shade and protection for fish and amphibians.

A. *Fit the stones at the edge of the pool or stream.*

©Charles Mann

TOOLS & MATERIALS

- 4-ft. level
- Rubber mallet
- Coping stones
- Concrete mortar
- Sponge
- Sump pump

HOW TO INSTALL COPING STONES

Step A: Position the Stones

1. Set the stones on top of the liner, positioned to rest 1 to 2" (25 to 50 mm) above the future water level.

2. Check the stones with a 4 ft. level: They should slope a quarter to half a bubble away from the pond.

Step B: Set the Stones

1. Working in small sections, remove each stone, create a bed of mortar, moisten the stone, and loosely seat it into the mortar bed.

2. Position the stones to hang 2 to 3" (50 to 75 mm) over the edge. Make sure the stones are level with one another and slope away from the pool. Tap them firmly into place in the mortar, using a rubber mallet.

Step C: Set Stones Around the Fixtures

1. Fit stones around skimmer boxes, filters, and other fixtures. Replace any utility covers and make sure they fit over the stones.

2. Working in a small section at a time, mix mortar and create a bed for the stones. Position the stones and tap them into place, using a rubber mallet. Be careful not to put mortar over pipe fittings or electrical connections.

Step D: Clean the Stones & Fill the Stream

1. Use water and a damp sponge to remove any mortar spills. Also, remove any excess mortar from the pond.

2. Allow the mortar to set for 24 hours.

3. Fill the pond or stream, using a sump pump to extract water contaminated with mortar or debris.

B. *Create a mortar bed and set the stones, hanging 2 to 3" over the edge, level with one another, and sloping away from the edge.*

C. *Set stones around the skimmer boxes, filters, and other fixtures.*

D. *Wipe away excess or spilled mortar, using water and a damp sponge, then let the mortar set for 24 hours. Fill the stream, then pump water through the stream until it runs clear.*

Lighting Systems

A well-designed lighting system remains concealed during the day and reveals itself only at night, extending your hours of water garden enjoyment.

A transformer and special sealed underwater lights are required for water garden lighting. A variety of options exist to alter intensity and color or to control the display. Place lighting fixtures under the surface of the water, highlighting submerged foliage, fish, rocks, and other features. The water surface will reflect the surrounding garden. Consider uplights placed in submerged planting containers, spotlights behind waterfalls to show the movement, and light fixtures attached to fountains.

A 12-volt DC system is usually used, extending from a transformer attached to a GFCI-protected outlet. Some new pond lights are powered by solar or photovoltaic (PV) cells and storage batteries, though such devices are larger than regular lighting fixtures.

Remember to use traditional garden lighting around your water feature, too. It helps blend the feature into your existing landscape. Position uplights beneath your trees, shrubs, and streamside grasses to gently accentuate branches and foliage, reflecting them on the moving water's surface.

WARNING

Electrical shock can cause fatal injury. Always meet or exceed all electrical code requirements and exercise caution when working with electricity.

Foliage lit from beneath with low-voltage lights draws attention to the water feature after nightfall.

12-volt Lighting System

The most commonly used lighting systems are 12-volt DC systems run from transformers attached to GFCI-protected outlets. These systems create the most desirable effects, have the widest options, and are safer than AC systems.

Always use an outdoor-rated transformer plugged into a GFCI-protected, weatherproof outlet (page 116 to 117). Use direct-burial cable without protective conduit below ground and within the water feature.

HOW TO INSTALL A 12-VOLT LIGHTING SYSTEM

Step A: Install the Transformer

1. Install a 12-volt DC, weatherproof transformer at a GFCI-protected outlet attached to a weatherproof junction box. Plug in the transformer.

2. Excavate a trench, 10" (25 cm) deep and 6" (15 cm) wide, between the edge of the water feature and the transformer.

3. Lay direct-burial 12-2 lighting cable in the trench.

Step B: Connect the Cable to the Transformer

Connect the direct-burial cable wire to the transformer, using weatherproof, outdoor-rated connectors and fittings.

Step C: Position the Lights & Set the Timer

1. Adjust and position one or more lights in hidden locations within the feature, directing light onto waterfalls or interesting surface plants.

2. Set the automatic timer on the transformer to turn the lights on at dusk and off later in the night.

TOOLS & MATERIALS

- Shovel
- 12-volt light fixtures
- 12-volt DC weatherproof transformer
- Direct-burial 12-2 lighting cable
- Outdoor-rated connectors and fittings
- Automatic timer

A. *Install the transformer at a GFCI outlet, then dig a trench and lay lighting cable between the transformer and the edge of the water feature.*

B. *Connect the cable to the transformer.*

C. *Adjust and position the lights (inset), then set the automatic timer.*

Planting Aquatic Environments

Now that you've installed your water feature, it's time to add plants. Planting aquatic environments may be a new experience for you, and while most aspects are similar to planting other gardens, there are a few differences to add interest and discovery.

There are four types of aquatic plants, each suited for a different section of your water environment. Some aquatic plants thrive near the water; others on, in, or below the surface of the water—most are rooted, while some are free-floating. This chapter presents the requirements and demonstrates the garden installation techniques for each type of aquatic plant. You'll find ideas for selecting healthy aquatic plants at the nursery or garden center and gain insight into the suggested planting ratios to achieve the best water quality. Information is provided on the specialty containers and optimum soil required for installing submerged plants as well as for the proper preparation and placement of your in-ground plants growing at the shoreline.

Before choosing plants for your water garden, look to your garden plan and the volume of your water feature to understand the space you have available for aquatic plants. Decide the number needed of each type of plant based on the planting ratios presented in this chapter. These ratios comply with most design aesthetics and, more importantly, will help maintain your feature's water quality.

Like many gardening endeavors, growing aquatic plants has some unique challenges. For instance, some grow quickly—the more exuberant varieties easily can overtake younger, weaker species in a matter of weeks—and shoreline plants may require more frequent watering than do your other garden plants. Deep-water submersibles, marginals, and floaters, however, often require less care than other plants. On the whole, an aquatic environment provides an opportunity to cultivate your gardening skills, imagination, and passion.

rapitest
POND TEST KIT
Test your pond to ensure healthy fish and plants
FERTILIZER SPIKES
AQUATIC PLANTS
MONROVIA

Aquatic Environments

PLANTING RATIOS

The correct ratio of aquatic plants to water area is key to achieving healthy water quality and a healthy environment for plants and fish. For each 50 square feet (4.6 m²) of water surface area:

Surface floaters = 6

Submerged oxygenators = 15 bunches

Shallow-depth marginals = 3

Deep-depth marginals = 3

Deep-water submersibles = 1

Aquatic plants are defined by where they grow: on the shoreline, on top of the water, or submerged. The first consideration is the same as for any garden: your site and climate conditions. You must choose plants that will thrive in your locale with the level of sun, shade, and wind found in your water garden. The United States Department of Agriculture (USDA) has divided the world into 11 zones base on their average minimum annual temperatures. These zones roughly predict which plants will survive in a given area. Choose plants that suit the plant hardiness zone of your water garden.

Plants require a certain pH from the soil or water in which they live. The pH scale measures acidity and alkalinity from 0 to 14, with 7.0 as neutral. Lower numbers indicate acidic conditions, higher numbers alkaline. Relative acidity affects a plant's ability to absorb nutrients. Test soil and water prior to introducing plants.

The staff at an aquatic nursery or garden center can help you discover plants that will thrive in your garden and meet your needs. Consult a good encyclopedia of aquatic plants for specifics on characteristics and care requirements of plants you're considering.

Select and cultivate aquatic plants in a careful ratio to achieve proper balance and a desirable appearance. Aquatic plants tend to colonize quickly. Because plants growing in the water play a role in maintaining water quality, they must be thinned and pruned constantly to maintain proper oxygen levels, to balance water quality, and to avoid algae blooms.

Aquatic plants are adapted by nature to live in different environments. In water gardens, risers are used to position plants at the proper depth. Aquatic plants include (left to right) deep-water submersibles, surface floaters, deep-depth marginals, above-water floaters, and shallow-depth marginals. Not shown: submerged oxygenator and shoreline plants.

Selecting Healthy Aquatic Plants

Use your garden plan, idea file, and the listings in this book to choose plants for your garden feature. If you are new to the world of aquatic plants, seek out a specialty nursery as a source of both plants and information about them. To choose healthy plants suited to your garden and climate, follow these steps:

A. *Make a list of plants for each aquatic category best suited to your theme, your garden's plant hardiness zone, and your garden plan.*

B. *Choose plants bearing attractive foliage and textures, and with vibrant colored blooms. They also should have several new buds or emerging leaves.*

C. *Avoid plants with discolored leaves or signs of pest infestation or disease. Choose only vigorous plants that appear strong.*

D. *Examine plants for clean, plump, and unstunted roots, often encased in a plastic bag with water to maintain an adequate moisture level.*

E. *Avoid plants that appear to be overly mature as these take longer to adjust to their new home in your water feature.*

135

Preparing to Plant

CHOOSING CONTAINERS

Containers specifically manufactured for aquatic plants are available at nurseries and garden centers. They usually are baskets made of rigid or flexible plastic.

Other options include terra-cotta pots, natural fiber and woven willow baskets, and polypropylene bags punctured with copious drain holes.

Avoid metal containers that might corrode or leach into the water feature's environment. Also avoid solid containers that would restrict the flow of water and dissolved gasses to the plant's roots inside the containers.

Container baskets should allow water to easily flow through the soil and roots of aquatic plants. Most are made of durable polypropylene plastic.

In a natural environment, aquatic plants grow in the soil at the bottom of a pond or stream, or along its shoreline. There's a method for growing submerged and shoreline plants in soil within the liner. In fact, some rigid liners are molded with depressions in them to hold soil. It's best, however, not to place soil directly onto the liner. Keeping soil out of the liner reduces the need for thinning and fertilizing, minimizes debris and loose soil that can clog pumps and filters, makes cleaning the liner easier for you and safer for your plants, and lets you easily isolate sick plants.

Plant shoreline plants in amended native soil outside the edge of the liner, watering frequently to keep them moist. Some shoreline plants can be invasive, and some have unique soil needs. The best idea is to install your plants in containers then place them—containers and all—in the shoreline soil.

To install marginals and deep-water submersibles, place prepared soil in special shallow containers, add the plants, and top the soil with a thin layer of gravel. Submerge the container to the depth required for the specific plant.

Pour floaters from their containers onto the water's surface; let them float freely or tether them with nylon fishing line.

After filling your pond or pool with water, wait 2 to 5 days before placing plants in it. This delay allows time for any water treatment chemicals to evaporate. The length of time necessary depends on the feature's volume. As the chemicals evaporate, the water may turn green with algae, signaling that the water is ready to support plant life. As your plants grow, they will shade and stifle the algae, controlling it. Milky green water will transform into clear, with a healthy brown tint.

The soil of aquatic plants submerged within the liner generally should have moderate fertility, a dense texture, and permit water to easily penetrate to the plants' roots. Shoreline plants outside the liner require moist garden loam.

Preparing Soil

Two distinctive soils are needed in and alongside water features. The soil for aquatic plants submerged within the liner generally should have moderate fertility, a dense texture, and permit water to easily penetrate to the plant roots. Shoreline plantings outside the liner require moist garden loam. To prepare your soil for planting, follow these steps:

Soil for Submerged Aquatic Plants

A. *Mix equal parts of humus, sand, and sterile potting soil. Add a double portion of dry clay to the mix. This is your base soil.*

B. *Line a submersible container with porous landscape fabric and fill it with the soil mix. Soak it until saturated, washing away the smallest particles.*

C. *Soak the soil overnight in a basin of water. Floating organic material will become saturated and sink. Gently mix it into the soil.*

Soil for Moist Shoreline Plants

A. *Use a soil test kit, available at most garden stores, to test the nutrients and acid-alkaline balance of the soil, following its package instructions.*

B. *Amend the soil as directed by the test results and your plant needs. Shoreline plants generally require an acidic 5.5–6.0 pH, achieved by adding peat or leafmold to overly alkaline soil. Improve texture by adding organic compost.*

C. *Complete your soil preparation by installing drip emitters around your feature. They will provide the regular irrigation needed to keep the soil moist.*

Preparing Containers & Baskets

Containers for aquatic plants serve a purely functional purpose. Unseen and submerged underwater, porous or woven plastic and fiber containers and baskets of various dimensions provide for constant water circulation, hold the soil in place, and maintain the plants at proper depth. To fill them with soil and protect them from erosion, follow these steps:

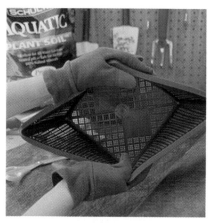

A. *Inspect containers for any cracks, voids, or other structural damage. Clean containers thoroughly to remove any contaminants.*

B. *Install clean porous burlap or landscape fabric mesh along the inside of the container to contain the soil while allowing adequate moisture flow.*

C. *Weight the base of the container with dense stone. Heavy containers will prevent movement in currents.*

D. *Fill with the soil mix, leaving space for the plant roots and a layer 1 to 2" (25–50 mm) thick of pea gravel. Soak the container for 24 hours to exhaust air trapped in the soil and to saturate the organic elements.*

Planting Submerged Aquatic Plants in Containers

All submerged plants—marginal and deep-water—are planted in specialized containers in a similar manner before being installed into the water feature. First prepare the planting container (see page opposite). Check your garden plan for the type, number of plants, and containers you'll need, and follow these steps:

A. *Remove the thoroughly soaked container and its soil from the water basin. Gently mix the soil to incorporate any waterlogged organics that have settled on the soil surface.*

B. *Open a hole in the soil for the roots of the plant, removing some soil if necessary. Spread the roots and gently transplant it into the soil as you would other plants.*

C. *Gently pack the soil around the roots, adding soil as needed to cover them. Immerse the container in the water bath for a few minutes until bubbling stops, then remove and drain it. Fill all voids and replace any soil that has settled.*

D. *Add a layer of washed pea gravel topdressing 1 to 2" (25 to 50 mm) thick to the top of the container. It will protect the soil and further weight the container to prevent movement.*

E. *Set the plant in place in the feature, at a depth appropriate to the species. Stabilize and secure the container, using cobblestone from the feature.*

F. *Place immature aquatic plants on adjustable stands with their foliage just below the water. As the plants grow and leaves reach the surface, progressively lower the stand until it's at its final depth.*

Planting Marginal Aquatics in the Liner

Plant all submerged plants in their specialized containers (page 139). Install the plants into your water feature to their specified depth: shallow-depth marginals to 6" (15 cm) or less, deep-depth marginals 6 to 12" (15 to 30 cm) deep, and deep-water submersibles more than 1 ft. (30 cm) deep. To install submerged plants, follow these steps:

A. *Install plants on the marginal shelves of the water feature, at the recommended depth for the species. Make sure the container is secure and stable on the shelf.*

B. *For shallow-depth marginals, place the container so that the rim is slightly showing, which will allow water to lap over the edge while avoiding constant soil saturation.*

C. *Plant invasive marginal plants in containers as you would other aquatic plants, then bury their containers inside separate liner pockets located at the edge of the feature (inset). Provide a reliable source of water other than that from the feature, such as with drip irrigation.*

D. *If necessary, especially on hot days when the water may evaporate quickly, provide supplementary water to the perimeter plants with adequate drainage away from the water feature. If this is a recurring problem, add a layer of mulch around these plants to help retain moisture.*

Planting Shoreline Plants

Shoreline plants thrive in constantly moist conditions outside the liner. In nature, they receive water from nearby ponds or streams. In a water garden, you must provide them with water. Test and prepare your soil. To plant them directly in the garden soil, follow these steps:

A. *Install shoreline plants outside the lining of the water feature. Place them on the site in their nursery containers, spacing them according to your garden plan.*

B. *Dig holes 1" (25 mm) deeper and ⅛ wider than the nursery container. Add 5–10–10 starter fertilizer to the bottom of the hole as directed on the package, adding covering soil to prevent direct root contact.*

C. *Gently remove the plant from its nursery container. Invert the plant while supporting it with your palm. Tap the container and slide out the plant.*

D. *Set the plant into the hole with the top of its rootball even with the surrounding soil. Use a spade handle to gauge when the depth is right.*

E. *Firm the soil around the plant, using your flattened palms. Water thoroughly, then repeat regularly until established. Maintain moist soil conditions with an irrigation system.*

F. *Plant invasive shoreline plants in containers as you would other aquatic plants, then bury their containers in the shoreline soil outside the liner. Provide a reliable source of water other than the feature, such as hand watering or a drip irrigation system.*

Fertilizing Plants

In a natural environment, plants growing in water receive nutrients from the natural decomposition of plant and animal life around them. In a typical water garden, marginal and deep-water submersible plants may require supplements of fertilizer or food until their ecosystem becomes balanced.

You have to be careful—adding too many nutrients may overwhelm the plants, fish, or wildlife, and may promote algae blooms. There are four times to consider fertilizing: when plants are being installed, when they're emerging from dormancy, after they're divided or thinned, and when an individual plant shows signs of distress.

If an individual plant is in need of fertilizer, it will become stunted, stop growing, or display discolored or limp foliage. Remove the troubled plant and its container from the water and care for it individually. Inspect it for signs of pests and disease before fertilizing or returning the plant to the water.

Another important note: as you fertilize or otherwise treat your surrounding landscape, avoid contaminating the feature's water with garden chemicals; they may alter or damage the delicate balance of the water and plants in your feature's ecosystem or cause algae to bloom.

©Derek Fell

TOOLS & MATERIALS

• Rubber gloves   • Fertilizer

HOW TO APPLY SLOW-RELEASE FERTILIZER
Step A: Remove the Plant & Insert Fertilizer Tablets
1. Wearing rubber gloves, remove the plant from the water feature and allow it to drain thoroughly. Use care to protect the foliage, especially when handling large plants.
2. Insert the tablet into the soil— below the gravel topdressing—as directed on the fertilizer package.

Step B: Replace the Plant
Replace the fertilized plant in the water feature. Fan its foliage, eliminating tangles or inverted leaves.

A. *Take the plant out of the water and let it drain. Brush back the gravel topdressing and insert the tablet into the soil.*

B. *Return the plant to the water feature and rearrange its foliage.*

Option: *To fertilize floating or standing foliage, apply liquid foliar fertilizer. Allow the foliage to dry completely before returning plants to the water feature.*

Testing & Treating Water

Balanced water quality is essential to maintaining a healthy water garden. Balance is achieved by establishing proper plant ratios, maintaining the water level, controlling debris and other organic matter, and testing regularly for the optimal pH and telltale nutrient levels of the water.

When your water turns from clear to green, algae is thriving in nutrient-rich water and sunlight. It signals a healthy, fertile aquatic environment ready to support more desirable plant life.

Use a reagent test kit to test your water regularly for its pH—the water's acid-alkaline balance—and nitrate, nitrite, and ammonia levels. Nitrite from plant decomposition converts by chlorophyll photo-

synthesis to nitrate, a stable form. Excess nitrite signals too much fertilizer in the water, a condition that causes algae to grow and quickly turn the water green. It's also important to check ammonia levels. Ammonia from fish and animal waste can stunt plants and kill fish. Test for ammonia and, if it is detected, take steps immediately to remove it from the water.

TOOLS & MATERIALS

• Pond test kit

HOW TO TEST & TREAT WATER

Step A: Collect Water Samples

1. Study the feature. Its water color and surface should be clear, tinted amber. Plants should be vital, green, and healthy. (Algae blooms or weakened plants denote excess nitrate in the water or high pH.)

2. If you suspect problems, purchase test kits from a garden center, water garden supplier, or aquarium store.

3. Collect several water samples according to the manufacturer's instructions.

Step B: Perform the Tests

1. Test the acid-alkaline balance of the water. Optimum pH levels are 6.5 to 7.5 on a scale of 14.

2. Test the water's nitrate and nitrite level. The relative balance reveals the feature's nutrients.

3. Test the water's ammonia content, which should be zero.

Step C: Adjust the Water as Necessary

1. If the tests indicate problems, remove and wash the feature's biologic filter media. Also clean the skimmer of accumulated debris. Exchange 20% of the feature's water. (It's generally not necessary to use chlorine or chloramine neutralizer for small water exchanges.) Retest after 24 hours.

2. If the test indicates that ammonia is present, exchange 10 to 20% of the feature's water every three to five days until the test is negative.

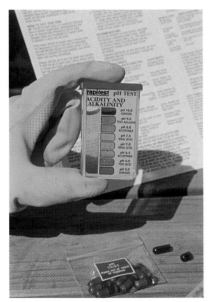

A. *Purchase a test kit and collect water samples.*

B. *Following manufacturer's directions, test the pH, nitrate and nitrite, and ammonia levels of the water.*

C. *If the tests indicate poor water quality, wash the filter and skimmer. Exchange some of the feature's water and retest.*

Cleaning a Pond

The pump, filter, delivery pipe, and housing of a water feature should be checked semi-monthly and may need to be cleaned out once a month. Check the pump manufacturer's recommendations. To clean the pump, use a garden hose spray nozzle to clean the housing and filter media; replace the filter and screen as necessary.

When the water quality, pump, and filters are well maintained, water features operate reliably for long periods. They need to be cleaned completely only every two to three years. When the water quickly becomes unbalanced and fails quality tests, the bottom is filled with sediment, or the liner is coated with algae, it's time for a thorough cleaning. Choose an overcast day in late spring or early summer, which allows time for plants to recover before going dormant for winter.

TOOLS & MATERIALS

- Screwdriver
- Drain hose
- Fish net
- Large buckets
- Pruning shears
- Rags and sponges

HOW TO CLEAN A POND

Step A: Pump Out the Water

1. Detach the pump discharge connection, leaving it in place. Replace the discharge connection with a temporary drain hose.

2. Use the pump to drain the feature. If the pump is in a skimmer box, relocate it to the main pond.

Step B: Remove Plants & Fish

1. Select containers capable of housing the feature's plants and fish for several days.

2. Gently remove plants, placing them nearby as the feature empties. Inspect the foliage for pest and disease damage. Thin or prune as necessary.

3. As the fish gather in the deepest areas of the remaining water, net them and put them in temporary containers. (Be sure to feed the fish and change the water as necessary while they are displaced.)

4. Once all plants and fish are removed, gently bail out the remaining water.

Step C: Clean the Feature

1. Use clean rags and soft sponges to remove all silt, debris, and other decayed matter from the bottom of the pond.

2. Wash off the protective gravel and boulders. Handle the liner gently as you work.

Step D: Inspect the Liner & Refill the Feature

1. Check for leaks, damage, and signs of wear. (See page 148 for information on repairing leaks.)

2. Reposition the protective gravel and the boulders.

3. Refill the pond with water. Allow two to three days for the chemical additives in your municipal water to dissipate and evaporate.

4. Replace the plants and then the fish.

A. *Detach the pump discharge connection and replace it with a temporary drain hose; drain the feature.*

B. *As the pond drains, relocate the plants and fish to temporary quarters. Remove any remaining water by hand.*

C. *Remove silt, debris, and decayed matter from the pond and liner; wash off the gravel and boulders.*

D. *Refill the water feature. Allow the chemical additives in the water to evaporate for two to three days, then replace the plants and fish.*

Repairing Liner Leaks

Liner leaks result from inadvertent punctures, sharp objects falling in the water, roots growing through the underlayment into the liner, animals trying to tunnel through it, and basic wear and tear.

Suspect a leak if you notice that the water is repeatedly and unexpectedly low, the soil outside the liner is saturated, or there's soil in the bottom of the feature. If you suspect a leak, quickly take action to repair it—the plants and fish depend on plenty of good quality water.

Even if you don't observe problems, inspect for leaks or wear points during regular maintenance checks of your water garden. Inspect the liner especially thoroughly when you drain and clean the feature.

TOOLS & MATERIALS

- Fish net
- Large buckets
- Drain hose
- Denatured alcohol or adhesive primer
- Patch kit
- Aquarium-grade silicone sealant

©Derek Fell

HOW TO REPAIR LINER LEAKS

Step A: Find & Expose the Damaged Area

1. Drain the water from the feature, remove the plants and fish, and clean the liner (see pages 146 to 147).

2. Remove the protective gravel, cobble, and boulders from the area suspected of leaks, exposing the liner.

Step B: Patch the Leak

1. Thoroughly clean the area around the puncture with clean water. Rinse and dry the area.

2. Clean the patch area with denatured alcohol or an adhesive primer.

3. Patch the affected area following the instructions from the repair kit. Extend all patches 2 to 4" (5 to 10 cm) beyond the immediate puncture area.

Step C: Reinforce the Patch

1. Apply a coat of an aquarium-grade silicone sealant over the repaired area to protect the patch and isolate it from the feature's water. Allow the patch and the sealant to dry thoroughly.

2. Reposition the protective gravel and boulders. Refill the pond with water, and allow two to three days for the chemicals in the water to dissipate and evaporate.

3. Replace the plants and then the fish.

A. *Drain the feature, remove the plants and fish, and inspect for the leak.*

B. *Clean the area with water, then with denatured alcohol or an adhesive primer. Patch the affected area, extending the patch 2 to 4" beyond the puncture.*

C. *Apply silicone sealant over the repaired area, and allow it to dry. Refill the pond, replacing the plants and fish.*

Winterizing in Cold Climates

As winter arrives in cold climates, your water feature requires protection from cold temperatures and ice. Hardy, dormant aquatic plants should remain in the water feature; tropicals should be removed to a warm location.

Before the first frost, take steps to protect the liner and the pump, pipes, and filters from damage due to ice or freezing temperatures. Remember that a natural exchange of air is essential to maintain water quality within the feature. Most fish species will congregate around an open water area. Dissolved oxygen supplies are most plentiful in those areas, and the circulating water carries oxygen to all the feature's areas and its plants.

TOOLS & MATERIALS

- Heat tape or insulation
- Small water heater or auxiliary submersible pump
- Plastic foam float blocks

HOW TO WINTERIZE A WATER FEATURE
Step A: Protect Pumps & Lines

1. Leave the submersible pumps operating in the feature—moving water resists ice formation.

2. Wrap above-ground recirculating lines with heat tape or insulation.

3. Turn off and drain above-ground pumps and lines.

Step B: Install a Heater

1. Install a small heater or auxiliary submersible pump near the surface of the water to prevent ice formation and to allow ample oxygen to enter the water.

2. If cold temperatures become extreme, add plastic foam float blocks to flex against ice expansion that otherwise would damage the liner. Leave at least 20% of the surface open.

A. *Protect above-ground recirculating lines with heat tape or insulation. Turn off and drain above-ground pumps and lines.*

B. *Install a small heater near the surface of the water. If necessary, add plastic foam float blocks to keep ice from damaging the liner.*

Healing Sick Plants

A watchful eye is first aid for healing plants. The sooner a pest infestation or disease infection is discovered, the sooner you can take action to control it. Accurate identification is key to effective pesticide and fungicide use.

Pest control begins with a healthy garden, both in the plant life and the water. Choose appropriate plants and provide them with consistent care. Although all aquatic plants have some natural resistance to infections, those varieties that are adapted to your USDA plant hardiness zone are most adept at naturally resisting your area's pests and illnesses.

Prevent infestations by using sterile containers and soil mixes every time you add a new plant; reused containers and garden soil often contain fungal spores that spread disease.

Maintaining overall plant health, ensuring water quality, and regularly removing debris in and around the water goes a long way toward prevention of the most common conditions.

If the pest infestation or disease infection is severe or spreading, consider applying pesticides and fungicides to the affected plants. Treat only the plants bearing signs of damage or disease, isolated outside the pond. If you keep fish or your feature supports other wildlife, keep the treated plants out of the pond as recommended by the manufacturer of the pesticide or fungicide.

Wear protective clothing when applying garden chemicals. Target the affected areas in package recommended doses and dilutions. Dispose of chemicals and applicators as recommended by the manufacturer when you're done. Clean your equipment and gloves after working on sick plants.

A. *Remove sick plants from the feature and isolate them in holding basins. Remove pests by hand.*

TOOLS & MATERIALS

- Temporary holding basin
- Small brush
- Plastic bags
- Appropriate pesticide or fungicide
- Protective clothing

HOW TO HEAL SICK PLANTS

Step A: Isolate the Plants & Remove the Pests

1. Create a temporary holding basin to isolate affected plants.

2. Remove sick plants from the water feature and place them in the holding basin.

3. Hand pick or use a small brush to remove insect pests from the foliage. This may be sufficient to control many pests.

Step B: Identify the Problem

If removing the pests did not solve the problem, collect a piece of damaged foliage in a plastic bag. Take the bag to a nursery, garden center, or county extension agent and ask for help identifying the issues at hand.

Step C: Select & Apply Chemical Controls

1. Based on the identification of the problem, choose a pesticide or fungicide that specifically lists that pest or disease. Wearing protective clothing and gloves, apply the control. Follow all package label instructions completely and exactly.

2. Once the plant is healthy and all chemical residue has abated as indicated on the product's label instructions, replace the plant in your water feature.

B. *Collect samples and take them to a garden center, nursery, or other expert source for identification.*

C. *Apply appropriate chemicals, following all manufacturer's recommendations. When the plant appears to be healthy and the chemical has abated, return the plant to the water feature.*

Garden Furnishings

When we began thinking of our yards as extensions of our homes, we radically revised our ideas about garden furnishings. Where once the standard may have been limited to a lounge chair and a picnic or other dining table, we've come to understand that well-furnished outdoor homes are more likely to be used and enjoyed. Seating, planters, and display pieces all play important parts in creating a comfortable and appealing atmosphere.

There's no reason to confine your furnishings to the deck or patio. Set a pergola in the middle of a rose garden or amidst a patch of wildflowers in the back corner of the yard. Add a couple of chairs and a small table, and you've created an outdoor breakfast nook or a special place for tea on leisurely afternoons. Or, suspend a swing beneath an elevated deck. Accessorize it with soft cushions, and place candles nearby to produce a gracious spot to relax at the end of a day.

You may have specific ideas about the furnishings you need or want to add to your garden. If not, invest some time in the garden, just thinking about the possibilities. Slow down, use your imagination, and make a plan. Then you'll be ready to build or acquire furnishings that work for the way you live. Or perhaps for the way you want to live.

Rose Bench

Every rose gardener deserves a quiet, restful place to sit and contemplate the beauty of the blossoms. This bench, which is both quick and easy to build, is ideal for compact mounding rose varieties or miniature rose trees.

A bench planter is an ideal starter project—all you need are simple construction skills and common carpentry tools. Allow a weekend to gather materials, cut, and assemble the bench.

TOOLS & MATERIALS

- Circular saw
- Power drill with ½" bit
- Adjustable wrench
- Hammer
- Cedar or pressure-treated lumber (see cutting list)
- Tape measure
- ½" (12 mm) threaded rods with nuts and washers
- Corrosion-resistant finishing nails
- Corrosion-resistant deck screws
- Clamps

Cutting List

Part	Name	Material	Size	Number
A	Inner rails	2 × 4 (5 × 10 cm)	57⅜" (38 × 89 × 1457 mm)	7
B	Outer rails	2 × 4 (5 × 10 cm)	93⅝" (38 × 89 × 2378 mm)	2
C	Spacers*	1 × 4 (2.5 × 10 cm)	6" (17 × 89 × 152 mm)	16
D	Ends	2 × 4 (5 × 10 cm)	16⅛" (38 × 89 × 410 mm)	2
E	Baseboards*	1 × 6 (2.5 × 15 cm)	16½" (17 × 140 × 419 mm)	6
F	Sleepers	2 × 4 (5 × 10 cm)	15½" (38 × 89 × 394 mm)	4
G	Sideboards*	1 × 6 (2.5 × 15 cm)	15½" (17 × 140 × 394 mm)	24
H	Corner braces	2 × 2 (5 × 5 cm)	17¾" (38 × 38 × 451 mm)	8
I	Bottom braces	2 × 2 (5 × 5 cm)	11¾" (38 × 38 × 298 mm)	8
J	Ledger trims*	1 × 3 (2.5 × 7.6 cm)	15¾" (17 × 64 × 400 mm)	16
K	Base trims*	1 × 3 (2.5 × 7.6 cm)	11½" (17 × 64 × 292 mm)	8
L	45° frame trims*	1 × 3 (2.5 × 7.6 cm)	16½" (17 × 64 × 419 mm)	8
M	Long fascia	1 × 4 (2.5 × 10 cm)	96" (17 × 89 × 2438 mm)	2
N	Short fascia	1 × 4 (2.5 × 10 cm)	19½" (17 × 89 × 495 mm)	2
O	Threaded rod with nuts and washers		½" (13-mm)	2

*Assumes all 1" (2.5 cm) lumber is planed ¹¹⁄₁₆" (17 mm) thick. Adjust measurements if you use ¾" (19 mm) lumber.

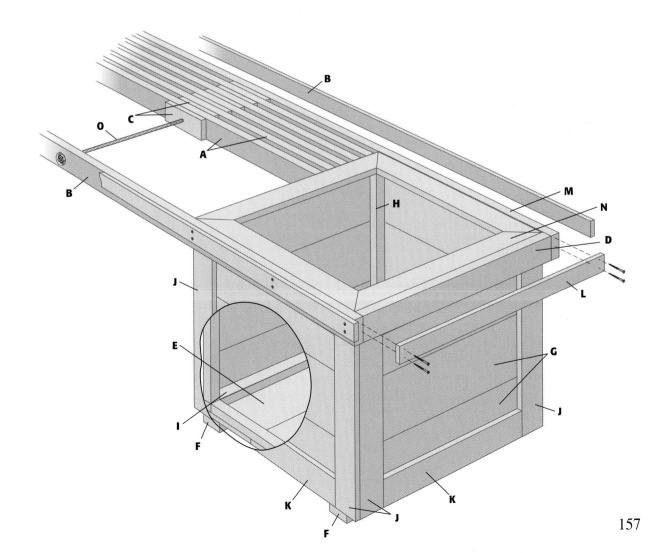

HOW TO BUILD A ROSE BENCH

Step A: Assemble the Seat

1. Cut the pieces as indicated on the cutting list.

2. Mark a point 15" (38 cm) from each end of each inner rail and at the center of each spacer. Drill a ½" (12 mm) hole at each mark.

3. Thread alternating inner rails and spacer blocks onto the threaded rods.

4. Center the outer rail on the assembly. Mark and drill ½" (12 mm) holes for the threaded rod. Mount the outer rails on the assembly and fasten them with washers and nuts.

Step B: Assemble the Planter Bases

1. Center three baseboards on top of two sleep-ers. Drill pilot holes and fasten the baseboards to the sleepers, using two deck screws at each end of each baseboard.

2. Drill three ½" (12 mm) drain holes in two of the baseboards.

3. Repeat with remaining baseboards and sleepers.

Step C: Build the Planter Sides

1. Fit four sideboards, four bottom braces, and four corner braces on the base in flush, progressive-over-lap corner joints.

2. Fasten the bottom braces to the baseboards, and the sideboards to the corner braces, using deck screws.

3. Add the remaining sideboards.

A. *Drill holes in the rails and spacers, and assemble them onto threaded rods.*

B. *Center three baseboards on top of a pair of sleepers and attach them with deck screws.*

C. *Assemble the sideboards, bottom braces, and corner braces in overlapping joints. Fasten the joints with deck screws.*

4. Repeat for the other planter assembly.

Step D: Attach the Trim

1. Butt two ledger trims at each corner and fasten them with finishing nails.

2. Fasten the base trims to the edge of the assembly with finishing nails.

Step E: Install the Top Trim

1. Miter 45° cuts at each end of each piece of top trim.

2. Fit the top trim to the top of each planter and fasten all trim with finishing nails.

Step F: Fasten the Planters to the Seat

1. Align the assemblies so that the ends of the planters are flush with the ends of the seat's outer rails.

2. Drill pilot holes and fasten the planters to the outer rails, using four deck screws at each end of each planter.

3. Position the fascia so it is flush with the tops and edges of the outer rails and planter assembly; clamp in place. Make sure the fascia obscures the hardware and fasteners.

4. Fasten the fascia in place, using finishing nails.

E. *Miter the top trim and nail it in place.*

D. *Attach two ledger trims and two base trims to each planter assembly.*

F. *Attach the planters to the outer rails of the seat, using deck screws. Fasten fascia with finish nails to hide deck assembly hardware and fasteners.*

Potting Table

If you are like many gardeners, your equipment expands into all available space—basement, garage, tool shed, closets, and spare rooms. A potting table can help you get organized by providing a convenient spot to store tools and materials during the off-season. Then, when the garden comes alive, you can move the potting table outdoors and use it to transplant seedlings, clean containers, mix fertilizer, and perform other messy tasks.

This potting table is broad enough to hold several pots and trays of nursery starts. Its open shelving is useful for storing materials, and the pegboards give you a great place to hang trowels, forks, and dibbles—in or out of season.

TOOLS & MATERIALS

- Circular saw
- Power drill
- Clamps
- Socket wrench
- Pressure-treated lumber
- Pegboard
- Corrosion-resistant deck screws
- ⅛" and ¼" drill bits
- Hex bolts, nuts, and washers
- Caster assemblies with wheel locks and fasteners
- Pegboard hooks
- Vinyl-covered hanger hooks
- Exterior wood glue
- Wood preservative
- Tape measure
- Framing square

Cutting List

Pressure-Treated Lumber:

Legs	2 × 6 (5 × 16 cm)	30" (75 cm)	4
Top crossbraces	2 × 6 (5 × 16 cm)	31" (79 cm)	2
Lower crossbraces	2 × 6 (5 × 16 cm)	32½" (83 cm)	2
Crossbrace blocks	2 × 6 (5 × 16 cm)	12" (30.5 cm)	4
Caster mount blocks	2 × 6 (5 × 16 cm)	5½" (14 cm)	4
Work surface planks	2 × 6 (5 × 16 cm)	72" (1.83 m)	6
Work surface supports	2 × 6 (5 × 16 cm)	31" (79 cm)	2
Lower shelf planks	2 × 6 (5 × 16 cm)	66" (1.68 m)	4

Lumber:

Front apron support	2 × 4 (5 × 10 cm)	52" (1.32 m)	1
Front apron	1 × 6 (2.5 × 16 cm)	66" (1.68 m)	1
Side aprons	1 × 6 (2.5 × 16 cm)	22" (55 cm)	2

Vertical supports	2 × 8 (5 × 20 cm)	18" (46 cm)	3
Top shelf	1 × 8 (2.5 × 20 cm)	72" (1.83 m)	1
Middle shelf	1 × 8 (2.5 × 20 cm)	34⅛" (86.5 cm)	1

Pegboard Pressboard Sheet ⅜" (10 mm):

Top shelf backing	22 × 72" (56 × 1.83 m)	1

Hardware and Materials:

Galvanized deck screws	No. 8 × 2½" (4 × 65 mm)	100
Hex bolts, nuts, washers	⁵⁄₁₆ × 3½" (8 × 85 mm)	16
Caster assemblies with wheel locks and fasteners		4
Pegboard hooks		6
Vinyl-covered hanger hooks (screw-in)		9
Bottle woodworker's exterior glue		1

HOW TO BUILD A POTTING TABLE

Step A: Build the Leg Assemblies

1. Cut the legs, crossbraces, crossbrace blocks, and caster mount blocks to size, following the cutting list on page 161. On a flat work surface, position a crossbrace block on each leg, flush with the sides and bottom edge of the leg. Drill pilot holes and attach the crossbrace blocks with glue and four deck screws for each leg.

2. Align the legs, parallel with one another and 33" (84 cm) apart. Set the lower crossbrace in place, the long edge tight to the crossbrace blocks and the ends flush with the outside edge of each leg. Place the upper crossbrace flush with the top corners of the front and back legs, allowing a 1½" (38 mm) setback from the front leg edge. Square up the assembly and clamp it in place; mark and drill two ¼" (6 mm) holes at each leg-crossbrace junction.

3. Thread a washer onto each bolt, then drive the bolts through the legs and crossbraces. Attach the final washer and nut on each bolt, then tighten them

just until the wood compresses. Release the clamps as each joint is secured.

4. Align a caster block at the foot of each leg and attach each with four deck screws.

5. Repeat #1 through #4 for the second leg assembly.

Step B: Assemble the Work Surface

1. Cut the work surface planks, work surface supports, and front apron support. Loosely align the six planks, squaring them into a rectangle. Apply glue to each edge of the four central planks, then square and clamp them tightly; allow to dry overnight.

2. Measure 4½" (11.5 cm) in and draw a line across each end of the assembly. Position a work surface support inside each line, flush with the assembly's back edge and 2" (50 mm) short of its front edge; clamp together.

3. Drill ⅛ × 2" (3 × 50 mm) pilot holes, two in each plank, through the support and into—but not through—the planks. Attach the supports to the assembly with deck screws.

4. Drill pilot holes and attach the front apron support

A. *Attach the crossbrace blocks to the ends of the legs, using deck screws, then attach the top and bottom crossbraces between the legs, using bolts and washers.*

B. *Glue together the planks of the work surface and let them dry. Attach the work surface supports and the apron supports, using deck screws.*

between the work surface supports, using deck screws.

Step C: Attach the Legs to the Work Surface

1. Place the work surface assembly face down on a level surface. Position a leg assembly on each end, aligning each flush with the back edge, parallel to and snug against a work surface support.

2. Drill ⅛" (3 mm) pilot holes horizontally through the top crossbrace into a work surface support and fasten the leg assembly with deck screws. Repeat for the other leg assembly.

3. Drill pilot holes and install a caster assembly on the caster mount block on the bottom of each leg. Use the hardware supplied with the casters to secure them.

Step D: Add the Bottom Shelf

1. Cut four bottom shelf planks. Using a circular saw, rip a plank to 5" (13 cm) wide.

2. Stand the potting bench on its legs, check it for square, then place the bottom shelf planks so they span the bottom crossbraces. Align each plank with the outer edge of the crossbraces; clamp in place

and drill two ⅛" (3 mm) pilot holes through each plank end into the crossbrace. Fasten with deck screws.

Step E: Install the Shelf Unit

1. Cut the vertical shelf supports, top, and middle shelf; cut the pegboard backing.

2. On two shelf supports, mark a line 8½" (21 cm) from an end. Set the supports and the middle shelf on a flat surface, with the middle shelf between the two shelf supports and lined up with the marks. Drill pilot holes through the supports and into the shelf, then attach the shelf with deck screws.

3. Add the upper shelf and the remaining shelf support, laying them out so the ends of the top shelf are flush with the sides of the shelf supports. Drill three pilot holes for each support and attach the shelf with deck screws.

4. Align the pegboard with the shelf assembly; the lower edge of the pegboard should extend 4" (10 cm) beyond the ends of the shelf supports. Fasten the pegboard to the shelf supports, using deck screws.

C. *Drill pilot holes and attach a leg assembly to each end of the work surface assembly. Add a caster to the bottom of each leg.*

D. *Cut four shelf planks; rip one plank to be 5" wide. Position the planks between the lower crossbraces and attach them, using deck screws.*

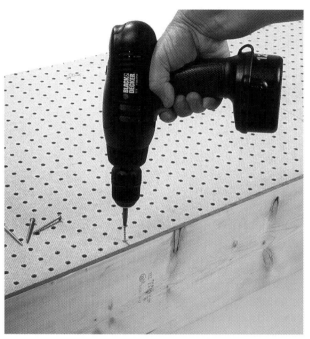

E. *Assemble the shelves and shelf supports, then attach the pegboard to the back of this upper shelf unit.*

Step F: Add the Aprons & Shelf Unit

1. Cut the side and front aprons. Fit the side aprons flush against the upper crossbraces, using the crossbraces as a stop. Drill pilot holes through the aprons and fasten them with deck screws.

2. Fit the front apron onto the apron support, drill pilot holes, and fasten the apron, using deck screws.

Step G: Install Hooks & Accessories

1. Position the shelf unit on top of the work surface and align the sides. Mark the locations of the shelf supports on the work surface, remove the shelf, and drill pilot holes through the work surface, two to each support.

2. Set the shelf unit back in place. Working from the underside, attach the shelf unit to the work surface with deck screws. Fasten the overhanging edge of the pegboard to the work surface, using deck screws.

3. Apply a coat of wood preservative to the entire assembly.

4. Hang hooks from the pegboard. Drill equally spaced ¼" (6 mm) pilot holes across the aprons and attach vinyl hooks for hand tools. If desired, attach wire baskets to the lower shelf unit.

F. *Attach the side aprons to the upper crossbraces and the front apron to the apron support. Secure the shelf unit to the top of the work surface.*

CONTAINER GARDENING

Planting in permanent containers requires care to ensure good results. First, picking the right container is a practical decision as well as a decorative one. You can use everything from a half-barrel to a wicker basket—the only requirement is that your pot or container have adequate drainage and be waterproof.

Inexpensive plastic pots are excellent for retaining water; set them inside more attractive containers if you wish, or dress them up by planting trailing annuals to cover the sides. Unglazed terra-cotta pots are quite porous, allowing soil to breathe and plant roots to cool; they're a good choice for plants that require thorough drainage. Overcome the need for frequent watering in terra cotta by painting the insides with waterproof latex sealant. Still other options are glazed clay pots and thick wooden planters, both of which hold moisture better than unglazed pottery.

G. Attach the sides and back of the shelf unit to the work surface. Install hooks and add accessories.

Birdhouse Plant Stand

Walk the aisles of any garden center, and you're bound to recognize how popular container gardening has become—there are literally hundreds of types and sizes of containers on the market. One of the many reasons is that container gardens can make the most of small spaces or create a feeling of intimacy in open areas. And in either case, a plant stand can help by providing a place to store and display container plants.

This plant stand also would be a charming addition to a patio, deck, or garden shed. Although they're very easy to produce, details like the shaped skirting, spindle supports on the shelves, and the birdhouse effect on the posts give it plenty of personality. And while we did a simple colorwashed finish on ours, you could use any paint or stain treatment that complements the style and tone of your yard.

By the way, dollhouse shingles might seem fragile, but the ones we used on the posts of a garden bench have survived ten years in the unforgiving climate of Minnesota. If you give the whole piece a coat of sealer/preservative every year or so, it should stand up to nearly any weather.

TOOLS & MATERIALS

- Drill with ¼" (6.35 mm) twist bit
- 1" (2.54 cm) spade bit
- Carpenter's square
- Reciprocating or circular saw
- Bar clamps
- Level
- Jig saw
- Ratchet wrench
- Caulk gun
- 8 ft. (2.44 m) cedar 4 × 4 (10 × 10 cm) (1)
- 10 ft. (3 m) cedar 2 × 4 (5 × 10 cm) (3)
- 8 ft. (2.44 m) cedar 1 × 4 (2.5 × 10 cm) (5)
- 8 ft. (2.44 m) cedar 1 × 3 (2.54 × 7.62 cm) (5)
- ¼" (6.35 mm) exterior plywood
- Cedar deck balusters (2)

- Latex paint
- Latex glaze
- 2½" (6.35 cm) corrosion-resistant deck screws
- 4" (15.25 cm) corrosion-resistant lag screws
- Exterior wood glue
- 6d (5 cm) corrosion-resistant finish nails
- 1½" (3.8 cm) corrosion-resistant deck screws
- 2" (5 cm) corrosion-resistant deck screws
- 8d (6.4 cm) corrosion-resistant finish nails
- 1"-dia. (2.54 cm) flexible PVC pipe (54" [1.37 m])
- Dollhouse shingles, cedar
- ¼" (6.35 mm) dowel
- Polyurethane sealer

Cutting List

Part	Lumber	Number	Size
Back supports	4 × 4	2	48" (1.22 m)
Shelf frame fronts & backs	2 × 4	4	42" (1.07 m)
Upper shelf sides	2 × 4	2	16" (40.64 cm)
Upper middle brace	2 × 4	1	13" (33.02 cm)
Lower shelf sides	2 × 4	2	20" (50.8 cm)
Lower middle brace	2 × 4	1	17" (43.18 cm)
Front legs	2 × 4	2	20" (50.8 cm)
Skirting front	¼" plywood	1	5½ × 45½" (13.97 cm × 1.16 m)
Upper side skirt	¼" plywood	2	5¼ × 16" (13.97 × 40.64 cm)
Lower side skirt	¼" plywood	2	5½ × 20" (13.97 × 50.8 cm)
Decking	1 × 4	9	46¼" (1.18 m)
Pickets	1 × 3	10	36" (91.44 cm)
Roofs	¼" plywood	2	4 × 4" (10 × 10 cm)
		2	4 × 4¼" (10 × 11.43 cm)

HOW TO BUILD A BIRDHOUSE PLANT STAND
Step A: Prepare the Lumber

1. Cut the parts as indicated on the cutting list. On each of the 4 × 4 posts (the back supports), center one mark 3½" (8.9 cm) and then another 5½" (13.97 cm) from the top end. Use a 1" spade bit to drill a 1½"-deep (3.8 cm) hole at the top mark, and then a ¼" twist bit to drill a ½"-deep hole at the bottom mark.

2. On the top edge of each post, mark the center. On each side, mark a point 3" (7.6 cm) down from the

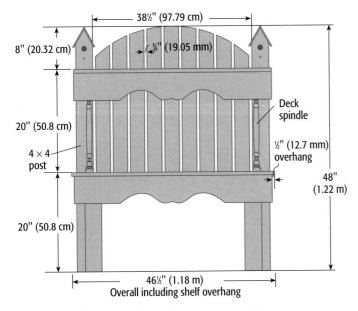

Skirting front template found on page 250

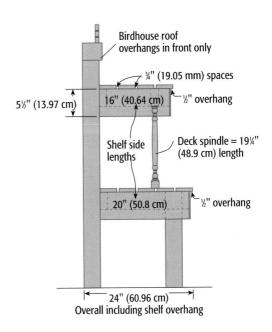

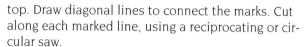

A. *Drill two holes in the face of each back support, then mark and cut the angles for the roof details.*

top. Draw diagonal lines to connect the marks. Cut along each marked line, using a reciprocating or circular saw.

3. Using the grid system or a photocopier, enlarge the pattern on page 250 and trace it onto the two pieces of ¼" plywood skirting. Cut along the marked lines, using a jig saw.

4. Mix paint and glaze in a 2:1 ratio and use it to wash all the pieces with color.

Step B: Construct the Shelf Frames

1. On a flat, level work surface, lay out the front, back, middle brace, and sides of the upper shelf frame. Drill pilot holes and secure the joints with 2½" deck screws. Repeat with the lower shelf frame.

2. Attach the front legs at the inside corners of the lower shelf frame, using two 2½" deck screws for each leg.

Step C: Attach the Shelf Frames to the Posts

1. On each 4 × 4 back support, mark one line 19¼" (48.9 cm) and another 39¼" (99.7 cm) from the bottom of the post.

2. Clamp the lower shelf frame to the back supports, aligning the top of the frame with the 19¼" marks. On each side, drill two ¼" pilot holes through the frame and into the post; countersink each ¼" deep, using a 1" spade bit. Insert a 4" lag screw and tighten it with a ratchet wrench.

B. *Construct the upper and lower shelf frames. Attach the front legs to the inside corners of the lower shelf frame.*

C. *Attach the shelf frames to the back supports, using lag screws and a ratchet wrench.*

3. Repeat #2 to attach the upper shelf frame at the 40" mark.

Step D: Complete the Shelves

1. Apply exterior wood glue to the backs of the skirting pieces and clamp them in place along the sides and front of each shelf frame. Make sure the top of the skirting is flush with the top of the shelf frame. Drive a 6d finish nail every couple of inches (5 cm) to secure the skirting to the sides and front.

2. Starting at the back of the frame, add the decking. Drill pilot holes and attach the decking with two 1½" deck screws at each side and at the middle brace. NOTE: The decking should overhang the ends and the front of the frame by ½" (12.7 mm).

3. Cut two deck balusters to 19¼", trimming an equal amount from each end. Clamp a baluster into position at one inside corner of the upper shelf; use a level to check adjacent sides of the baluster, and adjust until the baluster is plumb. Attach the top of the baluster to the side of the shelf frame, using two 2" deck screws. On the bottom, toenail two sides of the baluster to the decking, using one 6d finish nail on each side of the baluster. Repeat for the other baluster.

Step E: Add the Details

1. Mark the centers of the upper and lower shelf. Also mark a line down the center of one picket. Position the picket at the back of the plant stand, flush with the bottom edge of the lower shelf frame and all center marks matching. Drill pilot holes and attach the picket, using 1½" deck screws. Add the remaining pickets, spacing them ¾" (19.05 mm) apart.

2. On the outside edge of the last picket on each side, mark a point 3½" (8.9 cm) above the decking. At the center mark on the center picket, mark another point 8" (21.6 cm) above the decking. Tack a nail at each of these marks.

3. Cut a 54" (1.37 m) piece of flexible PVC pipe, and clamp it in place at each nail. Adjust the PVC until it creates a pleasing curve. Trace the curve, remove the PVC and nails, and then cut along the marked line, using a jig saw.

4. Spread exterior wood glue on top of the post and position the plywood roof pieces. Nail the pieces to one another at the peak, and then nail them into the post. Repeat on the other post. On each roof, add rows of dollhouse shingles, securing the shingles with exterior wood glue.

5. Cut two 2" pieces of ¼" dowel; glue one dowel into the small hole in each post.

6. Sand the cut edges of the pickets and touch up the finish. Apply a coat of polyurethane sealer to all surfaces, especially any exposed cut edges.

D. *Glue and nail the skirting in place, then install the decking. Attach the top of the balusters to the sides of the upper shelf frame.*

E. *Add the pickets and trim them to shape. Nail the roof sheathing to the posts, then add dollhouse shingles.*

Twig & Slat Bench

There are few things more important to a garden than really comfortable benches. Most of us think of benches in terms of providing places for visitors to relax. While that's true, it's only part of the story. The rest is that we, the gardeners, need places to rest, reflect, and take stock of our successes and our challenges. Place benches for your own pleasure and visitors are bound to enjoy them as well.

This bench combines the rustic appeal of branches with the more refined appearance of pickets. Because both trees and fences are common garden elements, the bench looks perfectly natural there.

We liked the contrast of crisp paint against the rough branches, but you might prefer to use an aging technique, such as crackling, a rubbed finish, or pickling on the painted portion of the bench.

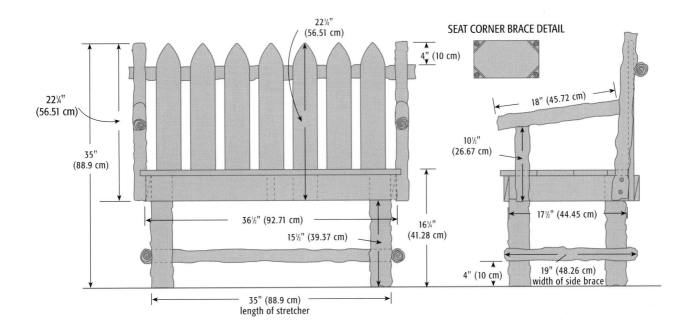

SEAT CORNER BRACE DETAIL

22¼" (56.51 cm)

4" (10 cm)

22¼" (56.51 cm)

35" (88.9 cm)

18" (45.72 cm)

10½" (26.67 cm)

36½" (92.71 cm)

15½" (39.37 cm)

16¼" (41.28 cm)

17½" (44.45 cm)

4" (10 cm)

19" (48.26 cm) width of side brace

35" (88.9 cm) length of stretcher

HOW TO BUILD A TWIG & SLAT BENCH
Step A: Gather & Prepare the Branches

1. Cut a supply of branches about 3" (7.6 cm) in diameter. You'll need one branch 6 ft. (1.83 m) long, one branch 5 ft. (1.5 m) long, and nine branches 3 ft. (91.44 cm) long. Remove any twigs and small branches, using loppers.

2. Following the cutting list, cut the pieces to size. When cutting branches, use a jig saw and make your cuts as square as possible. Shape the top of the pickets as desired.

A. *Gather branches and cut them to size. Cut the remaining pieces from 1 × 4 and 1 × 6 cedar.*

TOOLS & MATERIALS

- Loppers
- Jig saw
- Drill
- C clamps (2)
- Strap or bar clamp
- Level
- Branches
- 3½" (8.9 cm) corrosion-resistant deck screws

- Water-resistant sealer
- 2½" (6.35 cm) corrosion-resistant deck screws
- 1¼" (3.2 cm) corrosion-resistant deck screws
- 1½" (3.8 cm) corrosion-resistant deck screws

- 1 × 4 (2.54 × 10 cm) cedar lumber (5 8-ft. boards)
- 1 × 6 (2.54 × 15.25 cm) cedar (2 8-ft. boards)
- Exterior latex paint and brushes

Cutting List

Branches	Number	Size
Legs	4	16¼" (41.28 cm)
Leg braces	2	19" (48.26 cm)
Center stretcher	1	35" (88.9 cm)
Upper back brace	1	40" (1.02 m)
Side back braces	2	22¼" (56.51 cm)
Arm braces	2	10½" (26.67 cm)
Arms	2	18" (45.72 cm)
1 × 4 Cedar		
Front & back seat braces	3	36½" (92.71 cm)
Side & center seat braces	3	17½" (44.45 cm)
Pickets	7	21½" (54.61 cm)
Corner braces	4	10¾" (27.30 cm)
1 × 6 Cedar		
Decking	4	40" (1.02 m)

3. Paint the pieces cut from 1 × 4 cedar.

Step B: Construct the Seat

1. Lay out a pair of leg branches on a work surface. Position a brace across the legs, 4" (10 cm) from the bottom and centered horizontally. Holding this brace firmly in place, drill pilot holes through each end and into the legs. Secure each joint with 3½" deck screws. Repeat this process to construct a second pair of legs.

2. Drill pilot holes and use 2½" deck screws to

attach a side seat brace to each leg assembly. Align the top of the brace with the tops of the legs.

3. Place a pair of legs at either end of a front seat brace. Use two pairs of 2½" deck screws to attach the front brace to each leg assembly—drive one pair of screws into the leg and one pair into the side brace. Repeat to add a back seat brace to the assembly.

4. At the center of the seat assembly, attach the center seat brace, using a pair of 2½" deck screws at the front and at the back.

5. Center the center stretcher between the side leg braces, drill pilot holes, and secure the brace.

6. Cut four corner braces, beveling each end at 45°. Position one brace across each corner, and toenail it into place, using 1¼" deck screws.

Step C: Level the Legs

Place the base on a level floor and set a level across the seat. Shim the legs until the seat is level. Using a straight scrap of a 2 × 4, scribe each leg and then trim each, taking care to make square cuts.

Step D: Add the Bench Back

1. Starting 1½" (3.8 cm) from one edge and leaving 1½" between them, attach the pickets to the back brace, using 1¼" deck screws. The ends of the pickets should be flush with the lower edge of the back brace.

2. Clamp the brace and pickets into place. The

B. *Join pairs of legs with braces, and assemble the seat frame. Add the center brace and corner braces.*

C. *Shim the seat until it's level, then mark and trim the legs.*

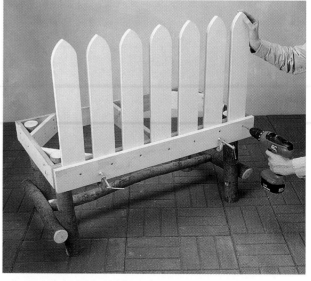

D. *Attach the pickets to the back brace, and clamp it in place. Secure the back brace to the back seat brace.*

bottom of the back brace should be flush with the bottom of the seat brace. Attach the back to the seat by driving screws through the back brace and into the seat brace.

Step E: Attach the Bench Back Braces

1. Drill pilot holes and attach the side back braces to the upper back brace. The top ends of the side braces should extend 4" (10 cm) past the upper back brace.

2. Clamp or band the brace assembly into position, with the top of the upper brace approximately 4" from the top of the pickets. Drill pilot holes and drive screws through the side braces and into the lower back brace, three screws for each side brace.

3. Attach each picket to the upper back brace, using a pair of screws for each.

Step F: Attach the Arms

1. Cut two arm braces. Drill pilot holes and attach one brace on each side of the seat assembly, using 3½" deck screws. Position the branches so the bottom of each is flush with the lower edge of the side brace.

2. Cut two arms. Position each arm against the side back brace and arm brace, drill pilot holes and attach with 3½" screws.

Step G: Add the Decking & Finish the Bench

1. Measure the side seat braces and notch the ends of a decking board to accommodate them. Attach the board to the seat assembly by driving

a pair of 1½" deck screws into each side brace as well as the center brace. Attach two more decking boards. Trim the final decking board, if necessary.

2. Touch up the painted portion of the bench if necessary, and put a coat of water-resistant sealer on the branches, especially on the cut ends.

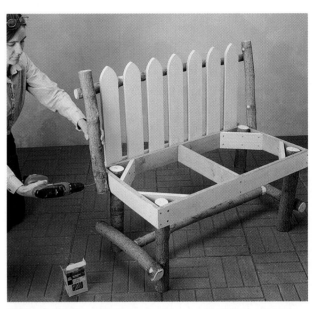

E. *Attach the side back braces to the upper back brace. Clamp this assembly into position and secure it to the lower back brace. Drill pilot holes and use pairs of screws to connect each picket to the upper back brace.*

F. *Attach the arm braces at the side of the seat, and then add the arms.*

G. *Notch each end of the first decking board and install it. Add two more boards, then trim, notch, and install the final decking board to fit.*

Porch Swing

When the siren song of privacy lured families to backyard decks, we all lost something important. In the years when we played out our day-to-day activities in full view of whoever happened to be on the front porch next door, we forged close connections with our neighbors. Even now, porches and porch swings conjure up images of first dates and furtive good-night kisses, frosty glasses of lemonade,

and waiting for the mail. It's easy to imagine that this swing recently held a grandmother piecing a quilt or a teenaged-girl in pincurls and pedal pushers, killing time while her nails dried.

If you're fortunate enough to have a porch or other place to hang a swing, build one and let it remind you to take time to watch the world go by. Maybe even talk with your neighbors.

TOOLS & MATERIALS

- Circular saw
- Router and chamfer bit
- Drill with ¾₆" (4.76 mm) twist bit and ⅝" (15.86 mm) spade bit
- Hammer
- Chisel
- Jig saw
- Belt sander
- 48" (1.22 m) flexible straightedge
- 1 × 6 (2.54 × 15.25 cm), 8 ft. (2.44 m) cedar (4)
- 1 × 4 (2.54 × 10 cm), 8 ft. (2.44 m) cedar (8)
- 1 × 2 (2.54 × 5 cm), 8 ft. (2.44 m) cedar (2)
- Latex paint
- Latex paint glaze
- Polyurethane sealer
- Paint brushes
- 3" (7.62 cm) galvanized deck screws
- 1½" (3.8 cm) galvanized deck screws
- 2" (5 cm) galvanized deck screws
- Deck balusters (2)
- Exterior wood glue
- C-clamps (2)
- Eye-bolts, nuts and washers
- Heavy chain, 32 ft. (9.75 m)
- 2" (5 cm) connecting links (4)

Cutting List

Key	Part	Lumber	No.	Size
A	Seat support	1 × 6 (2.5 × 16 cm)	2	37³⁄₁₆" (94.46 cm)
B	Front cross brace	1 × 6 (2.5 × 16 cm)	1	36" (91.44 cm)
C	Rear cross brace	1 × 6 (2.5 × 16 cm)	1	36" (91.44 cm)
D	Narrow seat slats	1 × 2 (2.5 × 5 cm)	4	37½" (95.25 cm)
E	Wide seat slats	1 × 4 (2.5 × 10 cm)	3	37½" (95.25 cm)
F	Center seat brace	1 × 4 (2.5 × 10 cm)	1	15½" (39.37 cm)
G	Seat stretcher	1 × 4 (2.5 × 10 cm)	1	37½" (95.25 cm)
H	Upper back brace	1 × 4 (2.5 × 10 cm)	1	30" (76 cm)
I	Middle back brace	1 × 4 (2.5 × 10 cm)	1	37¾" (95.88 cm)
J	Lower back brace	1 × 4 (2.5 × 10 cm)	1	36" (91.44 cm)
K	Back slats	1 × 4 (2.5 × 10 cm)	8	38" (96.52 cm)
L	Back support	1 × 4 (2.5 × 10 cm)	1	44¾" (1.14 m)
M	Arms	1 × 6 (2.5 × 16 cm)	2	29¾" (75.57 cm)
N	Arm facings	1 × 4 (2.5 × 10 cm)	2	13¾" (34.93 cm)
O	Front arm support	1 × 6 (2.5 × 16 cm)	2	15" (38.1 cm)
P	Rear arm support	1 × 6 (2.5 × 16 cm)	2	26" (66 cm)

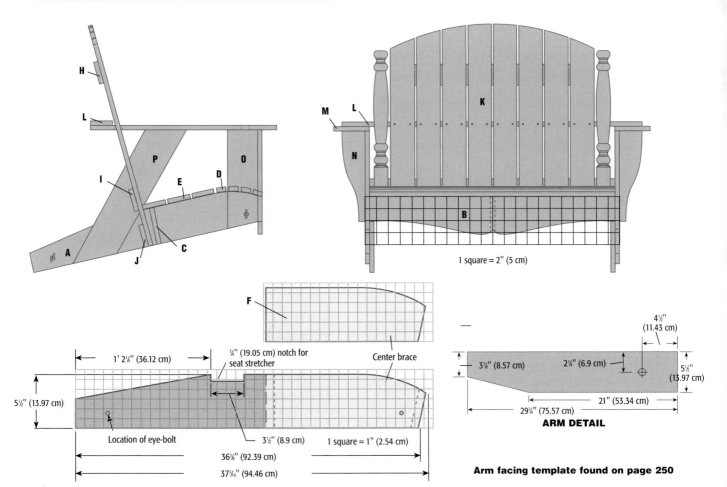

1 square = 2" (5 cm)

¾" (19.05 cm) notch for seat stretcher

Center brace

F

1' 2¼" (36.12 cm)

5½" (13.97 cm)

Location of eye-bolt

3½" (8.9 cm)

1 square = 1" (2.54 cm)

36⅜" (92.39 cm)

37³⁄₁₆" (94.46 cm)

SEAT SUPPORT (A) DETAIL

4½" (11.43 cm)

3⅜" (8.57 cm)

2¾" (6.9 cm)

5½" (13.97 cm)

21" (53.34 cm)

29¾" (75.57 cm)

ARM DETAIL

Arm facing template found on page 250

HOW TO BUILD A PORCH SWING

Step A: Prepare the Lumber

1. Cut the parts to length, as indicated on the cutting list. Using a router and a chamfer bit, chamfer the edges of all pieces, except those that require further shaping (the seat support, front cross brace, arms, and arm facings).

2. Mix paint and glaze in a 2:1 ratio and use it to wash all the pieces with color.

Step B: Shape the Pieces of the Seat Frame

1. Using the grid system or a photocopier, enlarge the shaping templates on page 175.

2. Trace the proper contour onto one of the seat supports (A), then cut along the cutting lines, using a jig saw. Use this piece as a template to mark and cut an identical seat support. Chamfer the edges and lightly sand each piece.

3. Transfer the placement marks for the front and rear cross braces onto the seat supports as indicated on the seat support template. Also mark the cutting lines for the mortise for the seat stretcher.

4. Set the depth gauge on a circular saw, then make ¾"-deep (19.05 mm) cuts along each of the cutting lines marked for the mortise. Make an additional cut every ¼" (6.35 mm) between those lines. Remove the waste material, using a hammer and chisel.

5. Trace the proper contour onto the front cross brace (B), and cut it to shape, using a jig saw. Chamfer the edges and lightly sand the piece.

Step C: Build the Seat Frame

1. Align the front cross brace with the placement marks, and attach it between the seat supports, using glue and 3" deck screws. The top of the pieces must be flush with one another.

2. Position the rear cross brace (C) between the seat supports, aligned with the placement marks; attach the seat support with glue and 3" deck screws. Again, make sure the tops are flush.

3. Using the seat support template on page 175, shape the center seat brace (F). Position the brace in the center of the seat and attach it to the front and

A. *Cut the lumber for the swing, and chamfer the edges of all the slats and arm pieces.*

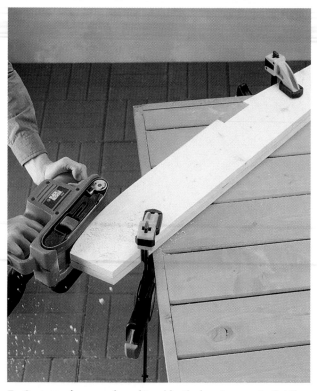

B. *Contour, shape, and sand two identical seat supports. Cut the mortises for the seat stretcher.*

rear cross braces, using counterbored 1½" deck screws.

4. Set the seat stretcher (G) into position in the mortises. Join these pieces, using a pair of 1½" deck screws on each side.

5. Arrange the seat slats on top of this assembly, using wood scraps to set ⅜" (9.5 mm) spaces between the slats. Start with the four 1 × 2 slats (D), and then add three 1 × 4 slats (E). The first slat should overhang the front of the frame by ¾" (19.05 mm). Drill counterbored pilot holes and drive 2" deck screws through the holes and into each of the seat supports as well as the center brace.

Step D: Construct the Seat Back

1. Trim two deck balusters to 26¾" (67.94 cm), and round the top of each one, using a belt sander.

2. Gang the back slats together and mark a straight line 22½" (57.15 cm) from the bottom of the slats.

3. Mark the centers of the upper (H), middle (I), and lower (J) back braces. Set the lower and middle

braces on a flat surface with the center marks matching and 1" (2.54 cm) of space between them. Position the balusters and back slats (K) on top of the braces, maintaining ½" (12.7 mm) spaces between them. Slide the upper brace into place beneath the slats, aligning it with the line marked across them at 22½". Make sure the ends of the slats are flush with the bottom edge of the lower back brace and their tops remain straight.

4. Drill pilot holes and attach the balusters and slats to the braces, using a pair of screws on each slat for each brace.

Step E: Shape the Back Slats

1. Mark the center of the back assembly, 36" (91.44 cm) from the lower edge of the slats. Mark the outside edge of each baluster on each side, 32½" (82.5 cm) from the lower edge. Tack a small nail at each of these marks.

2. Use the nails as reference points to bend a long, flexible straightedge into an arc. Trace that curve onto the slats, then cut along the marked line

C. *Construct the seat frame, using glue and 3" deck screws. Drill counterbored pilot holes and use 2" deck screws to attach the seat slats to the frame.*

D. *Attach the balusters and the back slats to the upper, middle, and lower back braces.*

E. *Trace a graceful curve onto the back slats and trim them to shape, using a jig saw.*

with a jig saw. Sand cut edges smooth with a belt sander.

Step F: Construct the Arms

1. Using the arm template on page 175 and the arm facing template on page 250, trace the appropriate contours onto one arm (M) and one arm facing (N), and use a jig saw to cut them out. Use each as a template to mark and cut the identical (mirrored) shapes on the other arm and arm facing. Chamfer the edges of each piece. On each arm, transfer the placement markings for the arm facings, front and rear arm supports, and back support, as well as for the front chain holes. Drill the front chain holes, using a ⅝" spade bit.

2. Drill pilot holes and attach a front arm support (O) to each arm at the placement marks, using 1½" deck screws.

3. Drill pilot holes and attach the back support (L) to each arm at the placement marks, using four 1½" deck screws.

4. Trim the top of the rear arm supports at a 60° angle. Drill pilot holes and attach a rear arm support (P) to each arm at the placement marks, using 1½" deck screws.

F. *Attach the front arm supports, the rear arm supports, and the back support to the arms.*

G. *Clamp the seat frame into position and connect it to the arm assembly by driving screws through the seat support and into the front and rear arm supports.*

Step G: Assemble the Seat & Arms

1. Set the seat assembly upright on your work surface, and use scrap lumber to prop it into a stable position. Clamp and prop the arm assembly into position, aligning the arm supports with the placement lines marked on the seat supports. Scribe a cutting line onto each front (O) and rear arm (P) support along the bottoms of the seat supports. Remove the arm assembly and trim the supports along the scribed lines, using a circular saw.

2. Reclamp the arm assembly into position, drill pilot holes, and attach the arm supports to the seat support, using pairs of screws.

3. Drill pilot holes and attach the arm assembly to the seat support by driving pairs of screws through the seat support into each front arm support from inside the seat frame.

Step H: Attach the Seat Back

1. Position the back so the lower back brace is between the seat supports, flush with their lower edges, and aligned with the placement lines. Clamp the back in place. On each side, drill pilot holes and attach the side supports to the lower back brace,

using three 2" deck screws on each side.

2. Drill pilot holes and attach each slat to the back support, using a pair of 1½" deck screws for each.

Step I: Apply Finishing Touches

1. Drill pilot holes and attach the arm facings to the arms and to the front arm supports, using glue and 2" deck screws.

2. Drill pilot holes and attach eye-bolts (as indicated on the diagram on page 175) on the seat supports and front arm supports.

3. Lightly sand all cut surfaces and retouch the finish as necessary. Apply a coat of polyurethane sealer to the swing.

4. Hook the chain to the bolts with connecting links and suspend the swing. Adjust the length of the chain and the position of the connection until the swing balances correctly. Mark the position and angle of the chain, then drill ⅝" (15.86 mm) holes through the back of the arms. Thread the chain through the holes and check the balance once again.

5. Hang the swing with heavy screw eyes driven into ceiling joists or into a 2 × 4 lag-screwed across ceiling joists.

H. *Set the back into position and attach the lower back brace to the seat support, then attach the back slats to the back support.*

I. *Install eye-bolts and suspend the swing with a heavy chain. Adjust the chain until the swing is balanced, then mark and drill the rear chain holes in the arms.*

Stained Glass Planter

Hypertufa—mainly a mixture of portland cement, peat moss, and perlite—is a wonderful medium for building all sorts of garden accents. It's as durable as concrete but without the weight. You can mold it into almost anything for which you can build a form.

While researching a book on garden-style decorating, we came across a poured-concrete planter that had a stained glass design embedded in it. It was beautiful, but extreme—extremely heavy and extremely expensive. We did a little experimenting and were delighted to find that stained glass could be embedded in our old favorite, hypertufa.

You have to be fairly careful as you pack the hypertufa around the stained glass. We tried several methods of holding the glass to the sides of the form, but found that double-stick carpet tape works best. Although it releases easily when the forms are removed, it holds the glass quite securely during the forming process.

It's important to tamp the hypertufa consistently throughout. Loosely packed hypertufa has many voids and air pockets, which are not especially attractive. Firmly packed hypertufa has an even, consistent, more appealing surface.

This project is fairly basic. Once you have some experience with these techniques, use your imagination and taste to adapt the basic project and create planters tailored to your personal style and your garden.

TOOLS & MATERIALS

- Glass cutter
- Breaker pliers
- Rotary tool or Carborundum stone
- Jig saw
- Straightedge
- Drill
- Hacksaw
- Wheelbarrow or mixing trough
- Hammer
- Chisel
- Paint scraper
- Wire brush
- Fine wire mesh
- Stained glass (two colors)
- 2"-thick (5 cm) polystyrene

- insulation board
- 3½" (8.9 cm) deck screws (40)
- Duct tape
- Double-stick carpet tape
- Scrap of 4"- dia. (10 cm) PVC pipe
- Dust mask
- Gloves
- Portland cement
- Peat moss
- Perlite
- Fiberglass reinforcing fibers
- Cement dye (optional)
- Plastic tarp
- Scrap 2 × 4 (5 × 10 cm)

Cutting List

Outer Form		Inner Form	
Floor 1	22" × 32" (56 × 81 cm)	Sides 2	7" × 24" (18 × 61 cm)
Sides 2	11" × 32" (28 × 81 cm)	Ends & Center Support	
Ends 2	11" × 18" (28 × 46 cm)	3	7" × 10" (18 × 25 cm)

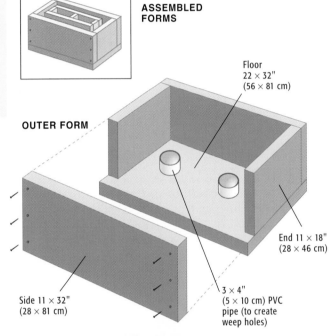

ASSEMBLED FORMS

Floor
22 × 32"
(56 × 81 cm)

OUTER FORM

End 11 × 18"
(28 × 46 cm)

Side 11 × 32"
(28 × 81 cm)

3 × 4"
(5 × 10 cm) PVC
pipe (to create
weep holes)

INNER FORM

End 7 × 10"
(18 × 25 cm)

Center support
7 × 10"
(18 × 25 cm)

Side 7 × 24"
(18 × 61 cm)

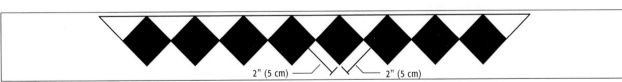

2" (5 cm)   2" (5 cm)

HOW TO BUILD A STAINED GLASS PLANTER

Step A: Make the Pattern and Cut the Glass

1. Mark twelve 2" (5 cm) squares onto one piece of the stained glass. Divide each square into two equal triangles.

2. Mark twenty-two 2" squares onto the second piece of stained glass.

3. Score the glass along the marked lines, using a glass cutter. Extend the score from one side of the glass to the other. Hold breaker pliers next to the score, and snap the glass apart. File the edges of each piece with a rotary tool or a Carborundum stone; rinse and dry each piece.

A. *Mark, score, and cut triangles and squares from stained glass.*

181

Step B: Build the Forms

1. Measure, mark, and cut pieces of 2"-thick polystyrene insulation board to the dimensions in the cutting list, using a jig saw.

2. Construct the inner form: Fit an end piece between the two side pieces and fasten each joint, using three 3½" deck screws. Repeat to fasten the other end and to add the center support. Wrap duct tape around the form at each joint.

3. Construct the outer form: Use deck screws and duct tape, as with the inner form. Set the bottom piece squarely on top of the resulting rectangle, and then screw and tape it securely in place.

4. Cut two 3" (7.6 cm) pieces of 4"-dia. PVC pipe, using a hacksaw, and set them aside.

Step C: Form the Floor

1. Center the pieces of PVC pipe in the floor of the outer form and press them into the foam, but not through the foam; these pipes establish the planter's drainage holes.

2. Mix the hypertufa, following the directions on pages 248 to 249. Be sure to wear a dust mask and gloves when handling dry cement mix; also wear gloves when working with wet cement.

3. Pack hypertufa onto the floor of the form, pressing down firmly and packing it tightly around the pieces of PVC. Continue adding hypertufa until you've created a solid, 2"-thick (5 cm)

floor. (Be careful not to get hypertufa inside the PVC pipe.)

Step D: Build the Walls

1. Attach double-stick carpet tape 2" from the top edge on the inside of the side and end pieces of the outer form. Remove the tape's backing, exposing the adhesive.

2. Arrange the stained glass pieces on the tape, positioned as planned for the design.

3. Center the inner form within the outer form. Add hypertufa between the forms. Using your gloved hands, pack it firmly. Make sure the walls will be solid—they need to withstand the weight and pressure of soil, moisture, and growing plants. Continue adding hypertufa until it reaches the top of the forms.

Step E: Allow to Dry & Remove the Forms

1. Cover the planter with a plastic tarp, and let it dry for two to three days. If the weather is extremely warm, remove the tarp and mist the planter with water occasionally during the curing process.

2. Remove the tape and screws from the outer form, and pull the polystyrene away from the planter. Work carefully so the form can be reused, if desired. If the walls appear to be dry enough to be handled, remove the inner forms. If not, let the planter cure for another day or two, and then remove the inner form.

B. *To construct the forms, fasten the joints with 3½" deck screws; then reinforce them with duct tape.*

C. *Pack hypertufa onto the floor of the form; press it down firmly to create a level, 2"-thick floor.*

Step F: Complete the Curing Process

1. If you want to give the planter a rustic appearance, this is the time to create it. Working carefully with a hammer and chisel, knock off the corners and sharp edges.

2. Next, add texture to the sides by using a paint scraper or screwdriver to scrape grooves into the hypertufa.

3. Finally, brush the surface with a wire brush. Avoid the areas immediately surrounding the stained glass, but be bold in other areas. The more texture you create, the more time-worn the planter will appear to be.

4. Cover the planter with plastic, and let it cure for about a month. Uncover it at least once a week, and mist it with water to slow down the curing process. Although it's natural to be impatient, don't rush this step. The more slowly the hypertufa cures, the stronger and more durable the planter will be.

5. Unwrap the planter and let it cure outside, uncovered, for several weeks. Periodically wash it down with water, inside and out, to remove the alkaline residue of the concrete (which would otherwise endanger plants grown in the container). Adding vinegar to the water speeds this process somewhat, but it still takes several weeks. Again, this step is important, so don't rush it.

6. After the planter has cured outside for several weeks, put it inside, away from any sources of moisture, to cure for several more weeks.

NOTE: Before filling the planter with potting soil, cover the drainage holes with fine wire mesh.

D. *Center the inner form within the walls of the outer form. Pack hypertufa between the forms to create the planter's walls.*

E. *After the planter has dried for two to three days, remove the screws and carefully disassemble the forms.*

F. *Round the corners and texture the surface of the planter with a hammer and chisel, paint scraper, and wire brush. Work carefully so you don't dislodge the stained glass.*

183

Accessories

Webster's Dictionary tells us that an accessory is an object or device "not essential in itself but adding to the beauty, convenience, or effectiveness of something else." When it comes to garden accessories we respectfully disagree. Beauty—appeal to the eyes, ears, nose, and soul—is the garden's whole reason for being. That which adds beauty is essential.

Accessories have more than aesthetic appeal: They give gardeners something to work on and play with once the basic structure of the garden is in place. We always face seasonal tasks, such as dividing and transplanting, and like Hope, weeding springs eternal; but there are limits to the number of major borders or beds that can be added to one garden. Fortunately, when we're in the mood to create, there's almost always room for accessories. And if your own garden's already well appointed, remember this: Garden accessories make wonderful gifts.

Copper Sprinkler

This copper sprinkler combines a simple but ingenious mechanism with a simple head shape and design.

The swivel mechanism incorporates parts from some unexpected sources, but they're all widely available. Copper pipe and fittings are available at virtually any home center. The round brass tubing (made by K&S Engineering) is sold at many hardware stores as well as hobby and crafts centers. The hinge pin bushings (manufactured by Motormite) are available at many auto parts stores.

The spacing of the holes on this square head is critical, but quite simple. On the sides of the head, the holes face in opposite directions, which creates the directional force that makes the head spin. As water is pushed out of the holes, the pressure rotates the head. The holes on each side need to be centered on the pipe. There are holes in the top as well, but they're merely decorative—they play no part in the sprinkler's action.

Unlike many of our copper projects, this one must have watertight solder joints. That means the soldering involved here is a little more delicate than in some of our other projects, but if you work slowly and carefully, it won't be difficult. If necessary, review the soldering techniques described on pages 246 to 247.

TOOLS & MATERIALS

- Tubing cutter
- Wire cutters
- Center punch
- Bench grinder or rotary tool
- Propane torch
- Drill with ¹⁄₁₆" (1.6 mm) twist bit
- Clamp
- Markers, black and red
- ½" (12.7 mm) Type L copper pipe
- ¹¹⁄₃₂" (8.7 mm) brass tubing
- ⁵⁄₁₆" (8 mm) brass tubing
- Wire brush or emery cloth
- Hinge pin bushings (4)
- Solder
- Flux and flux brush
- Pliers

- ½" (12.7 mm) copper tee
- ½" (12.7 mm) copper 90° elbows (4)
- ¼" (6.35 mm) copper tubing (39" [99 cm])
- 1-gallon (4-l) paint can
- 1-quart (1-l) paint can
- Flat washers (4 or 5)
- 10-gauge (3-mm) copper wire (65" [165 cm])
- ½" (12.7 mm) brass shower ell
- 6" (15.25 cm) galvanized wicket
- Machine screws and nuts (2)
- Spray paint, copper color
- ½" (12.7 mm) threaded copper adapter
- Teflon tape
- Hose connector

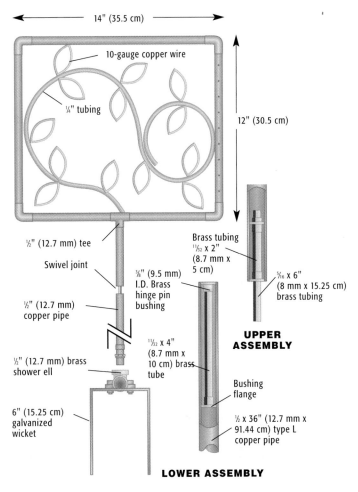

14" (35.5 cm)

10-gauge copper wire

¼" tubing

12" (30.5 cm)

½" (12.7 mm) tee

Swivel joint

½" (12.7 mm) copper pipe

⅜" (9.5 mm) I.D. Brass hinge pin bushing

½" (12.7 mm) brass shower ell

6" (15.25 cm) galvanized wicket

¹¹⁄₃₂ x 4" (8.7 mm x 10 cm) brass tube

LOWER ASSEMBLY

Brass tubing ¹¹⁄₃₂ x 2" (8.7 mm x 5 cm)

⁵⁄₁₆ x 6" (8 mm x 15.25 cm) brass tubing

UPPER ASSEMBLY

Bushing flange

½ x 36" (12.7 mm x 91.44 cm) type L copper pipe

HOW TO BUILD A COPPER SPRINKLER
Step A: Make the Assemblies for the Swivel Joint

1. Cut one 5" (12.7 cm) piece and one 36" (91.44 cm) piece of ½" copper pipe, using a tubing cutter. Also cut one 2" (5 cm) and one 4" (10 cm) piece of ¹¹⁄₃₂" brass tubing, and one 6" (15.25 cm) piece of ⁵⁄₁₆" brass tubing. Deburr the pieces, being careful not to flare the ends; use a wire brush or emery cloth to polish the ends.

2. Test-fit the hinge pin bushings inside the 5" piece

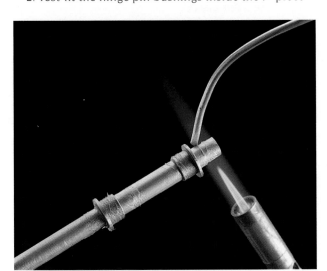

A. *Solder the upper assembly, connecting the ⁵⁄₁₆" tube, the ¹¹⁄₃₂" tube, and the bushing. Heat all three pieces; first feed solder into the joint between the brass tubes, then into the bushing joint.*

of copper. If necessary, use a bench grinder or a rotary tool to slightly shape the flanges of the hinge pin bushings so they fit snugly within the pipe. NOTE: To help you create a uniform edge, use a scrap of the ¹¹⁄₃₂" tubing as a spindle.

3. To form the upper assembly, slide a bushing onto each end of the 2" length of ¹¹⁄₃₂" brass tubing, with the flanges facing the ends of the tube. Set the flange of one bushing back ⅛" (3 mm) from the end of the tube. Position the other bushing flush with the opposite end. Slide the 6" length of ⁵⁄₁₆" brass tubing inside the ¹¹⁄₃₂" tube, positioning the inner tube to protrude ⅜" (9.5 mm) beyond the top (set back) bushing.

4. To form the lower assembly, slide a bushing onto each end of the 4" piece of ¹¹⁄₃₂" brass tubing, flanges facing outward, flush with the ends of the tube.

5. Begin soldering at the top of the upper assembly (see pages 246 to 247 for soldering techniques). Heat all three pieces—the ⁵⁄₁₆" tube, the ¹¹⁄₃₂" tube, and the

bushing. Feed solder into the joint between the two brass tubes first. Next, feed solder into the bushing joint, approaching that joint from the side opposite the flange.

6. Solder the three remaining bushing joints, each time feeding the solder into the joint from the side opposite the flange.

Step B: Construct the Swivel Joint

1. Flux the inside of the 5" piece of ½" copper and the flange of the bushing on the upper assembly. Slide the assembly inside the copper pipe, positioning the lower bushing to be flush with the end of the copper pipe.

2. Flux the inside of the 36" piece of copper and the

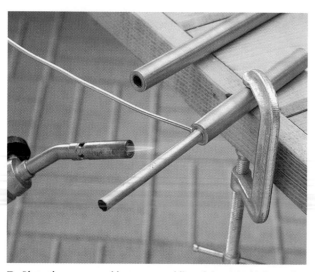

B. *Place the upper and lower assemblies of the swivel joint at the edge of a work surface and solder the joints. Feed the solder from the bottom so the solder doesn't run into the brass tubes.*

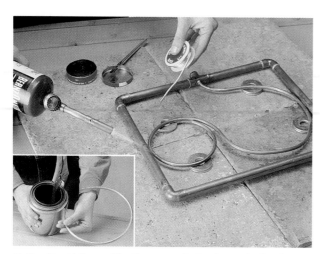

C. *Dry-fit and then solder the rectangle that forms the head. Shape ¼" tubing for the vine (inset), and solder it in place.*

shoulder of one bushing on the lower assembly. Slide the assembly inside the pipe, positioning the bushing flange to be flush with the top of the pipe.

3. Place the assembled pieces at the end of a protected work surface, and solder each one. Be careful not to displace the bushings. Concentrate the flame on the copper pipe as you heat the joints, and feed the solder from the bottom. Don't let the solder run into the brass tube.

Step C: Form the Head

1. Clean and flux all the pieces of the head. On a heatproof surface, lay out the head sides, top, and bottom pieces, along with four ½" copper 90° elbows and a ½" copper tee to form a rectangle roughly 12 × 14" (30.5 × 35.5 cm) (see diagram on page 187).

2. Cut a 39" (99 cm) piece of ¼" copper tubing and slightly flatten each end. Clamp one end of the tube to a 1-gallon paint can and wrap almost one whole revolution. Remove the tubing and clamp the opposite end to a 1-quart paint can. Wrap the tubing, in the opposite direction, 1¼ rotations, or just until the two loops intersect one another. Unclamp the tubing and place it on a flat, level soldering surface. Refine the shape until both loops lie flat and the small loop wraps inside itself. Form a slight bend on the open end of the large loop.

3. Lay the shaped tubing inside the copper rectangle, and use large, flat washers to shim the tubing into position. Adjust the tubing until it touches the edge of the frame at the open end of the large loop and at the outer edges of both loops. Clean, flux, and solder these points.

Step D: Add the Leaves

1. Cut a 65" (1.65 m) length of 10-gauge copper wire

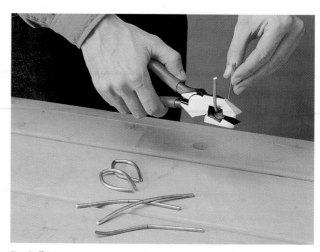

D. *Coil 10-gauge copper wire around a quart paint can, and then cut the wire into 5" pieces. Shape each piece into a leaf; file or grind the end of each leaf until it's flat.*

and mark every 5" (12.7 cm) with a black marker. Using a red marker, place another mark 2½" (6.35 cm) from one end and every 5" from that mark.

2. Clamp and wrap the wire around a 1-quart paint can. Remove the coil and use wire cutters to cut the coil at each black mark, yielding thirteen 5" pieces of curved wire.

3. Lightly crimp each piece of wire at the red mark. Use pliers to fold each wire in half to form a leaf shape. File or grind the end of each leaf to form a flat surface where the leaf can be soldered to the vine.

4. Clean and flux the contact spots, then use large, flat washers to shim the leaves into position around the copper tubing. Solder the leaves to the vine.

Step E: Insert the Stem & Drill the Holes

1. Insert the 5" stem into the tee, and shim the open end of the stem to be even with the other pieces. Solder each joint and let the assembly cool.

2. Place the head on a flat surface. Along the surface of one side of the head, mark nine points, 1" apart. Repeat on the other side of the head, so the marks face the opposite direction. Finally, lay out five marks, one every 2", along the top of the head.

3. Centerpunch and drill one ¹⁄₁₆" (1.6 mm) hole at each mark. Be sure to drill the holes through only one wall of the pipe.

Step F: Add the Swivel Joint

Dry-fit the upper assembly of the swivel joint to the tee at the bottom of the sprinkler head (be sure the brass tube is extending down). Flux the mating surfaces and solder the joint.

Step G: Build the Stand & Assemble the Sprinkler

1. Center a ½" brass shower ell on top of a 6" galva-nized wicket, and mark the holes. Drill holes in the wicket, and then secure the ell to it, using machine screws and nuts. Spray paint these pieces to match the copper color of the sprinkler. Let the paint dry.

2. Solder a ½" threaded copper adapter to the open end of the stand pipe. When the piece is cool, wrap the threads of the adapter with Teflon™ tape. Screw the adapter into the top of the shower ell and a hose connector to the other.

3. Set the hoop into the stand pipe, mating the upper and lower portions of the swivel joint. Attach a garden hose to the hose connector.

E. *Mark the placement, then drill holes along the sides and at the top of the head. (Drill through only one wall of each pipe.)*

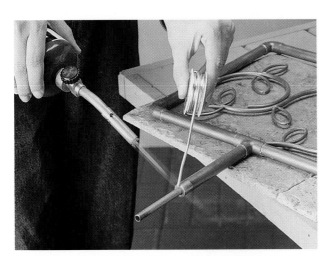

F. *Solder the swivel joint to the tee at the base of the head.*

G. *Assemble the standpipe. Connect a shower ell to one end and a garden hose connector to the other.*

Clay Pot Birdbath

To attract birds to your yard and garden, you need to provide sources of clean water for drinking and for bathing. It may be surprising, but good hygiene is just as important to birds as it is to people. Regular baths discourage parasites and help the birds stay warm—clean feathers actually offer better insulation than dirty ones.

A simple birdbath can be just as effective and attractive as a more elaborate version. This one is merely clay pots and saucers stacked and then secured with a threaded rod and a combination of washers and nuts. Just for fun, we used a texturized paint technique on the clay pots and saucers. Then we added sugar glass beads because—like many people—birds are drawn to a little bit of sparkle.

Place your birdbath in an area that offers resting spots and perches for the birds, but without providing hiding places for predators. An area with trees and bushes nearby is good, for example, as long as there are no low-hanging branches from which a cat could pounce upon the unsuspecting birds.

Birds are creatures of habit. Once they are familiar with sources of food or water, they begin to count on their presence, so keep your birdbath clean and filled throughout the season.

TOOLS & MATERIALS

- Terra-cotta pots: 14" (35.5 cm), 12" (30.5 cm), 9½" (24 cm)
- Terra-cotta saucers: 18" (46 cm), 16" (41 cm), 12" (30.5 cm)
- Large container of sand
- Drill with ½" (12.7 mm) masonry bit
- Duct tape
- Ruler
- Permanent marker
- Conical rasp bit
- Water-based masonry paint
- Paint brushes
- Acrylic glaze
- Acrylic paint
- Plastic wrap
- Sparkle dust
- Waterproof sealer/glue/finish, such as Mod Podge Outdoor
- Sugar glass beads
- Rubber washers (5)
- Large flat metal washers (5)
- Threaded rod (48" [1.22 m])
- Nuts (5)
- Silicone caulk
- Acorn nut

HOW TO BUILD A CLAY POT BIRDBATH

Step A: Drill Holes in the Saucers

1. Put duct tape on the bottom of each saucer, then center and mark an X on each saucer, using a ruler and permanent marker. Soak the saucers in water for at least an hour.

2. Fill a large bucket or other container with sand. Set a saucer upside down in the sand so the edges of the saucer are supported by the sand. At the center mark, drill a hole, using a ½" (12.7 mm) masonry bit. Drill slowly, using light pressure. If necessary, use a conical rasp bit to enlarge the hole. Repeat with each saucer.

A. *Drill a ½" hole at the center of each saucer.*

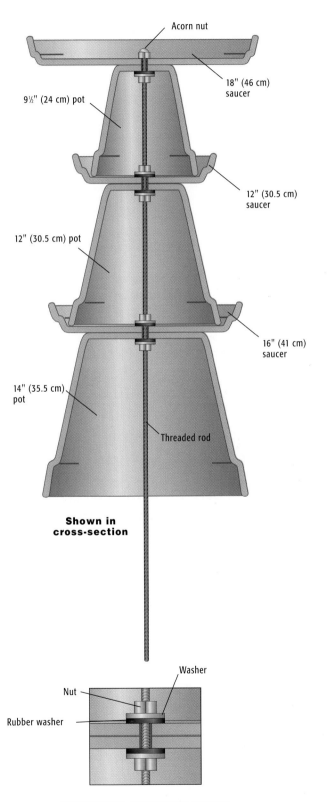

Acorn nut

18" (46 cm) saucer

9½" (24 cm) pot

12" (30.5 cm) saucer

12" (30.5 cm) pot

16" (41 cm) saucer

14" (35.5 cm) pot

Threaded rod

Shown in cross-section

Washer

Nut

Rubber washer

HARDWARE ASSEMBLY DETAIL
(shown in cross-section)

Step B: Paint the Pots & Saucers for the Base

1. Start with clean, dry terra-cotta pots and saucers. Paint a coat of water-based masonry paint on the outside of each piece and the interior of the 18" saucer. After the first coat is dry, apply a second. Let all the pieces dry.

2. Mix a slightly darker or lighter color of acrylic paint and an acrylic glaze, at a ratio of about 10:1. Roughly paint the glaze onto one of the pots. Scrunch up a handful of plastic wrap and use it to pat the wet glaze to produce a crazed texture over the entire pot. Repeat with each pot and saucer, and let them dry overnight.

3. Seal each piece with a coat of waterproof sealer/glue/finish. Mix a little sparkle dust into the finish when you seal the interior of the 18" saucer.

Step C: Embellish the Saucers

Paint the rim of the 12" and 16" saucers with waterproof sealer/glue/finish, and roll them in sugar glass beads.

Step D: Assemble the Base

1. Mark the rod 32½" (82.5 cm) from one end. Slip a rubber washer and a flat washer on the threaded rod and add a nut. Position the washers and nut at the marked location. Slide the 14" pot onto the rod, facing down. Top it with the 16" saucer, facing up.

2. Continue alternating pots and saucers, using rubber washers as bumpers, and metal washers and nuts to hold the pots in place.

Step E: Install the Basin

1. Set the base in position in the garden, carefully pressing down to push the rod into the soil. (The buried rod provides stability for the birdbath.)

2. Add the 18" saucer to create the basin. Put a dab of silicone caulk at the edges of the hole to seal any gaps surrounding the threaded rod. Top the threaded rod with an acorn nut.

B. *Paint a base coat on each pot and saucer, and let it dry. Add a glaze and texture it with plastic wrap.*

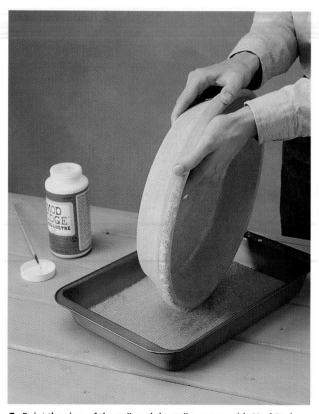

C. *Paint the rims of the 12" and the 16" saucers with Mod Podge Outdoor, and roll them in sugar glass beads.*

TIP: CLEANING A BIRDBATH

Providing a birdbath is the first step; keeping it clean is the second. A well-used birdbath can quickly fill up with debris, such as leaves, feathers, and bits of food. Depending on how much use your birdbath gets, it may need to be cleaned as often as once a week, but certainly every two weeks.

To clean a birdbath, rinse the basin thoroughly, then scrub its surface with a stiff brush. Next, fill the basin with a 10:1 solution of hot, soapy water and bleach, and let it soak for about 15 minutes. (Chlorine is toxic to birds, so set the birdbath inside or cover it with a tarp while the solution soaks.) After it has soaked, rinse the bath and scrub it with a brush once again. Finish with a very thorough rinse, then fill the bath with fresh water.

If you prefer not to use chemicals, use sand to scrub out your birdbath. Just dip a damp cloth into a bag of clean sand, and then scour away the grime. Rinse and refill the bath.

D. *Use a threaded rod, rubber washers, flat washers, and nuts to secure the stack of pots and saucers.*

E. *Top the stack with the 18" saucer, then use silicone caulk to seal any gaps between the hole and threaded rod. Add an acorn nut to secure the basin.*

Millstone Fountain

In New England, gardeners often use antique well covers for fountains of this type. In the Midwest, people sometimes use antique millstones. Neither type of stone is easy to find these days, and they're quite expensive when you do happen across one. But we found that hypertufa (a versatile mixture that includes portland cement and peat moss) provides a practical, inexpensive alternative. If you're looking for a simple, elegant fountain for an existing garden pond, this could be perfect.

Before you begin this project, read the background information on working with hypertufa, found on pages 248 to 249. There you'll find recipes, mixing instructions, and directions for curing hypertufa.

Although you could use either one, we prefer Recipe #2 for projects that will be constantly exposed to water, such as this one.

On this project, timing is critical. Cast the stone at least two months before you plan to put it into a pond. The curing process includes a month of drying time (which is essential) and then another two to three weeks to wash the alkalinity of the portland cement out of the stone. Skipping this final step won't affect the structural integrity of the stone, but the excess alkalinity could change the water in your pond enough to kill the fish or aquatic plants. Avoid the whole problem by allowing plenty of time for the curing process.

TOOLS & MATERIALS

- Jig saw
- Drill with ⅛" (3 mm) twist bit and 1½" (3.8 cm) spade bit
- Hammer
- Circular saw
- Compass
- Tape measure
- Straightedge
- Aviation snips
- Chisel or paint scraper
- Wire brush
- ⅛" (3 mm) hardboard (at least 2 × 4 ft. [61 cm × 1.21 m])
- 2 × 4 (5 × 10 cm) (at least 2 ft. [61 cm])
- 2 × 2 (5 × 5 cm) (at least 2 ft. [61 cm])
- ¾" (19.05 mm) plywood (4 × 6 ft. [1.22 × 1.82 m])
- 1" (2.54 cm) wallboard screws

- 2 × 2 lumber (at least 24" [61 cm])
- ¼" (6.35 mm) plywood (scrap at least 12" [30.5 cm] long)
- 1" (2.54 cm) brads
- 2½" (6.35 cm) wallboard screws (4)
- 1½" (3.8 cm)-dia. PVC pipe (6" [15.25 cm])
- Release agent
- Hypertufa recipe #2 (page 248)
- Dust mask
- Rubber gloves
- ¼" (6.35 mm) hardware cloth
- Plastic tarp
- Concrete blocks
- Submersible pump with water delivery tube
- Bricks (2)

A. *Secure two strips of hardboard to cleats, using 1" wallboard screws.*

HOW TO BUILD A MILLSTONE FOUNTAIN

Step A: Build the Walls of the Form

1. Cut two 12 × 47½" (30.5 × 1.21 m) strips of ⅛" hardboard. Along one edge and both ends of each strip, mark and drill an ⅛" hole every 4" (10 cm).

2. Cut a 12" (30.5 cm) cleat from a 2 × 4 and two 12" cleats from a 2 × 2. Butt the ends of the hardboard strips together, center them over the 2 × 4 cleat, and fasten them with 1" wallboard screws. Fasten a 2 × 2 cleat flush at each of the other ends, using wallboard screws.

Step B: Build the Base of the Form

1. Cut two 27½"-diameter (70 cm) circles from ¾" plywood, using a jig saw.

2. Stack the circles, carefully align them with one another, then join them, using 1" wallboard screws. Drill a 1½"-diameter (3.8 cm) circle at the center of this base.

3. Make a mark every 14⅜" (36.5 cm) around the circumference of the base. Lay a straightedge so the end touches a mark, and the edge touches a tangent point on the side of the drilled circle. Draw a line along the straightedge. Repeat with each point along the outer circumference of the form. Cut six ¼ × 12" (6.35 mm × 30.5 cm) strips of ¼" plywood;

B. *Cut and join two circles of ¾" plywood. Mark placement lines and tack strips of ¼" plywood to the face of the base.*

C. *Attach the hardboard wall to the base of the form, and then screw the 2 × 2 cleats together to close the circle.*

D. *Mix the hypertufa and pack a 2" layer onto the floor of the form. Insert a piece of hardware cloth, and add hypertufa until the stone is about 4" thick.*

fasten one strip to each line, using 1" brads.

Step C: Assemble the Form

1. Bend the hardboard wall around the base. Starting midway between the cleats, attach the wall to the base, using 1" wallboard screws.

2. To close the ends, screw the cleats together, using 2½" wallboard screws.

3. Set the piece of 1½"-diameter PVC pipe into the hole in the center of the base. Apply release agent to the outside edges of the pipe, the base (including the ¼" strips), and the inside wall of the form.

Step D: Cast the Stone

1. Mix the hypertufa, following the directions on pages 248 to 249. Be sure to wear a dust mask and gloves when handling the dry cement mix and wear gloves when working with wet cement.

2. Pack hypertufa onto the floor of the form, pressing it down firmly and packing it tightly around the PVC. Continue to add hypertufa until you've created a solid, 2"-thick (5 cm) layer.

3. Using aviation snips, cut a piece of hardware cloth to fit within the form. Settle the hardware cloth into place, then add and pack down the hypertufa until it's approximately 4" (10 cm) thick.

Step E: Allow to Dry & Remove the Forms

1. Cover the form with a plastic tarp, and let the hypertufa dry for at least 48 hours. If the weather is warm, remove the tarp and mist the hypertufa with water occasionally during the curing process.

2. Remove the screws from the form, working carefully so the form can be reused, if desired. If the stone appears to be dry enough to handle without damaging it, remove the PVC pipe in the center. If not, let the hypertufa dry for another 24 hours, then remove the pipe. Turn the stone over and pull away the plywood base.

Step F: Complete the Curing Process

1. If you want the stone to have a weathered look, now is the time to create it. Working slowly and carefully, use a hammer to rough up the edges of the stone. To add texture, gouge grooves on the surface, using a chisel or paint scraper. Complete the aging process by brushing the entire stone with a wire brush.

2. Cover the stone with plastic, and let it cure for about a month. Uncover it at least once a week, and mist it with water to slow down the curing process. Although it's natural to be impatient, don't rush this step. The more slowly the hypertufa cures, the stronger and more durable the stone will be.

3. Unwrap the stone and let it cure outside, uncovered, for several weeks. Periodically wash it down with water to remove some of the alkaline residue of the concrete (which would otherwise endanger the plants or fish in your pond). Adding vinegar to the water speeds this process somewhat, but it still takes several weeks. (See page 249 for more details on the curing process.)

Step G: Install the Pump & Stone

1. Place concrete blocks in the pond, positioned to support the stone and bring it slightly above the surface of the water. Between the blocks, set two bricks to support the pump. Center the pump on top of the bricks, then extend the electrical cord up over the bank and out to the nearest GFCI receptacle.

2. Turn on the pump and adjust the flow valve, following manufacturer's instructions. Test and adjust until the bubbling effect or spray appeals to you. Keep in mind that the first 4 to 5" (10 to 13 cm) of spray are covered by the stone.

3. Center the hole in the stone over the water delivery tube of the pump, and lower the stone onto the blocks in the pond.

4. Arrange plants and stones on the bank to disguise the electrical cord as it exits the pond.

E. *When the hypertufa has cured for at least 48 hours, remove the form walls, the PVC pipe, and the plywood base.*

F. *Using a wire brush, chisel, and hammer, remove the stone's sharp edges and create a weathered texture.*

G. *Stack bricks and concrete blocks to support the stone and the pump. Place and adjust the pump, and set the stone on top of the blocks, centered over the pump.*

Wire Rabbit Bean Cage

No matter how much we resent the damage rabbits sometimes do, few of us can resist the image of one bounding through our garden. This wire rabbit is more appealing than the live version in one way: It has no interest whatsoever in nibbling at your lilies or your lettuces.

We contrived a way to attach the rabbit to a widely available type of bean cage, which looks great covered by pole beans, morning glories, or sweet peas. Another option is to create a sturdy plant stake to support the rabbit, using a length of ½" copper pipe joined to an upper stem of ¼" flexible copper tubing with a ¼ × ½" reducing coupling. Or, you could make the stem itself 24 to 36" long and stick it directly into a large pot of ornamental grass—your rabbit will appear to be leaping over a field or meadow.

You can find 8-gauge bare copper wire in the electrical department of most hardware stores and home centers. It's typically sold by the foot, measured out from large spools. If you straighten and then coil the wire before you begin to shape it, you'll find it more malleable.

You can buy bell wire in the electrical department, too. It, however, comes with a plastic covering that needs to be stripped away. You can use a utility knife to strip wire, but it's much easier and safer to use an inexpensive tool known as a wire stripper.

TOOLS & MATERIALS

- Pliers
- Wire stripper
- Drill and ⁵⁄₁₆" (8 mm) twist bit
- Propane torch
- Permanent marker
- 8-gauge (4 mm) copper wire
- Masking tape
- Bell wire (144")
- Solder
- Flux and flux brush
- Wire cutter
- Copper pot scrubber
- ¼" (6.35 mm) flexible copper tubing (2 ft. [61 cm])
- ⅜" (9.5 mm) flexible copper tubing (1 ft. [30.5 cm])
- ⁵⁄₁₆" (8 mm) threaded rod (6" [15.25 cm])
- ⁵⁄₁₆" (8 mm) nuts (2)
- Wire bean cage
- Rubber mallet

HOW TO BUILD A WIRE RABBIT BEAN CAGE
Step A: Prepare Pattern & Wire

1. Using the grid system or a photocopier, enlarge the pattern shown below. (Our rabbit is 24" [61 cm] from the tip of the hind leg to the tip of the front leg.) Tape the pattern to a smooth, flat work surface.

2. Measure the perimeter of the pattern to determine the necessary lengths of wire. (We needed 82" [208.28 cm] for the rabbit's profiles and 32" [81.28 cm] for the center loop.)

A. *Measure the perimeter of the pattern and cut wire to length.*

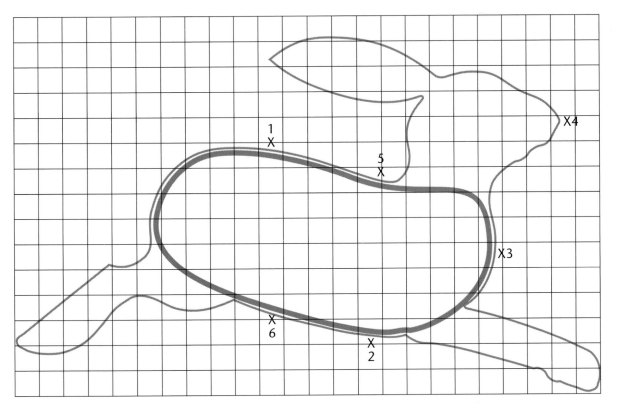

1 square=1" (2.54 cm)

3. Cut 8-gauge wire to length. Partially coil the wire to make it easier to shape.

Step B: Form the Pieces

1. Starting at the mid-back (#1 on the pattern), shape the wire along the contours of the rabbit pattern, using a pair of pliers to create the sharp bends. At the intersection, overlap the ends of the wire, leaving the ends loose.

2. Starting at the mid-bottom (#2), form a second rabbit shape, as described above.

3. Make a center loop for the body of the rabbit, starting at the mid-front (#3).

Step C: Refine the Shapes & Mark the Joints

1. Lay the first rabbit shape on the work surface. Add the center loop and the second rabbit shape. Adjust the pieces until the shapes are as similar as possible. Tape the pieces together at several locations, using masking tape.

2. At each intersection, trim the overlapping wire, and use a permanent marker to indicate the remaining joints as indicated on the pattern.

Step D: Solder the Joints

1. Cut and strip eight 18" (45.72 cm) lengths of bell wire.

2. At the first joint (#4 on the pattern), flux the 8-gauge wire, then wrap a piece of bell wire tightly around all three pieces to join them. Flux and solder the joint. Repeat with the remaining joints (#5 and #6).

3. Flux and solder the wire intersection of each shape. Let the joints cool completely.

Step E: Embellish the Rabbit

1. Bend the legs and ears away from the center loop to add dimension to the rabbit.

2. Thread a piece of bell wire through a copper pot scrubber, and put the scrubber in place along the center loop, positioning it for the tail. Wrap the wire around the center loop to secure the tail, then flux and solder the wire as described in Step D.

Step F: Build the Mounting Frame

1. Cut two 20" (50.8 cm) pieces of ¼" flexible copper tubing. Using a rubber mallet, flatten the first ½" (12.7 mm) of each end of each piece of tubing. At the center of each flattened end, drill a ⁵⁄₁₆" (8 mm) hole.

2. Bend each flattened end out, then shape the tubing into identical, gentle arcs. Lay out the arcs in an X, and mark the centers of the intersection. Drill

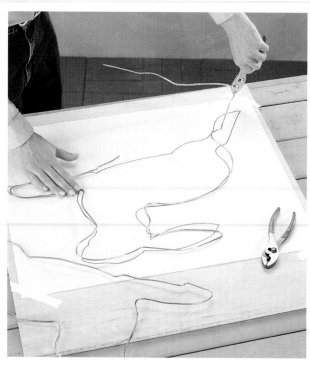

B. *Shape the wire along the contours of the pattern, using pliers to bend sharp angles or curves. Make two rabbit shapes and one center loop.*

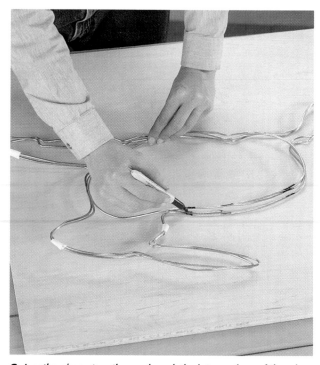

C. *Lay the pieces together and mark the intersections of the wire as well as the joining spots.*

a ⁵⁄₁₆" hole at each mark.

3. Put a nut approximately 1" (2.54 cm) from the end of a 6" length of threaded rod. Stack the tubing in an X and slide that end of the threaded rod through the center holes. Add a nut on the bottom and tighten it until the tubing is held securely together.

4. Cut a 9" (22.86 cm) length of ⅜" flexible copper tubing for the stem. About 2" (5 cm) from one end, bend the tubing at about a 120° angle. Flux the bent portion of the stem. Join the stem to the rabbit shape by wrapping the joint with about 8" (20.32 cm) of bell wire. Flux the wire and solder the stem to the rabbit shape.

5. Attach the mounting frame to the top of the bean cage, inserting the wire ends into the holes in the mounting frame. Set the rabbit's stem onto the threaded rod. Adjust the angle of the stem until the rabbit appears to be leaping over the bean cage.

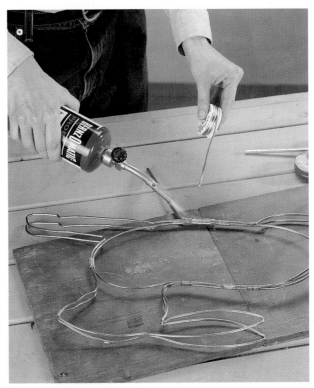

D. *Flux the joints and wrap them with bell wire. Flux the bell wire and solder the joints.*

E. *Pull the layers away from one another at the ears and legs, giving the rabbit dimension. For the tail, use a piece of bell wire to attach a copper pot scrubber to the center loop.*

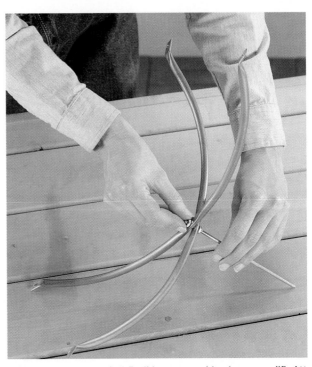

F. *Shape two pieces of ¼" flexible copper tubing into a modified X and drill holes through the center. Use two nuts to secure a threaded rod to this frame.*

Placemat Bird Feeder

With a sense of style and a touch of humor, this whimsical bird feeder charms human visitors even as it welcomes feathered guests. It also reminds us that all creatures have a place at Nature's table.

Once again, we've used plumbing materials in somewhat surprising ways. The bird-feeder stand is a simple combination of galvanized pipe and base flanges, which are available in the plumbing department of most hardware stores and virtually all home centers. You should be able to find 48" (1.22 m) lengths of pipe that are precut and prethreaded. If not, most stores will cut pipe to length and thread the ends for you, free of charge.

When we've used expanded metal grate in the past, we've purchased it at a steel yard and used a reciprocating saw to cut it to size. However, the idea for this birdfeeder really got off the ground when we discovered that precut 12 × 24" (30.5 × 61 cm) pieces are widely available at hardware stores and home centers. Typically used for vents and grills, they can be found in the area where sheet metal and flashing is displayed. NOTE: Even on precut pieces, the edges of metal grate can be sharp. Wear heavy gloves when handling it.

Remember that birds are creatures of habit and will quickly come to rely on your feeder as a food source. Keep it well stocked throughout the season, and they will return year after year.

TOOLS & MATERIALS

- Drill
- Reciprocating saw or jig saw with metal-cutting blade
- Grinder or rotary tool
- Shovel
- Pewter or aluminum plate & cup
- 1¼" (3.2 cm) galvanized pipe (48" [1.22 m], threaded at each end)
- Base flanges (2)
- Quick-setting cement
- Caulk gun
- Galvanized bucket or empty paint can
- Soil tamper
- Screwdriver
- ¾" (19.05 mm) expanded metal mesh (12 × 24" [30.5 × 61 cm])
- Panhead machine screws and nuts (2 sets)
- Flat washers (2)
- Locking pliers
- Silicone caulk or Liquid Steel
- Stainless steel knife, fork, and spoon
- Pewter or aluminum napkin ring
- Decorative wire mesh
- Heavy gloves
- Mixing bucket
- Permanent marker
- Sand

HOW TO BUILD A PLACEMAT BIRD FEEDER
Step A: Assemble the Base

1. Thread a base flange onto the bottom of a 48" piece of 1¼" galvanized pipe.

2. Mix a small batch of quick-setting cement. Set the pipe into a galvanized bucket or empty paint can, make sure the pipe is plumb, and fill the container with quick-setting cement. Let the cement dry according to manufacturer's directions.

A. *Thread a base flange onto a 48" galvanized pipe, and set that assembly into a bucket or can. Fill the container with quick-setting cement and let it dry.*

FLANGE/PLACEMAT ASSEMBLY

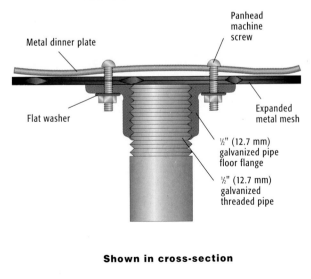

Metal dinner plate

Panhead machine screw

Flat washer

Expanded metal mesh

½" (12.7 mm) galvanized pipe floor flange

½" (12.7 mm) galvanized threaded pipe

Shown in cross-section

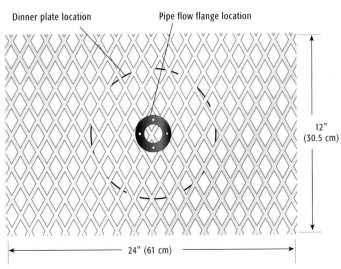

Dinner plate location

Pipe flow flange location

12" (30.5 cm)

24" (61 cm)

Step B: Prepare the Plate

Center a base flange on the back of the plate you've selected; mark two of the holes onto the back of the plate, using a permanent marker. Carefully drill a ⅜" (9.5 mm) hole at each mark. Drill two or three additional holes (beyond the area of the base flange) for drainage.

Step C: Attach the Placemat & Plate

1. If necessary, cut the expanded metal mesh to size, using a reciprocating saw or a jig saw with a metal-cutting blade. Use a grinder or a rotary tool with an abrasive disk to soften the edges of the mesh.

2. Center the plate on top of the mesh. Through each hole in the plate, thread a panhead machine screw through the mesh and the holes in the base flange; add flat washers and nuts, and tighten carefully.

Step D: Add the Details

1. Using silicone caulk or Liquid Steel, secure the silverware and napkin ring to the mesh.

2. Fold a piece of decorative wire mesh into a napkin-like shape. Insert the mesh into the napkin ring, and secure it with a dab of silicone caulk.

3. Drill several drainage holes in the bottom of the cup. Position the cup as for a place setting, and secure it with silicone caulk.

Step E: Install the Feeder

1. Dig a hole 2 to 3" (5 to 7.62 cm) wider and 4" (10 cm) deeper than the bucket of the stand. Keep the edges of the hole fairly straight and the bottom as level as possible. Add 1" (2.54 cm) of sand to the hole.

2. Set the stand into position, then thread the feeder assembly onto it. Add or remove sand until the feeder is level.

3. Fill in the hole; tamp the dirt to hold the feeder level and keep it stable.

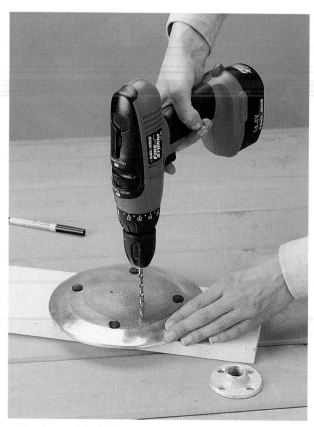

B. *Mark two of the holes of a base flange onto the back of the plate. Drill a hole at each mark.*

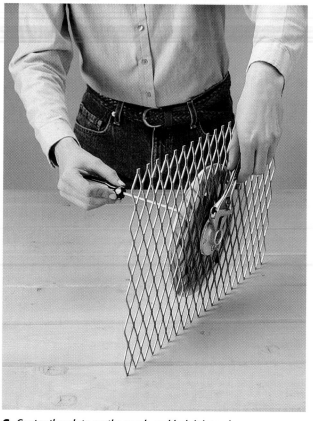

C. *Center the plate on the mesh and bolt it into place.*

TIP: FEEDING BIRDS

Wherever you live, this unique feeder is sure to attract lots of seed-loving birds. And no matter where you place it on your property, the birds will soon find it.

Your feeder will be easier and safer for the birds to use if you place it near sheltering trees, such as alder, birch, maple, or poplar. Shrubs with thick foliage, such as barberry, evergreens, and shrub roses, are also good places for birds to nest. Providing some natural seed plants, such as purple coneflower or black-eyed Susan, will help attract birds to the area as well. Include a source of water nearby, and the birds are sure to return again and again.

A good birdseed mixture may contain sunflower seed, safflower seed, cracked corn, and millet. It will attract sparrows, chickadees, finches, buntings, and many others. Some finches and siskins also like thistle (niger) seed.

Cardinals, jays, and grosbeaks especially like sunflower seeds. These are big birds with big appetites, so always keep a supply of food on hand.

Eastern bluebirds may be attracted by peanut butter mixes and raisins. Baltimore orioles may even visit a feeder if orange halves are available.

And don't forget winged visitors such as mourning doves and juncos. Even though they won't usually come to the feeder tray, they happily eat seeds dropped to the ground by other birds.

D. *Glue the cup, silverware, napkin ring, and decorative mesh into place.*

E. *Dig a hole, add a layer of sand, and adjust until the bucket is level. Refill the hole and tamp the soil to keep the bucket stable.*

Carved Stones

Carved stones give voice to a garden. They can express welcome, encouraging words—even humor. One easy way to carve stones involves using a rotary tool and diamond-tipped bit. The equipment, which is available at hobby and home improvement stores, costs approximately $40 to $50. We've carved dozens of stones with only a small handful of bits.

We've had tremendous fun scattering carved stones along walking paths, in parks, and other public places. We typically place them in slightly unusual spots, where only observant folks with sharp eyes will see them. We've also found that personalized carved stones are warmly received gifts. We like to surprise people with clever messages or unusual symbols.

On-line, Internet sites can be a good place to find designs. There are sites dedicated to Native American and Celtic hieroglyphs, or Asian language symbols. It's best to avoid intricate designs that would be difficult to follow with the rotary tool.

The best stones for carving have even coloration, a relatively smooth texture, and flat or uniformly rounded surfaces. Crystalline rocks, such as quartz and granite, are somewhat difficult to carve, but if you're patient, the results can be spectacular. Dark stones work well because the interior layer revealed by the bit usually contrasts well with the surface.

When carving, set the rotary tool at a fairly high speed at first. Higher speeds generally work best, though this does vary with the type of stone. You may have to experiment a bit—some stones may carve best at slightly slower speeds.

TOOLS & MATERIALS

- Stones
- Variable-speed rotary tool
- Diamond bits
- Transfer paper (sold at fabric stores)
- Stylus
- Particle mask
- Safety goggles
- Artist's brush
- High-gloss enamel or permanent marker

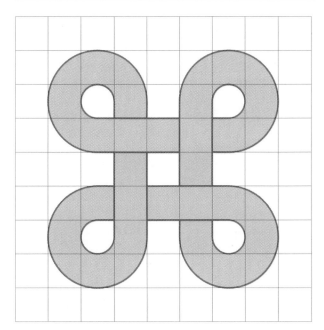

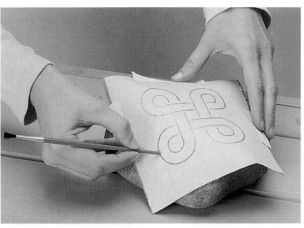

A. *Transfer the design or words to the surface of the stone, using transfer paper and a stylus or gently pointed tool.*

B. *Follow the lines of the design with the rotary tool, using a light touch. Retrace the lines until they're clearly visible.*

C. *Paint the grooves with high-gloss enamel to emphasize the contrast between the design and the stone.*

HOW TO MAKE CARVED STONES

Step A: Transfer the Design

Copy or trace the design on paper, then use transfer paper and a stylus or other gently pointed tool to reproduce the design on the stone.

Step B: Carve the Design

1. Gently score a preliminary groove along the lines of the design, using very light hand pressure with a rotary tool and a diamond bit. Wear safety goggles and a particle mask. It's best to clamp small stones in a vise or workbench while you carve.

2. Retrace the lines until they're deep enough to show well. Never force the tool into the stone, which would overtax the motor and dull the bit.

Step C: Highlight the Carving

1. Wash the stone with mild soap and water and let it dry.

2. Using a fine artist's brush, apply a high-gloss enamel to the carved area. Or use a permanent marker to highlight the carving.

Flower Bed

Antique loving gardeners often use iron beds as raised-bed planters. That's great if you happen to have an old bed on hand and plenty of space in your garden. If not, a miniature version might be the answer. With a wood frame for a planter, it really is perfect—inexpensive, just the right size, easy to build, and clever as can be.

The best plants for this flower bed are spreading types that will mimic the way a bedspread or coverlet drapes over the edge of a bed. Here we show firefly impatiens, but you could try sweet alyssum, lobelia, or even nasturtium.

If you want to carry the idea to its fullest, add a 10 × 24" (25.4 × 61 cm) layer of dirt to the head end of the 2 × 4 bed frame. The extra height in that area will create the impression of pillows on the bed.

TOOLS & MATERIALS

- Circular saw
- Tubing cutter
- Drill
- Propane torch
- Locking pliers
- Hammer
- Shovel
- Center punch
- 1¼" (3.2 cm) rigid copper (8 ft. [2.44 m])
- ½" (12.7 mm) rigid copper (8 ft. [2.44 m])
- ¾" (19.05 mm) rigid copper (4 ft. [1.22 m])
- ½" (12.7 mm) flexible copper (5 ft. [91.44 cm])
- ¼" (6.35 mm) flexible copper (5 ft. [1.5 m])
- 1¼ × ½" (3.2 cm × 12.7 mm) reducers (4)

- 1¼" (3.2 cm) tees (4)
- Wire brush
- Rotary tool (optional)
- Flux and flux brush
- Solder
- 12-gauge (2 mm) copper wire
- 1-gallon (4-l) paint can
- Scrap of 1½" (3.8 cm) PVC pipe
- 2 × 4 (5 × 10 cm) rough-cut cedar (four 2-ft. [61 cm] boards and four 36" [91.44 cm] boards)
- 10d (7.6 cm) nails
- Rebar (2 ft. [61 cm])
- Copper strapping tape
- Potting soil
- Trailing plants
- 1" (2.54 cm) corrosion-resistant deck screws (4)

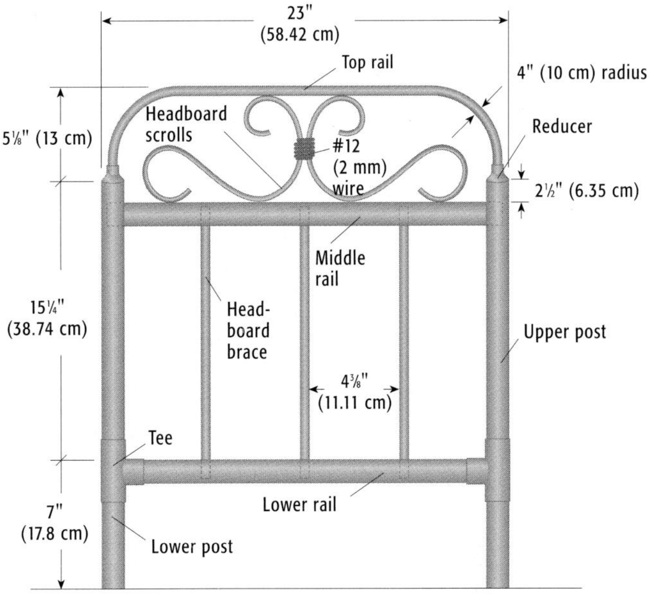

Cutting List

Rigid copper

	Pipe	Number	Size
Headboard upper post	1¼" (3.2 cm) pipe	2	15¼" (38.74 cm)
Footboard upper post			
Lower post		4	5½" (13.97 cm)
Lower rails		2	20¼" (51.44 cm)
Middle rails	¾" (19.05 mm) pipe	2	22⅜" (56.8 cm)
Headboard braces	½" (12.7 mm) pipe	3	14¾" (37.46 cm)
Footboard braces		3	10¾" (27.31 cm)
Flexible copper			
Top rail	½" (12.7 mm) tubing	2	30" (76.2 cm)
Headboard scrolls	¼" (6.35 mm) tubing	2	30" (76.2 cm)

Diagram labels: 23" (58.42 cm), Top rail, 4" (10 cm) radius, Headboard scrolls, Reducer, 5⅛" (13 cm), #12 (2 mm) wire, 2½" (6.35 cm), Middle rail, 15¼" (38.74 cm), Head-board brace, Upper post, 4⅜" (11.11 cm), Tee, Lower rail, 7" (17.8 cm), Lower post

HOW TO BUILD A FLOWER BED

Step A: Prepare the Posts & Rails

1. Following the cutting list and diagrams, cut all the rigid copper pieces for the headboard and footboard. Mark the holes on the middle and lower rails; center-punch and drill ½" (12.7 mm) holes through only the first wall of each rail.

2. On each upper and lower post, mark the holes for the middle rail. Center punch the hole locations, then drill a ¾" (19.05 mm) hole through only the first wall of each post.

Step B: Construct the Frames

1. For the headboard, lay out the middle and lower rails, and fit the braces between them. If necessary, use

A. *Cut the copper pipe for the headboard and footboard. Mark and drill holes on the upper posts and the middle and lower rails.*

B. *Connect the braces to the middle and lower rails, then add the posts.*

C. *Form the top rail from ½" flexible copper. Make sure the arcs are equal on each side.*

D. *Clean the pipe and fittings and then dry-fit the assemblies. Solder the joints of each, working from the bottom.*

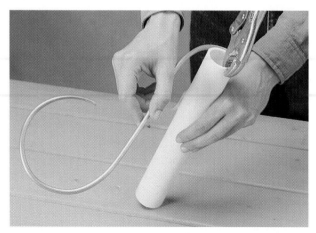

E. *Cut two 30" pieces of ¼" copper tubing. Shape each piece into an S-shaped scroll.*

a rotary tool to tailor the holes until the pieces fit securely. Make sure the braces extend as far as possible into the rails.

2. Construct each post, placing a 1¼" tee at the lower rail location on the upper and lower post pieces. Connect the rail and brace assemblies to the posts. Insert the middle rail into the hole on each post and the lower rail into the tee on each side. Make sure the middle rail extends as far as possible into the posts.

3. Top each post with a 1¼ × ½" reducer.

Step C: Add the Top Rails

Cut a 30" (76 cm) piece of ½" flexible copper for the top rail of the headboard. Form a 4"-radius (10 cm) arc at one end; insert the end of the arc into the reducer at the top of one of the headboard posts. At the other end, shape an arc that brings the end of the rail down to meet the reducer fitting on top of the second post. Trim the ends so the legs of the arcs are of equal length and the rail sits level across the headboard.

Step D: Solder the Assemblies

1. Clean and flux the joints, then dry-fit the pieces of the headboard on a flat, flame-resistant surface. Solder the joints of each, working from the bottom and alternating from side to side. Check from time to time to make sure each assembly remains square and flat. (For more information on soldering, see pages 246 to 247.)

2. Repeat Steps B through D to build the footboard.

Step E: Form the Scrollwork for the Headboard

1. Cut two 30" pieces of ¼" copper tubing. Flatten both ends of each piece of tubing.

2. Use locking pliers to clamp one end of a piece of tubing to the top edge of a 1-gallon paint can. Wrap the tubing about three-quarters of the way around the paint can, then remove it and reclamp the end to a piece of 1½" PVC pipe. Rotate the pipe to curl about 4" of the tubing toward the center of the larger curve.

3. Clamp the opposite end of the tubing to the PVC pipe. Rotate the pipe away from the curve formed in #2, curling about 4" of the tubing around the pipe in the opposite direction, creating an S-shaped scroll.

4. Repeat the process with the second piece of tubing, checking after each step to make sure it matches the first.

Step F: Add the Scroll to the Headboard

1. Mark the centerpoint of the top and middle rails on the headboard, and set the first scroll between them. Adjust the tubing into a graceful curve that allows the large curve of the scroll to align with the centerpoint of the headboard and the smaller curve to contact the middle rail about 2½" (6.35 cm) from the post. Repeat this process to position the opposite scroll.

2. Clean and flux the contact spots on the scrolls and on the top and middle rails. Solder the scrolls into position. When the center joint cools, wrap it with 12-gauge wire.

Step G: Construct the Planter Frame

1. From rough-cut cedar 2 × 4s, cut four 24" (61 cm) pieces and four 36" (91.44 cm) pieces. At each end of each piece, cut a 1½" (3.8 cm) notch; stagger the position of the notches so that each board is notched at the top on one end and at the bottom on the other.

2. Lay out four boards in a rectangle, interlocking the notches. Drive a 10d nail into each joint, angling the nail slightly. Add the second course, offsetting the orientation of the notches to produce an alternating pattern.

3. At 18" (45.72 cm) from one end of the planter frame, drill a ⅜" (9.5 mm) hole completely through the bottom course and half-way through the top one. Repeat on the opposite side of frame.

Step H: Install the Flower Bed

1. Dig a flat, 2"-deep, 6"-wide (5 × 15.25 cm) trench around the perimeter of a 24 × 36" (61 × 91.44 cm) area. Loosen and, if necessary, amend the soil.

2. On each side of the trench, 18" (45.72 cm) from one end, drive a 12" (30.5 cm) piece of rebar 7" (17.8 cm) into the ground. Insert the rebar into the holes in the frame and settle the frame into position.

3. Cut and shape copper tape into straps for the 1¼" pipe. Position the straps, drill pilot holes, and screw the straps into place with deck screws to attach the headboard and then the footboard to the planter frame.

4. Fill the frame with potting soil and add plants.

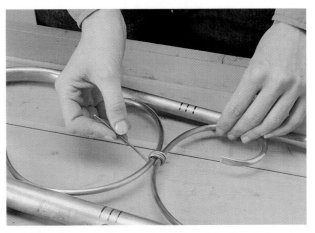

F. *Position the scrolls, flux the pipe at the points of contact, and solder the scrolls into place. Use wire to conceal the joint between the two scrolls.*

G. *Cut, notch, and interlock cedar 2 × 4s to form a frame for the planter. Nail each joint, angling the nails slightly. Make two courses, and offset the orientation of the notches.*

H. *Attach the headboard and footboard to the planter with copper tape and 1" deck screws.*

211

Copper Chandelier

Imagine this: Dinner on the patio, fragrance waltzing on the evening breeze, candles flickering from a gleaming chandelier. Sounds like something out of a magazine article, right? Not necessarily. In just a few hours, you can make this beautiful chandelier out of a roll of copper tubing, a handful of plumbing stand-offs, and a little bit of copper wire. Then all you need is a warm evening and a patio.

This project may look complicated, but it's absolutely doable. All you have to do is read and follow the directions carefully. Almost before you know it, you could be dining by candlelight and soaking up compliments.

A copper chandelier makes a wonderful gift for almost any occasion—birthday, anniversary, wedding, Mother's or Father's Day, Christmas. Anyone with a patio, deck, or garden would be delighted to receive such a unique, handcrafted gift. There's no reason to limit its use to the outdoors, either—it would look just as lovely indoors.

As you'll see in the diagram on the opposite page, we used screws to attach the candle cups. Those screws serve a second purpose as well: They help candles stand securely in the cups. You can thread larger or soft candles, such as beeswax, directly onto the screws, but it's much easier to insert the type of small candles shown here if you drill ⅛" (3 mm) pilot holes in them first.

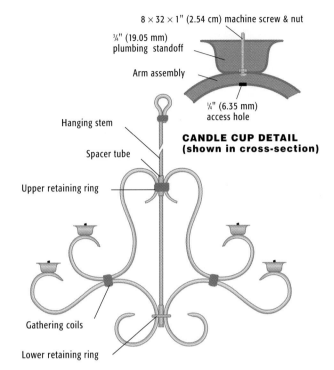

8 × 32 × 1" (2.54 cm) machine screw & nut

¾" (19.05 mm) plumbing standoff

Arm assembly

¼" (6.35 mm) access hole

**CANDLE CUP DETAIL
(shown in cross-section)**

Hanging stem

Spacer tube

Upper retaining ring

Gathering coils

Lower retaining ring

TOOLS & MATERIALS

- Tubing cutter
- Rubber mallet
- Locking pliers
- Drill
- Wire nippers
- Channel-type pliers
- Band saw or hacksaw
- Propane torch
- ⅜" (9.5 mm) flexible copper tubing (22 ft. [6.4 m])
- 2"-dia. (5 cm) PVC pipe (18" [45.72 cm])
- Foamboard
- Center punch
- Utility knife
- Flaring tool

- 12-gauge (2 mm) copper wire (8 ft. [2.44 m])
- ¾" (19.05 mm) plumbing standoffs (10)
- 8 × 32 × 1" (2.54 cm) roundhead machine screws & nuts (10)
- 1"-dia. (2.54 cm) PVC pipe (18" [45.72 cm])
- ¼" (6.35 mm) flexible copper tubing (3 ft. [91.44 cm])
- Flux and flux brush
- Solder
- Compass
- Protractor
- Masking tape

HOW TO BUILD A COPPER CHANDELIER

Step A: Form the Arms

1. Cut ten 24" (61 cm) lengths of ⅜" flexible copper tubing. Flatten the first 2" (5 cm) of one end of a piece of tubing, using a rubber mallet. Flatten the end completely, then gradually taper up to full size. (One side of the tubing will be flat and the other will remain somewhat convex.) Turn the tubing over and flatten the opposite side of the other end. Repeat this process to flatten the ends of the remaining pieces.

2. Cut an 18" (45.72 cm) piece of 2"-dia. (5 cm) PVC pipe; clamp the first 12" (30.5 cm) of the PVC into a workbench. Clamp one end of a piece of tubing to the end of the PVC pipe with locking pliers. (Make sure the flat side of the tubing is facing the PVC.) Slowly wrap the tubing around the PVC, making almost one complete revolution; take care not to crimp the copper. Remove the tubing, clamp the opposite end to the PVC (again, the flat side of the tubing should face the PVC), and wrap the tubing around the PVC in the same manner. Repeat with each of the nine remaining pieces of tubing.

3. Unwrap the ends of each piece of tubing and refine each piece into an elongated S shape. One end should remain rather tightly curved and the other should be somewhat more open. When you're satisfied with the shape, refine the other pieces, using the first as a pattern.

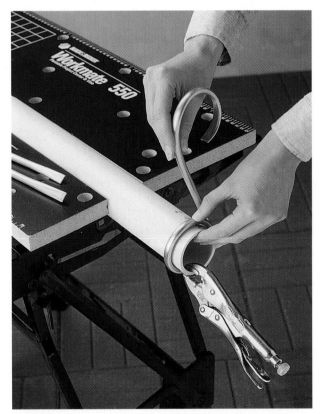

A. *Flatten the ends of ten pieces of copper tubing, then shape each piece into an S curve.*

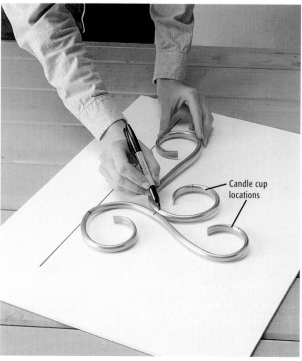

B. *Arrange pairs of arms and mark the contact points; mark the candle cup locations at the apex of each outer curve.*

Step B: Mark the Contact Points

1. Draw an 18" (45.72 cm) straight line on a large piece of foamboard. Lay out two S-shaped arms along the line, and adjust the relationship between the arms until they form a pleasing shape. Mark the contact points between each arm and the line, and between the two arms. Also, mark the locations for the candle cups at the apex of the curve of the two outer ends of the tubing.

2. One by one, lay the remaining pairs of arms over the first pair and duplicate the marks onto each set of arms.

Step C: Prepare for the Candle Cups

Slide the ends of each arm back onto the PVC pipe. Center punch and drill a ⅛" (3 mm) hole at each mark; drill all the way through the tubing. Remove the arms from the PVC and enlarge the holes on the inside of the curves only, using a ¼" (6.35 mm) bit.

Step D: Connect the Arms

1. Clamp two 6" (15.25 cm) sections of ⅜" copper tubing next to each other in a small bench vise. Cut five 10" (25.4 cm) lengths of 12-gauge copper wire. Wrap each length of wire tightly around the copper tubing at least four times, creating five coils of wire. Trim the coils to the same size, using wire nippers.

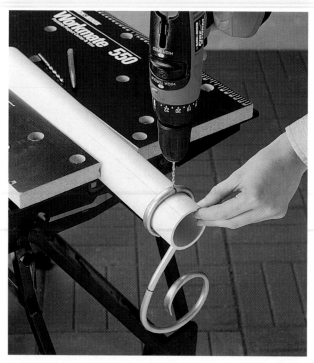

C. *On each arm, slip the outer curve back onto the PVC and drill a hole through the tubing at the cup marks.*

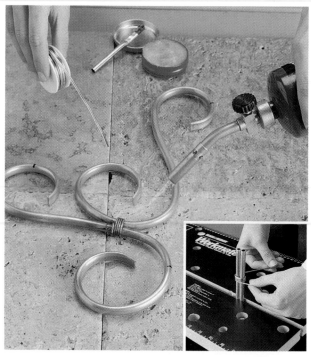

D. *Make five coils of 12-gauge wire (inset). Place the coils at the marked spots and solder the arms together.*

2. Slip the large ends of two S-shaped arms into a coil. Arrange the arms and align the layout marks you made in Step B. Adjust the coil and flux it thoroughly. Solder the coil in place, making sure it's completely full of solder. (For more information on soldering, see pages 246 to 247.) Repeat this process to join the remaining four pairs of arms.

Step E: Add Candle Cups

Remove the base portion from ten ¾" standoffs, using channel-type pliers. Thread a 1" 8 × 32 roundhead machine screw up through the hole in each arm and through a standoff. Fasten the standoff in place, using a nut.

Step F: Construct the Spacing Jig

1. Draw a line through the center of an 18 × 20" (45.72 × 50.8 cm) piece of foamboard. Mark the center of the line, and use a compass to draw an 8⅜"-dia. (21.27 cm) circle at the center of the foamboard.

2. Using a protractor, draw a line every 72° to divide the circle.

3. Use a utility knife to cut a ¼"-wide (6.35 mm) slot centered over each line.

Step G: Form the Retaining Rings

1. Clamp 12" (30.5 cm) of an 18" (45.72 cm) piece of 1"-dia. PVC tubing into a workbench. Wrap 12-gauge

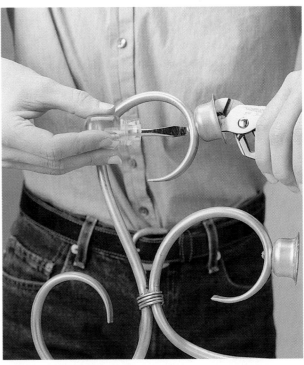

E. *Remove the bases from ten plumbing standoffs. Attach a standoff to each outer curve, using machine screws and nuts.*

F. *Draw an 8⅜"-dia. (21.27 cm) circle on a piece of foamboard. Equally divide the circle with five lines, then cut out a ¼" slot along each line.*

G. *Use 1"-dia. (2.54 cm) PVC pipe as a form to shape an upper retaining ring from 12-gauge wire and a lower ring from ¼" (6.35 mm) tubing.*

copper wire tightly around the form at least five times. Remove the coil and trim it with a wire nipper. This is the upper retaining ring.

2. Wrap ¼" copper tubing around the PVC three times. (You'll use only the complete circle formed at the center.) Cut through the tubing, using a band saw, to produce a single, slightly offset ring. This is the lower retaining ring.

3. Cut two 1½" (3.8 cm) pieces of ⅜" copper tubing and flare one end of each. These are the spacers.

Step H: Assemble the Chandelier

1. Slip the tops of all five arms into the 12-gauge wire retaining ring. Center the assembly over the spacing jig and adjust the arms along the five lines. Tape the arms

SPACER TUBE DETAIL

Hanging stem

Lower retaining ring

⅜" (9.5 mm) flexible copper tubing

into position within the spacing jig.

2. Slip one of the spacers into the center of the ring formed at the top of the assembly.

3. Use two pairs of pliers to spread apart the arms of the lower retaining ring. Remove the assembly from the spacing jig, and slip the second spacer into the center of the ring formed at the bottom of the chandelier. Use a large pair of channel-type pliers to crimp the ring back into a circle. Flux each area thoroughly and solder the spacers in place. Make sure each retaining ring is saturated with solder.

Step I: Add the Hanging Stem

1. Cut a 30" (76 cm) piece of ¼" copper tubing for the hanging stem. Wrap the first 6" (15.25 cm) of the tubing around the piece of 1"-dia. (2.54 cm) PVC, forming a slightly elliptical loop. Wrap the joint with 12-gauge copper wire, at least four times. Solder the joint.

2. Straighten the remaining portion of the stem and thread it through both ⅜" spacers in the center of the chandelier. Flare the bottom of the stem, which will lock it in place.

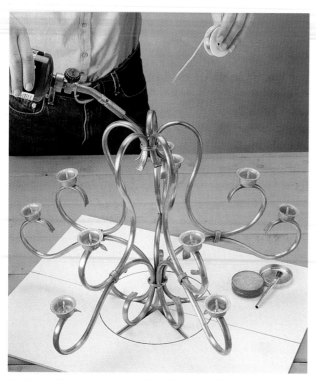

H. *Gather the arms and hold them in place with ⅜" tubing spacers and the retaining rings.*

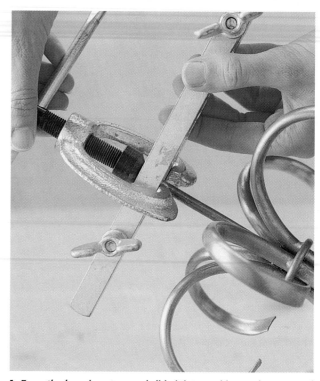

I. *Form the hanging stem and slide it into position at the center of the chandelier. Flare the bottom of the stem to hold it in place.*

Decorative Birdhouse

Birdhouses are popular in garden decorating, both indoors and out. This particular version is strictly decorative—its simple design makes it impractical for actual habitation. In fact, the holes are covered with screen to keep birds from trying to make themselves at home. You could make a habitable version, though—just add floors to subdivide the sections and hinge the back so it can be opened for cleaning.

The tin roof is made from galvanized flashing. It's easy to work with, but the edges are quite sharp—wear heavy gloves when cutting and bending it.

The finishing technique used here creates a weathered, worn appearance. If you're not fond of that look, skip the stain, wax, and distressing steps—simply paint the lumber. Since the birdhouse is meant to be ornamental rather than functional, you can use any color or combination of colors you like, rather than limiting yourself to colors that attract birds. You could even use some decorative painting techniques to brighten or embellish it, if that suits the style of your garden.

While you can set this birdhouse on a table or other piece of furniture, you might prefer to mount it on a stand. An old newel post from a porch or deck works beautifully for this. Start by toenailing the newel post to a base large enough to give it stability. Next, drill a hole in the bottom of the birdhouse and tap in a T-nut. Install a furniture bolt in the top of the newel post, then screw the bolt into the nut.

Voilà!

TOOLS & MATERIALS

- Hammer
- Straightedge
- Circular saw
- Miter box
- Drill and ¼" (6.35 mm) twist bit
- 1" (2.54 cm) spade bit
- Clamps
- Heavy-duty stapler and staples
- Aviation snips
- Heavy-duty awl or flat file
- 1 × 6 (2.54 × 15.25 cm) pine (4 ft. [1.22 m])
- 1 × 1 (2.54 × 2.54 cm) pine (5 ft. [1.5 m])
- 1 × 2 (2.54 × 5 cm) pine (2½ ft. [76.2 cm])
- 2 × 6 (5 × 15.25 cm) pine

- (at least 5½" [13.97 cm])
- Foam brush
- Exterior wood glue
- 4d finish nails
- 2" (5 cm) corrosion-resistant deck screws
- Water-based stain
- Beeswax
- Latex paint
- Polyurethane sealer
- Fine wire mesh or screening
- 18-gauge (1.25 mm) galvanized sheet metal (at least 18" [45.72 cm] square)
- Wooden drapery finial
- Heavy gloves
- Awl
- Foam brush

Cutting List

Lumber	Number	Size
1 × 6	4 (front, back & sides)	21" (53.34 cm)
1 × 1	8 (trim)	7" (17.8 cm)
1 × 2	4 (base trim)	7" (17.8 cm)
2 × 6	1 (roof support)	5½ × 5½" (13.97 × 13.97 cm)

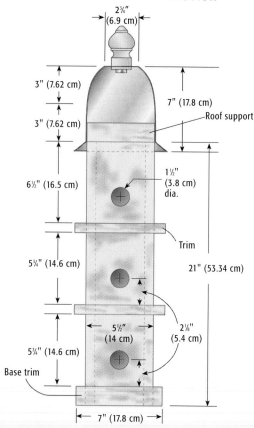

ROOF SHOWN IN CROSS-SECTION

2¾" (6.9 cm)

3" (7.62 cm)

3" (7.62 cm)

7" (17.8 cm)

Roof support

6½" (16.5 cm)

1½" (3.8 cm) dia.

Trim

5¼" (14.6 cm)

21" (53.34 cm)

2⅛" (5.4 cm)

5½" (14 cm)

5¼" (14.6 cm)

Base trim

7" (17.8 cm)

HOW TO BUILD A DECORATIVE BIRDHOUSE

Step A: Assemble the Tower

1. Cut the lumber as indicated on the cutting list. Rip two side pieces to 4" (10 cm) wide.

2. On the front piece, mark three centerpoints as indicated on the diagram. Drill a hole at each mark, using a 1" spade bit. Lightly sand the faces and edges of each piece, then mark placement lines for the trim pieces.

3. Cut three 2" (5 cm) squares of fine wire mesh or screening. Staple one piece of mesh across the back of each hole on the front piece.

4. Spread exterior wood glue along the back edges of the front piece, then clamp it to the two side pieces. Nail the front to the sides, using 4d finish nails. When the glue is dry, attach the back piece to the sides, using glue and nails.

5. Cut 45° miters on the ends of the trim pieces. (Each trim piece should be 7" [17.8 cm] long at the long edges of the miter.) Tack these pieces in position at the marked lines, using 4d finish nails.

Step B: Add the Finish

1. Distress the surface of the tower by gouging small holes here and there with an awl.

2. Brush water-based stain over the entire tower assembly, using a foam brush. (We used golden oak.) Let the stain dry overnight.

3. Rub beeswax onto areas that would naturally show wear—around the holes, edges, and sides. Paint the

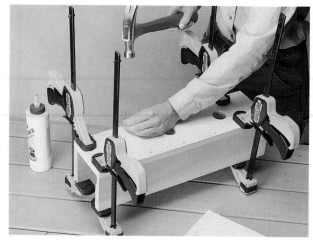

A. *Glue and nail the front to the sides. When the glue is dry, add the back and then the trim.*

tower assembly. (We used antique white.) The moisture in the paint will lift some of the stain, discoloring the paint and creating a weathered, aged effect. While the paint is still wet, use a clean, dry rag to rub some of it off, especially in the waxed areas. Let the paint dry thoroughly.

4. Apply a coat of polyurethane sealer to the entire tower.

Step C: Prepare the Roof

1. Using the grid system or a photocopier, enlarge the roof pattern shown on page 250. Cut out the pattern, then trace it onto a piece of galvanized sheet metal.

2. Use aviation snips to cut along the outline, then use a straightedge and a heavy-duty awl or the tail of a flat file to score the texture lines. Again using aviation snips, cut along the dotted lines. If necessary, use a rotary tool to smooth the cut edges. Finally, score the metal along the fold lines.

3. Fold down the sides of the roof along the marked, scored fold lines at the top, and then fold the lower edges up at the marked, scored lines.

4. Mark and drill a ¼" (6.35 mm) hole at the center of the roof. Insert a 2" deck screw through the hole in the center of the roof piece, and use it to secure a finial to the top of the roof.

Step D: Install the Roof

1. Set the 2 × 6 roof support on top of the tower assembly and, on each side, drill two angled pilot holes

up through the tower and into the roof support. Drive a 2" deck screw into each pilot hole, attaching the roof support to the tower assembly.

2. Line up the folded edge of each side of the roof with the lower edge of the corresponding side of the roof support. Nail the roof to the roof support, using evenly spaced 4d finish nails.

B. *Distress the wood, then stain, paint, and finish the tower.*

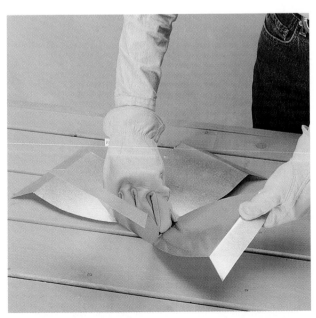

C. *Trace the pattern onto the sheet metal, then cut and shape the tin roof.*

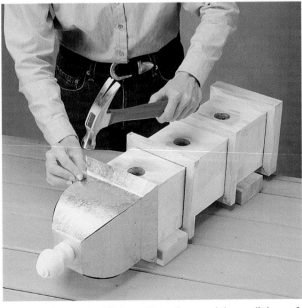

D. *Screw the 2 × 6 roof support into place, and then nail the roof to that support.*

Candle Tree

Imagine the flickering light of dozens of candles dancing with the foliage and flowers in the evening breeze, weaving a magical spell upon the garden. A candle tree is a wonderful way to transform that image into reality. It's so inexpensive and easy to build that you could make several to line a pathway or to light an entertainment area.

A candelabra like this looks great in a container planted with medium-height flowers and trailing foliage. Just insert the stem into the soil and push it down until it's stable. However, to install one in a planting area or other open ground, it's best to provide an anchor. An easy way to do that is to drive a

36" (91.44 cm) piece of rebar 18" (45.72 cm) into the ground, then fit the candelabra's stem over the rebar.

By varying the length of the hanging loops, you can arrange the candle cups at various heights in much the same way you would arrange flowers in a vase. If necessary, adjust the curve of individual branches to create a pleasing arrangement.

A note of caution: Never leave candles burning unattended. And although the candelabra is quite stable when properly installed, it's a good idea to remove the glass candle holders during storms, just to be on the safe side.

TOOLS & MATERIALS

- Locking pliers
- Rubber mallet
- Band saw or hacksaw and metal-cutting blade
- Pliers (2 pairs)
- Ball-peen hammer
- Center punch
- Drill and ³⁄₆₄" (2.38 mm) twist bit
- Propane torch
- Aviation snips
- Wire brush
- Tubing cutter
- 8-gauge (4 mm) copper wire (27 ft. [2.74 m])

- Anvil
- 5-gallon (19-l) metal bucket
- Flux and flux brush
- Solder
- ¾ × ½" (19.05 × 12.7 mm) reducer coupling
- ½" (12.7 mm) copper pipe (5 ft. [1.5 m])
- ¾" (19.05 mm) copper pipe (5" [12.7 cm])
- 16-gauge (1.5 mm) galvanized wire (27 ft. [8.2 m])
- Hot glue gun and glue
- Glass votive holders (9)

HOW TO BUILD A CANDLE TREE

Step A: Curve the Branches

1. Cut 8-gauge copper wire into three 9 ft. (2.74 m) sections. Lay out the sections and mark each every 3 ft. (91.44 cm).

2. Using locking pliers, clamp a section of wire to a 5-gallon metal bucket and wrap the wire around the bucket. Use a rubber mallet to tap the wire into shape. Repeat this step with the other sections of wire to produce three coils, approximately 12" (30.5 cm) in diameter.

A. *Clamp one end of a 9 ft. (2.74 m) piece of copper wire to a bucket and form a coil. Cut the coil into 3 ft. (91.44 cm) sections.*

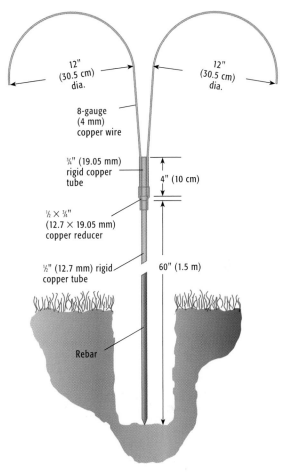

12" (30.5 cm) dia.

12" (30.5 cm) dia.

8-gauge (4 mm) copper wire

¾" (19.05 mm) rigid copper tube

4" (10 cm)

½ × ¾" (12.7 × 19.05 mm) copper reducer

½" (12.7 mm) rigid copper tube

60" (1.5 m)

Rebar

Shown in cross-section

3. Cut each coil at each mark, using a band saw and a metal-cutting blade, if possible. If you don't have a band saw, use a hacksaw and a gentle touch.

Step B: Tailor the Branches

1. Mark each of the nine branches, 12" (30.5 cm) from one end. Straighten the first 12" of each branch, using two pairs of pliers—with one pair of pliers, grip the wire at the 12" mark, and use the other pair to straighten the wire from the mark to the end.

2. On the opposite (still curved) end, flatten the first 1½" (3.8 cm) of the wire, using a ball-peen hammer and an anvil or other durable, flat surface. Continue striking the wire until the end is approximately ⁵⁄₁₆" (8 mm) wide. On each branch, mark, center punch, and drill a ³⁄₆₄" (2.38 mm) hole in the center of the flattened area, ¼" (6.35 mm) from the end.

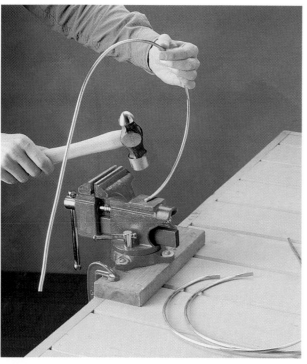

B. *Shape each branch, then use a ball-peen hammer to flatten the curved end. Drill a ³⁄₃₂" hole in each flattened end.*

Step C: Assemble the Branches

1. Clean and flux the first 2" (5 cm) of the straightened end of each branch. Cut a 1" (2.54 cm) piece of ¾" copper pipe to use as a temporary gathering band. (If possible, use a band saw to cut this nipple—using a tubing cutter may crimp the pipe.)

2. Slip the fluxed ends of eight of the branches into the gathering band, and turn the assembly upside down so the curved portions rest on a level, heat-resist-ant work surface. Fan the branches out evenly, and then fit the last branch into the band. Position the gathering band 4" (10 cm) from the ends of the branches; make sure the ends are even and that they fit tightly into the band.

3. Using a propane torch, heat a pair of branches and feed a bit of solder between them. Continue this process until all of the branches are connected to one another. Cut the gathering band away, using aviation snips, then clean up the soldered area with a wire brush.

Step D: Complete the Branch Assembly

Slip the soldered end of the assembly into a 4" length of ¾" copper pipe. If necessary, use a rubber

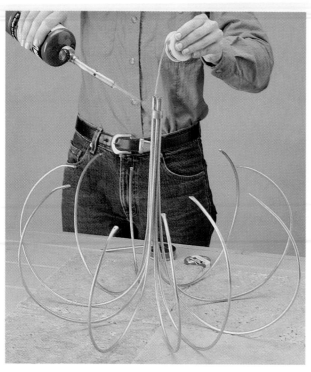

C. *Gather the branches together and temporarily hold them in place with a 1" piece of ¾" copper. Solder the branches together and cut away the gathering band.*

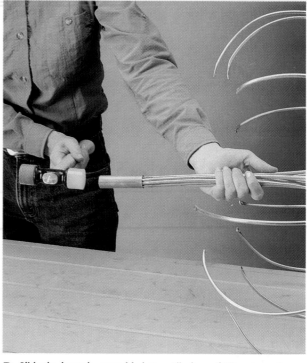

D. *Slide the branch assembly into a 4" piece of ¾" copper pipe. Gently tap it into place with a rubber mallet, if necessary.*

mallet to tap the assembly into place, but be careful not to distort the shape of the branches. At this point, you can reshape the curves of the branches if you like. The goal is to slightly vary the heights of the branches as you would flowers in a bouquet.

Step E: Add the Base

1. Clean, flux, and solder a ¾ × ½" reducer coupling to one end of a 60" (1.5 m) length of ½" copper pipe.

2. Clean, flux, and solder the branch assembly to the reducer fitting.

Step F: Add the Candle Cups

1. Form an open loop at each end of a 12" (30.5 cm) piece of 16-gauge galvanized wire. Use a dab of hot glue to hold the wire in place at each side of a glass votive holder. Cut a wire about 20" (50.8 cm) long, and wrap it around the votive holder three or four times, securing the hanging wire in position. Tuck the end of the wrapped wire behind the hanging wire and trim it so the loop ends neatly.

2. Cut nine 1¼" (3.2 cm) pieces of 16-gauge wire, and form each into an S-shaped hook. Insert one end of each hook into the hole of a branch, then suspend a votive holder from each.

TIP: MAKE YOUR OWN CANDLES

Tealights work well for this candelabra, but they burn quickly. For longer lasting candles, you can make your own. You'll need glass votive holders, small papercore wick, plastic stir sticks, small wick sustainers, needlenose pliers, and paraffin wax.

Prime a length of wick by dipping it into melted wax for a few seconds and allowing it to dry.

Stick the end of a wick into the hole in a wick sustainer. Use needlenose pliers to crimp the metal around the wick. Tie the other end of the wick to a stir stick, then set the stick across the mouth of the votive holder, centered and as straight as possible.

Melt the paraffin wax over indirect heat, using a double boiler. Heat the wax slowly and watch it closely.

When the wax is melted, carefully pour it into the votive holders, filling each one about ⅔ full. When the wax has cooled and solidified, trim the wicks to extend approximately ⅝" (15.86 mm) above the surface of the candles.

NOTE: Do not pour melted wax or any clean-up water containing melted wax into a sink. Wax solidifies quickly and will clog the drain.

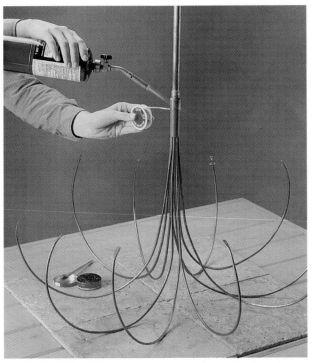

E. *Solder a reducer coupling to a 60" piece of copper pipe, and then to the branch assembly.*

F. *Form a wire loop over a votive holder. Wrap wire around the holder to secure the hanging loop.*

Tealight Candelabra

The vine theme and the shape and scale of this candelabra make it appropriate for a garden, porch, patio, or deck. Placed slightly behind or to the side of a seating area, it provides a warm glow for summer evening get-togethers. With citronella candles, it might even help keep timid mosquitoes away from the party.

Don't be intimidated by the shaping of the vine. It's simple if you follow the directions carefully. And, just in case you're not familiar with standoffs, you'll find them at hardware stores and home centers in areas where other plumbing materials are sold. They're bell-shaped parts that are used to hold plumbing lines away from framing members, such as floor or ceiling joists and wall studs.

HOW TO BUILD A TEALIGHT CANDELABRA

Step A: Shape the Tops

1. Cut three pieces of ½" flexible copper, 60" (1.5 m), 54" (1.37 m), and 48" (1.22 m). Mark a point 3" (7.62 cm)

TOOLS & MATERIALS

- Channel-type pliers
- Aviation snips
- Tubing cutter
- Rubber mallet
- Locking pliers
- Carpenter's square
- Center punch
- Drill and ³⁄₁₆" (4.76 mm) twist bit
- Flat file
- Compass
- Reciprocating saw or hacksaw
- Propane torch
- Protractor
- Two-part epoxy
- Tealight cups (3)
- ½" (12.7 mm) flexible copper (20 ft. [6 m])
- Clamps
- Foamboard or plywood scrap

- 10-24, ¾" (19.05 cm) brass machine screws and nuts (3)
- ½" (12.7 mm) copper standoffs (3)
- ¼" (6.35 mm) flexible copper tubing (6 ft. [1.82 m])
- 10-gauge (3 mm) copper wire (4 ft. [1.22 m])
- Duct tape
- Flux and flux brush
- Solder
- Toilet flange
- Scrap 2 × 4 (5 × 10 cm)
- 1¼"-dia. (3.2 cm) PVC pipe or dowel (scrap)
- 3½"-dia. (8.9 cm) PVC pipe (scrap)
- Markers, red & black

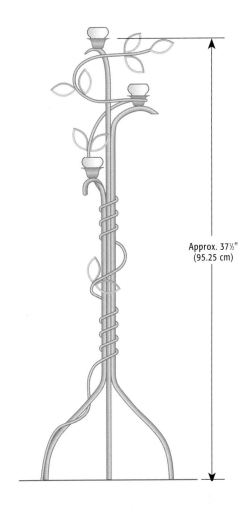

Approx. 37½"
(95.25 cm)

from one end and another mark 20" (50.8 cm) from the opposite end of each piece. Using a rubber mallet, shape the first 3" (7.62 cm) of each piece of copper; completely flatten the ends, then taper up to the full shape at the 3" mark.

2. Screw a toilet flange to a scrap 2 × 4, and clamp

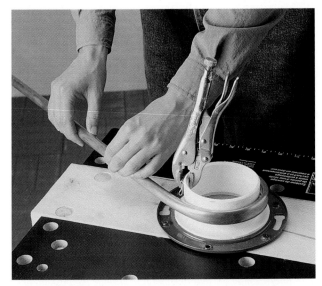

A. *Clamp flexible copper tubing to a toilet flange and wrap it around the flange, shaping the tops of the candelabra legs.*

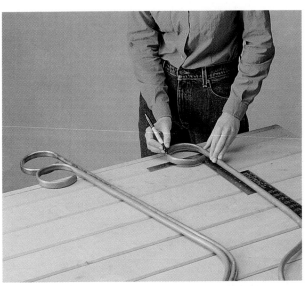

B. *Shape the ends of the legs into gradual S curves, then mark the tops of the legs and cut them to shape.*

the 2 × 4 into a workbench. Clamp the flattened end of one piece of copper tubing to the toilet flange, and wrap the pipe around the flange. Work slowly, and be careful not to kink the tubing as you wrap it. Repeat the process with the other two pieces.

Step B: Shape the Legs & Trim the Tops

1. Starting at the 20" mark on one of the legs, curve the pipe out and down to form a very gradual S shape. Lay a second leg next to the first, and align the 20" marks. Form an S shape that duplicates the first leg. Repeat to shape the third leg.

2. Lay each of the legs flat on a work surface. Using

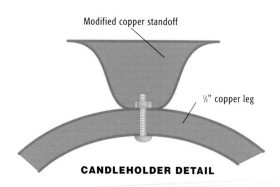

Modified copper standoff

½" copper leg

CANDLEHOLDER DETAIL

a carpenter's square, mark a cutting line on the outside edge of the curve, directly across from the point at which it intersects the straight portion of the leg. Trim the tubing at an angle, using a reciprocating saw or hacksaw.

Step C: Shape the Vine

Cut a 6 ft. (1.83 m) piece of ¼" copper tubing. Starting at a point 18" (45.72 cm) from one end, wrap the tubing around a piece of 1¼" PVC pipe or a dowel; wrap the tubing around the pipe or dowel five times. Slide the tubing off the pipe or dowel. Leave 10" (25.4 cm) of the tubing straight, then wrap it around the pipe three more times.

Step D: Join the Legs & Add the Vine

1. Stack the legs, align them with one another at the 20" mark, and slide the coiled tubing onto them.

2. Draw a circle on a scrap of plywood or foamboard, then use a protractor to draw lines that divide the circle every 120°. Arrange the legs so one foot rests on each line, and tape the tubing together with duct tape. Apply flux just below the first coil, then solder the legs together.

3. Pull the coiled areas apart and position the tubing in a vine-like arrangement around the candelabra. Solder the vine into place.

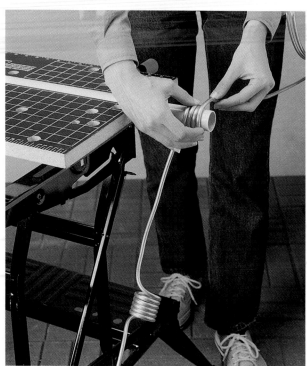

C. Wrap ¼" tubing around a piece of 1¼"-diameter PVC pipe to shape the vine.

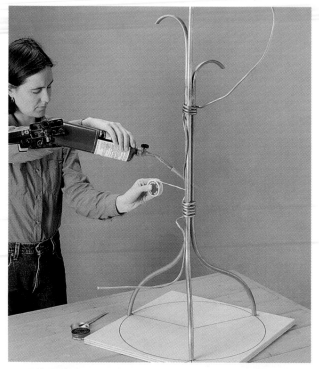

D. Slide the vine onto the legs, then arrange the legs so they're 120° apart. Solder the legs together and arrange the position of the vine.

Step E: Shape the Leaves

1. Cut a 45" (1.14 m) piece of 10-gauge (3 mm) copper wire. Along the length of the wire, make a red mark every 5" (12.7 cm) and a black mark every 2½" (6.35 cm).

2. Clamp the end of the wire around a scrap of 3½"-dia (8.9 cm). PVC pipe; wrap the wire around the pipe tightly. Remove the coil from the pipe, pulling the coils apart. Snip the wire at each black mark, using aviation snips. At each red mark, crimp the wire; bend each piece of wire into a leaf shape.

Step F: Embellish the Vine

Tailor the ends of each leaf with a flat file or a grindstone so the ends are flat. Flux the wire and tubing, and solder each leaf into place.

Step G: Add the Candleholders

1. Remove the base portion from three ½" standoffs, using channel-type pliers.

2. Mark, center punch, and drill a ³⁄₁₆" (4.76 mm) hole at the apex of the curve at the top of each leg. Insert a machine screw from a standoff up through the hole and into the tealight cup. From the top, add a nut to secure the standoff to the tubing.

3. Attach one tealight cup onto each standoff, using two-part epoxy.

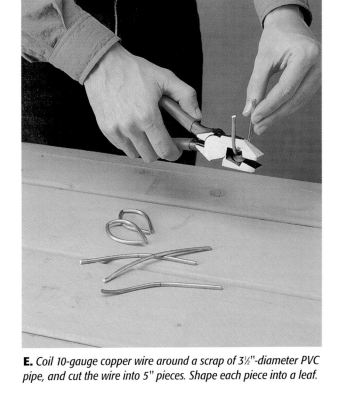

E. *Coil 10-gauge copper wire around a scrap of 3½"-diameter PVC pipe, and cut the wire into 5" pieces. Shape each piece into a leaf.*

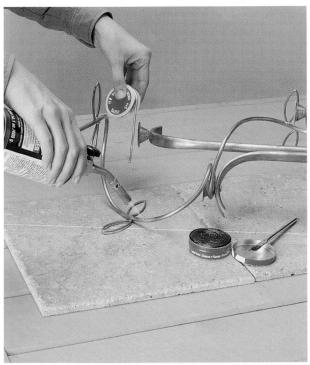

F. *File the ends of the leaf shapes until they're flat enough to sit squarely on the vine. Flux the leaves and the tubing, and solder each leaf in place.*

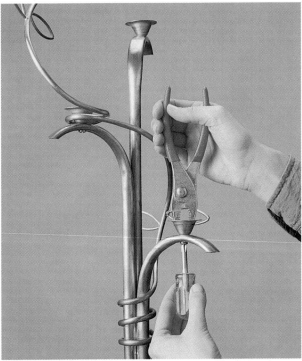

G. *Drill a hole at the apex of the curve on the top of each leg. Disassemble three plumbing standoffs and secure each to a leg, using a machine screw and nut.*

Door Spring Bug

Put away the pesticide. These bugs are not just adorable—they're useful, too: Flying at the top of a metal rod, they can be put to work as plant stakes.

The bug shown below sat in a friend's garden through one winter and one summer before we photographed it—just enough time to develop a lovely layer of rust and character. If you prefer a clean, crisp look, spray your bug with a coat of polyurethane sealer before putting it outside.

TOOLS & MATERIALS

- Drill and ¼" (6.35 mm) and ³⁄₁₆" (4.76 mm) twist bits
- Aviation snips
- Propane torch
- Flat file
- Hot glue gun
- ½" (12.7 mm) threaded flare plug
- 10-32 knurled nut, brass
- 10-32 × 1" (2.54 cm) slotted roundhead machine screw, brass
- ¼"-dia. (6.35 mm) extension spring

- Center punch
- Wire stripper
- Flux and flux brush
- Solder
- Spring-style door stopper, antique brass
- ⅜" (9.5 mm) glass beads (3)
- Glass seed beads (6)
- 12-gauge (2 mm) copper wire
- ⅜" (9.5 mm) brass tube
- ¼" (6.35 mm) rod (36" [91.44 cm])
- Bell wire

HOW TO BUILD A DOOR SPRING BUG

Step A: Construct the Body

1. Mark and center punch holes on a ½" (12.7 mm) threaded flare plug, one in the center of the flat cap end and one in the center of the main body of the plug. Drill ¼" (6 mm) holes at each of these locations.

2. Using aviation snips, cut away the loop from one end of the ¼" (6.35 mm) extension spring. Insert the remaining loop end of the spring into the ¼" hole in the center of the body.

A. *Center punch and drill two ¼" holes in a ½" threaded flare plug—one hole in the center of the flat cap end and one in the body of the plug.*

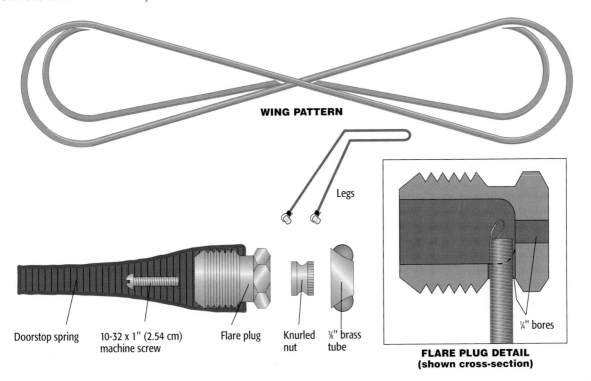

WING PATTERN

Legs

Doorstop spring

10-32 x 1" (2.54 cm) machine screw

Flare plug

Knurled nut

⅜" brass tube

¼" bores

FLARE PLUG DETAIL
(shown cross-section)

229

Step B: Assemble the Body

Thread a 10-32 × 1" machine screw into the open end of the flare plug, through the spring loop, and through the ¼" hole at the end of the plug. Lock this screw in place with a 10-32 knurled nut.

Step C: Add the Wings

1. Following the diagram on page 229, shape the legs and wings from 12-gauge copper wire.

2. Flux the contact points and solder the wings to the top of the flare plug body.

Step D: Add the Stem & Legs

1. Thread a spring-style door stopper onto the threaded end of the flare plug.

2. Flux the contact points and solder the legs to the bottom of the flare plug body.

Step E: Construct the Head

1. Use a flat file to shape a bevel on the end of a 2" (5 cm) piece of ⅜" brass tube.

2. On the long side of the bevel, mark a point ⅜" (9.5 mm) from the end of the tube, and then center punch and drill a ³⁄₁₆" hole.

3. Mark the tube ¾" (19.05 mm) from the long side

of the bevel, and cut the tube to length. Bevel this end of the tube, again using a flat file.

Step F: Assemble the Head

Shape the antenna from 12-gauge copper wire. Flux the contact points and solder them to the top of the ⅜"-tube head (9.5 mm).

Step G: Embellish the Bug

1. Strip some bell wire and cut six 2" (5 cm) lengths. Wrap each piece around a length of 12-gauge wire to form tight coils with ¼" (6.35 mm) tails. Thread a glass seed bead onto the tail of each coil, and bend the wire down to secure the bead.

2. Trim the legs and antenna to final lengths and add a beaded coil to each.

3. Thread the head onto the end of the machine screw at the cap end of the body. (Be careful not to overtighten it.) For eyes, hot glue ⅜" glass beads into the open ends of the head, then glue a bead to the open end of the spring to complete the tail.

4. Insert a 36"-long ¼" rod into the open end of spring at the bottom of the bug.

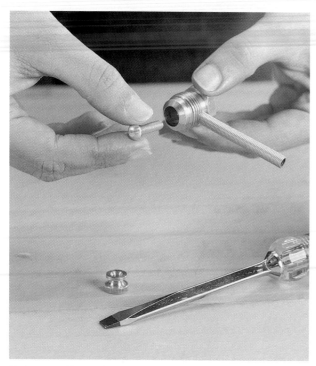

B. *Insert a ¼" extension spring into the hole in the body of the flare plug. Thread a machine screw through the spring's loop and then through the hole in the end of the plug. Secure the screw with a knurled nut.*

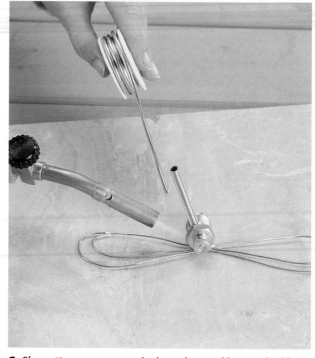

C. *Shape 12-gauge copper wire into wings and legs, and solder these wire shapes to the flare plug body.*

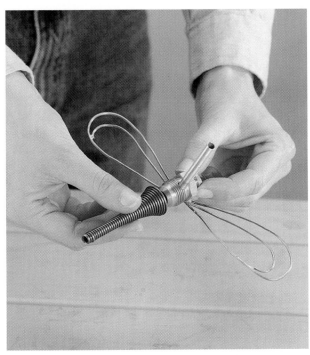

D. *Thread a spring-style door stopper onto the threaded end of the flare plug.*

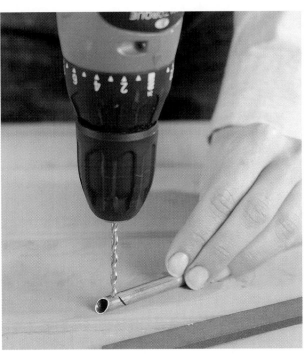

E. *File a bevel at one end of a piece of ⅜" brass tube. Drill a hole ⅜" from the long side of the bevel, and cut the tube to length. File a bevel at the cut end of the tube to complete the shape of the head.*

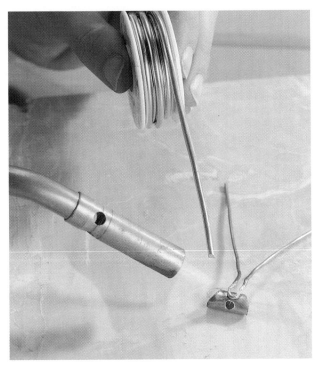

F. *Solder the antennae to the top of the brass-tube head.*

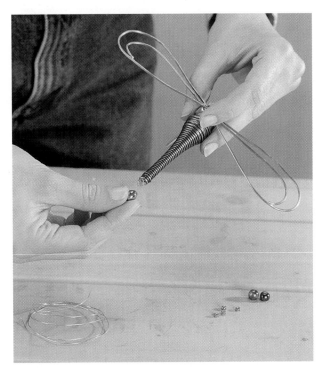

G. *Hot glue beaded coils to the legs and antennae. Attach two larger beads to the brass-tube head for the eyes and one to the end of the tail.*

Rose Arbor

Garden arbors have returned to popularity. The sight of this graceful arch, laden with sprays of colorful blossoms, will provide a stunning complement to your garden and landscape.

The best time to install an arbor is well before planting, even before you've picked the specific flowers to grow. Arbors are ideal for climbing, pillar, or rambling roses or perennial climbers such as honeysuckle, clematis, or white jasmine. Even annual climbers such as morning glories will drape themselves elegantly over an arbor; sweet peas will scramble up its sides. For a special, old-fashioned touch, plant mounds of lavender on both sides of the arbor, just in front of the climbers.

Building this arbor requires average skills, common carpentry tools, and a free weekend. We made ours from clear heart redwood; cedar or hemlock are good alternatives.

TOOLS & MATERIALS

- Jig saw or band saw
- Drill and ⅛" (3 mm) and ⅜" twist bits
- Hammer
- Level
- Shovel
- Cedar lumber, see cutting list
- 4" (10 cm) decorative finials (4)
- 8d galvanized finish nails
- 6d galvanized finish nails
- 3d galvanized finish nails
- #8 × 3½" (4 × 89 mm) tempered weatherproof deck screws
- #6 × 1½" (3.5 × 38 mm) corrosion-resistant wood screws
- ⅜ × 6" (10 × 100 mm) corrosion-resistant carriage bolts
- Exterior carpenter's wood glue
- Exterior wood filler
- Pea gravel
- Quick-setting concrete mix
- Exterior primer/sealer and paint or varnish
- Tape measure
- Circular saw
- Sandpaper
- Clamps
- Paint brush
- Framing square

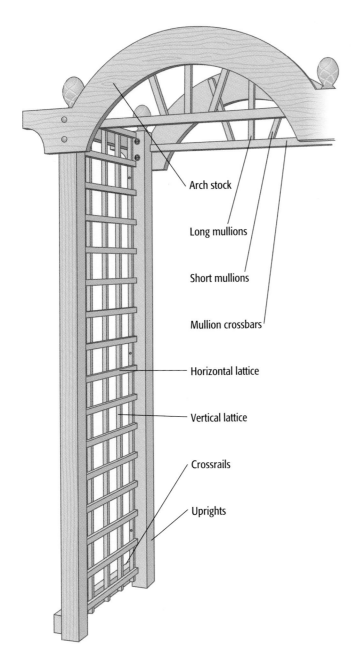

Arch stock

Long mullions

Short mullions

Mullion crossbars

Horizontal lattice

Vertical lattice

Crossrails

Uprights

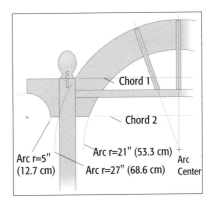

Chord 1

Chord 2

Arc r=5"
(12.7 cm)

Arc r=21" (53.3 cm)

Arc r=27" (68.6 cm)

Arc
Center

HOW TO BUILD A ROSE ARBOR
Step A: Prepare Pieces

1. Cut pieces as indicated on cutting list at left.

2. Each arch is made from two 2 × 12s edge-glued together. Rip a fillet from one edge of each piece of arch stock. Sand smooth. Apply glue to the ripped edge, align the edges, and clamp the pieces together. Allow to dry for 24 hours.

3. Apply a coat of wood sealer to all lumber, including the sides and cut edges of each piece. Let the preservative dry for 24 hours.

CUTTING LIST:

Uprights	4 × 4 (10 × 10 cm)	10 ft. (3 m)	4
Crossrails	2 × 4 (5 × 10 cm)	36½" (90 cm)	4
Vertical lattice	1 × 1 (2.5 × 2.5 cm)	7 ft. (2.13 m)	5
Horizontal lattice	1 × 1	28" (74 cm)	20
Mullion crossbars	2 × 2 (5 × 5 cm)	41" (1.04 m)	2
Short mullions	1 × 1	6" (15 cm)	4
Long mullions	1 × 1	8" (20 cm)	2
Arch stock	2 × 12 (5 × 30.5 cm)	5 ft. (1.5 m)	4

A. *Cut the lumber and laminate the stock for the arch.*

233

Step B: Lay Out & Cut the Arches

1. On paper, draw two concentric arcs with radii of 21" (53.3 cm) and 27" (68.6 cm). Draw parallel chord lines 12" (30.5 cm) and 20" (50.8 cm) from the outer arc. Mark two points along each side of the top chord: 10½" (26.7 cm) from the large arc, and along the bottom chord, 8½" (21.6 cm) from the small arc.

2. Use a framing square to draw a 3" (7.6 cm) line down from the upper mark. Join the line to the bottom chord with a 5" (12.7 cm) radius circle.

3. Transfer the pattern to the laminated arch stock. Use a jig saw or band saw to cut the arch.

Step C: Reinforce the Arch Joint

1. Drill ⅛" (3 mm) pilot holes through each lamination joint, top and bottom. Use a ⅜" (9 mm) twist bit to enlarge the first inch (25 mm) of each pilot hole.

2. Drive a #8 deck screw through each hole and into the joint.

Step D: Fit the Mullions

1. Mark a line 4" (10 cm) above and parallel to the bottom of the back of each arch. Align the bottom of the crossbar to the line; glue and nail it in place.

2. Mark the centerpoint of the crossbar and measure left and right 4½" (11.5 cm), marking the two points. Mark the centerpoint of the arch top and points 9½" (24 cm) to each side of the curve. Extend lines through the marks.

3. Center a mullion on each line, flush to the arch top. Mark the short mullions' bases and cut the bevels. Glue and toenail the mullions to the arches; glue them to the crossbar.

4. Reinforce the joints between the crossbar and the mullions by drilling ½" (0.8 mm) pilot holes through the crossbar and into each mullion; fasten each with an 8d finish nail.

Step E: Assemble the Lattice

1. Cut 8 spacers, each one 5⅛" (13 cm) long.

2. On a layout table, use the spacers to position the vertical lattice parallel with one another and flush at the top. Tack the lattice to the work surface.

3. Aligned with the top of the vertical lattice pieces, nail the first horizontal lattice piece, using 3d finish nails. Use two spacer blocks to position and nail each subsequent course.

4. Repeat to create the lattice for the opposite side of the arbor.

B. *Draw the arches on paper, transfer the pattern to the laminated stock, and cut out the arch.*

C. *Drill pilot holes and drive screws through the lamination joints to reinforce them.*

D. *Custom-fit the mullions to the arch. Fasten them to the arch and crossbar.*

E. *Lay out the vertical lattice pieces and attach the horizontal lattice pieces to them.*

Step F: Assemble the Lattice Frame

1. Set the uprights at the edges of the lattice and position the crossrails flush with the ends of the uprights, checking the assembly for square.

2. Drill four ⅛" (3 mm) pilot holes in each corner joint and fasten the crossrails to the uprights, using deck screws.

3. Turn the assembly over and fasten the lattice frame to the uprights, using #6 deck screws. Fasten the lattice frame to the crossrails with 6d finish nails.

4. Repeat #1 to #3 to complete the remaining lattice assembly.

5. Drill a pilot hole on top of each upright and add a finial.

6. Tack a temporary diagonal brace between each pair of uprights to support the lattice frame as you install it.

Step G: Erect the Sides of the Arbor

1. At the site, position the lattice frames and mark the location of each upright. Dig four 22" (56 cm) deep postholes and backfill each with 4" (10 cm) of pea gravel.

2. Stand the lattice frames upright in the post-holes; set the final height, shim, level, and square the frames to one another.

3. Secure the assembly by tacking temporary diagonal braces between the lattice frames.

Step H: Set the Uprights in Concrete

Fill each posthole with concrete mix and add water according to the manufacturer's instructions. Allow the concrete to cure for 24 hours.

Step I: Install the Arch

1. With an assistant, align the arch assembly with the tops of the uprights. Using the mullion crossbar as a spacer, square and level the assembly; clamp it in place.

2. Drill two ⅜" (10 mm) holes through each joint. Bolt the arch assembly in place, using carriage bolts.

3. Install the finials and, if desired, putty, prime and paint the entire arbor.

F. *Insert deck screws in pre-drilled holes to fasten the crossrails to the uprights.*

G. *Position the lattice frames and mark the postholes. Set the uprights into the postholes and adjust their positions as necessary.*

H. *Fill the postholes with concrete mix and add water. Allow the concrete to cure for 24 hours.*

I. *Clamp the arch assembly in position. Drill holes and use carriage bolts to fasten the arch to the sides of the arbor.*

Mailbox Planter

This weekend project combines building skills and love of flowering perennial plants. In addition to the building materials, visit a salvage yard to find an interesting rectangular planter to suspend below the mailbox. We used a brass planter with an antique patina.

TOOLS & MATERIALS

- Circular saw
- Jig saw
- Drill, 1" (25 mm) paddle bit and ⁵⁄₁₆" (8 mm) spade bit
- Carpenter's square
- Clamps
- Rubber mallet
- 4 × 4 (89 × 89 mm) cedar post, 8 ft. (243 cm)
- 2 × 4 (38 × 89 mm) cedar boards, 8 ft. (243 cm) (2)
- 2 × 6 (38 × 140 mm) cedar board
- 2 × 8 (39 × 184 mm) cedar board
- 1 × 2 (19 × 38 mm) cedar board, 8 ft.
- ¼ × 5½" (6 × 140 mm) bolts, nuts, and washers (6)

- #8 × 2" (4 × 50 mm) brass wood screws (6)
- #6 × 1½" (3.5 × 40 mm) brass wood screws (16)
- Decorative post cap (1)
- Exterior wood glue
- Mailbox
- Rectangular planter box
- Nylon rope, cord, or chain
- Potting soil
- Plants
- Tape measure
- Hammer
- Chisel
- Sandpaper
- Wooden buttons (12)
- Cabinet pulls (8)

CUTTING LIST:

Post	4 × 4 × 96"	(89 × 89 mm × 243 cm)	1
Side rails	2 × 4 × 47"	(38 × 89 mm × 119 cm)	2
Spacers	2 × 4 × 10¾"	(38 × 89 × 273 mm)	2
Box shelf	2 × 6 × 17½"	(38 × 140 × 445 mm)	1
Brace	2 × 8 × 16½"	(38 × 184 × 419 mm)	2
Long frames	1 × 2 × 27"	(19 × 38 × 686 mm)	2
Short frames	1 × 2 × 6¼"	(19 × 38 × 159 mm)	2

HOW TO BUILD A MAILBOX PLANTER

Step A: Cut Mortises & Shape the Side Rails

1. Cut the side rails as indicated on the cutting list.

2. On one end of each side rail, make a mark at 14" (35 cm) and another at 17½" (44.3 cm). Set the depth on a circular saw to ½"; starting at the first mark and working to the second, make a series of cuts ¼" apart.

3. Using a hammer and chisel, remove the waste material between the cuts. Sand the face of the mortise as necessary.

4. On each end of each side rail, use a jig saw to cut an arc 3" (75 mm) in diameter.

Step B: Shape the Braces

1. Cut two braces as indicated on the cutting list.

2. Use a jig saw to cut an arc 5½" (13.97 cm) in diameter in each end of each brace.

Step C: Assemble the Post and Rails

1. Cut the spacers.

2. Lay out one side rail, and set the post into the

A. *Cut 3½" (90 mm) mortises into each side rail, then cut a 3" (75 mm) arc in each end of each rail.*

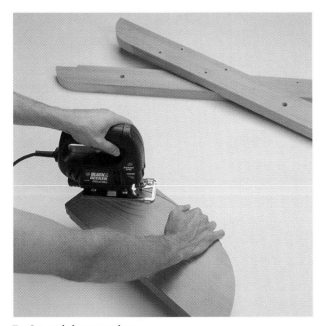

B. *Cut and shape two braces.*

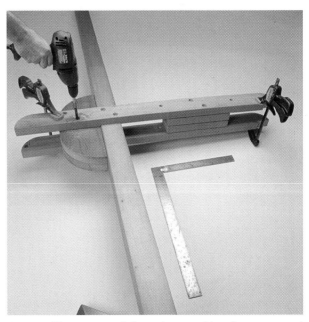

C. *Assemble, square, and clamp the post, side rails, spacers, and brace.*

mortise. Position the spacers and the braces and add the second side rail. Square and clamp the assembly.

3. Use a 1" paddle bit to drill 6 holes, ½" (13 mm) deep, centered at the site of each bolt (see diagram). Turn the assembly over and drill holes on the other side.

Step D: Fasten the Assembly

1. Use a ⁵⁄₁₆" spade bit to through-drill the six bolt holes.

2. Fasten the assembly with bolts, washers, and nuts. Set the nuts finger tight, plus ½ turn.

Step E: Add Buttons

Use exterior wood glue and a wooden button to plug each bolt hole. Tap each button into place, using a rubber mallet wrapped with a soft cloth.

Step F: Add Cabinet Pulls

1. Drill four receiving holes for the four cabinet pulls that will support the planter (see diagram for placement).

2. Use exterior wood glue to fasten the cabinet pulls into the side rails. Glue the decorative cap onto the top of the post.

Step G: Attach the Box Shelf

1. Cut the box shelf as indicated on the cutting list.

Position the shelf on top of the side rails, 2½" (6 cm) from the front.

2. Drill pilot holes and attach the box shelf to the side rails, using six #8 wood screws.

Step H: Attach the Mailbox

Fasten the mailbox to the box shelf with eight #6 wood screws. Adjust the box position to allow the door to open freely.

Step I: Make the Planter Hanging Frame

1. Cut two long frame pieces and two short frame pieces. Drill pilot holes for four cabinet pulls. (Align the pilot holes with the cabinet holes in the side rails.)

2. Position the short frame pieces between the long frame pieces. Drill pilot holes and fasten the frame with two #6 wood screws at each corner.

3. Glue the cabinet pulls into their pilot holes. Allow the assembly to dry overnight.

Step J: Install the Planter Box

1. Fill the planter box with potting soil and plants. Water thoroughly.

2. Insert the planter box into the support frame and suspend it from the cabinet pulls with nylon rope, cord, or chain.

D. *Drill through the assembly and fasten it with nuts and bolts.*

E. *Glue a wood button into each bolt hole.*

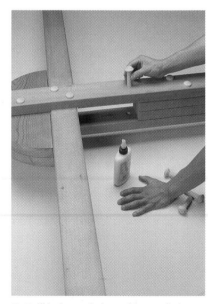

F. *Drill holes and glue cabinet pulls into the side rails. Add the decorative cap on top of the post.*

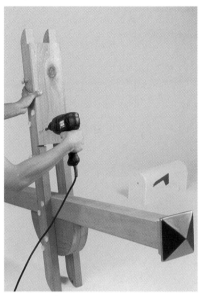

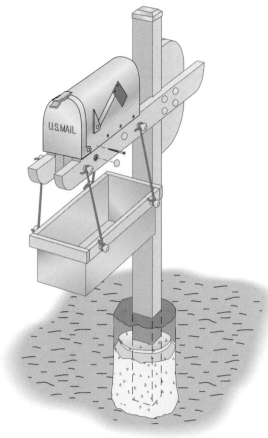

G. *Drill pilot holes and attach the box shelf to the side rails.*

H. *Drill pilot holes and attach the mailbox to the box shelf.*

I. *Fasten the planter hanging frame with 2 #6 wood screws at each corner. Drill and attach 4 cabinet pulls with wood glue.*

J. *Fill the planter box with potting soil and plants. Insert the planter box into the support frame and suspend it from the side rails with nylon rope, cord, or chain.*

Post-mounted Birdhouse

This droll mansion will house a flock of wrens, martins, or other small songbirds—and look great doing it. Once you've assembled the materials, it should take only about 8 hours to build this little charmer.

TOOLS & MATERIALS

- Drill
- 1½" (3.8 cm) & ⅝" (16 mm) drill bits
- Hammer
- Rubber mallet
- Circular saw
- Table saw
- Sheet metal shears
- Socket wrench
- Steel straightedge
- Copper flashing
- Decorative molding
- Half-round molding
- Mounting fixture
- Bolts, nuts and washers (4)
- ½" (13 mm) plywood
- ¾" (19 mm) plywood
- ⅝" (16 mm) dowel
- 6d corrosion-resistant finishing nails
- Exterior wood glue
- Waterproof panel adhesive
- Primer
- Paint
- Tape measure
- Nail set
- Sand paper
- Clamp
- Gloves

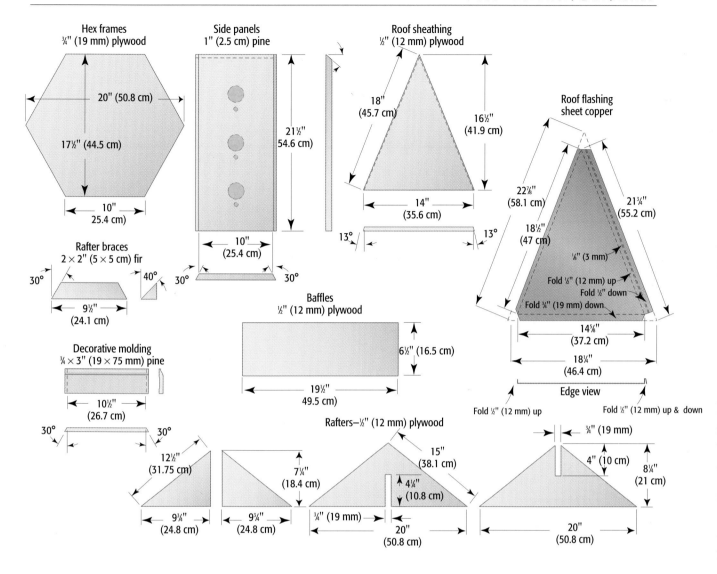

Hex frames
¾" (19 mm) plywood

20" (50.8 cm)

17½" (44.5 cm)

10"
25.4 cm)

Side panels
1" (2.5 cm) pine

21½"
54.6 cm)

10"
(25.4 cm)

Roof sheathing
½" (12 mm) plywood

18"
(45.7 cm)

16½"
(41.9 cm)

14"
(35.6 cm)

13°   13°

Roof flashing
sheet copper

22⅞"
(58.1 cm)

21¾"
(55.2 cm)

18½"
(47 cm)

⅛" (3 mm)

Fold ½" (12 mm) up
Fold ½" down
Fold ¾" (19 mm) down

14⅝"
(37.2 cm)

18¼"
(46.4 cm)

Edge view

Fold ½" (12 mm) up   Fold ½" (12 mm) up & down

Rafter braces
2 × 2" (5 × 5 cm) fir

30°   40°

9½"
(24.1 cm)

30°   30°

Decorative molding
¾ × 3" (19 × 75 mm) pine

10½"
(26.7 cm)

Baffles
½" (12 mm) plywood

6½" (16.5 cm)

19½"
49.5 cm)

30°   30°

12½"
(31.75 cm)

Rafters—½" (12 mm) plywood

7¼"
(18.4 cm)

15"
(38.1 cm)

4¼"
(10.8 cm)

¾" (19 mm)

4" (10 cm)

8¼"
(21 cm)

9¾"
(24.8 cm)

9¾"
(24.8 cm)

¾" (19 mm)   20"
(50.8 cm)

20"
(50.8 cm)

HOW TO BUILD A POST-MOUNTED BIRDHOUSE

Step A: Cut the Pieces

1. Cut four 17½ × 20" (44.5 × 51 cm) pieces of ¾" plywood. Mark and cut the hexagons as indicated on the diagram above.

A. *Cut and shape the pieces of the birdhouse.*

Cutting List

Part	Material	Size	Number
Hex frame	¾" (19 mm) plywood	17½ × 20" (44.5 × 50.8 cm)	4
Beveled side panels	1 × 10" (2.5 × 25 cm) pine	21½ × 10" (54.6 × 25.4 cm)	6
Roof sheathing panels	½" (12 mm) plywood	14 × 18 × 16½" (35.6 × 45.7 × 41.9 cm)	6
Baffles	½" (12 mm) plywood	19½ × 6½" (49.5 × 16.5 cm)	3
Rafters	½" (12 mm) plywood	9¾ × 12½" (24.8 × 31.75 cm)	1
		9¾ × 7¼" (24.8 × 18.4 cm)	1
		20 × 15" (50.8 × 38.1 cm)	1
		20 × 8¼" (50.8 × 21 cm)	1
Decorative molding		2 × 2 × 9½" (38 × 38 mm × 24.1 cm)	6
Roof flashing	Sheet copper	18¼ × 22⅞ × 22⅞" (46.4 × 58.1 × 58.1 cm)	6
Hole frames	Half-round moldings	2" (5 cm)	12
		4" (10 cm)	12
Perches	⅝" dowel	2"	6

2. Cut six side panels, six rafter braces, six pieces of roof sheathing, and six pieces of decorative molding. Bevel the edges of each piece as indicated on the diagram.

3. Cut the rafters. On the two largest rafters, cut ¾" (19 mm) notches as indicated on the diagram.

Step B: Assemble the Rafters

Assemble the rafters on one of the hex frames, then fit the rafter braces as spacers. Fasten the rafters to the hex frame with 6d finishing nails and wood glue.

Step C: Attach the Side Panels to the Hex Frames

1. Mark a 1½" entrance hole and a ⅜" hole for a perch on each side panel; vary the position of the holes so that two panels have holes at the top, two have holes in the center, and two have holes at the bottom.

2. Place the first hex frame flush with the bottom of a side panel, then position two more hex frames so the four hex frames are attached along the side panel at 6½" (16.5 cm) intervals. Drill pilot holes and fasten the side panel to the hex frame with glue and nails.

3. Attach a second and then a third side panel to the assembly. Position panels so the placement of the entrance holes is staggered.

Step D: Add the Baffles

Fit the baffles in place to divide each floor in half.

Step E: Attach the Post-mounting Fixture

1. Mark the center of the base hex frame and position the post-mounting fixture over it.

2. Mark the holes of the post-mounting fixture onto the hex frame and drill holes for the bolts.

3. Fasten the post-mounting fixture to the base with bolts, nuts, and washers, using a socket wrench to tighten the nuts until snug.

Step F: Add Remaining Side Panels & the Rafter Assembly

1. Attach the three remaining side panels as before, alternating them to stagger the placement of the entrance holes.

2. Align the top hex frame/rafter assembly and attach it, using 6d finishing nails and glue.

3. Sink all surface nails with a nail set.

Step G: Attach the Roof Sheathing Panels

1. Sand the edges of the rafters as necessary to create flat nailing surfaces for the roof sheathing panels.

2. Align the roof sheathing panels on the rafter assembly. Drill pilot holes and fasten the panels, using 6d finishing nails.

Step H: Shape the Roof Flashing

1. Wearing gloves and using metal shears, cut the roof flashing panels to size.

2. Clamp a flashing piece to a work surface. Use a metal straightedge and a rubber mallet to fold the edges of the flashing as indicated by the diagram on page 243. Repeat with remaining roof flashing pieces.

Step I: Install the Roof Flashing

1. Apply panel adhesive to one section of the roof sheathing. Fit a roof flashing panel to the roof and clamp it in place. Repeat with remaining flashing pieces. Let the adhesive cure.

2. Bend the bottom of each flashing panel to fit under the eaves of the roof.

Step J: Add the Finishing Touches

1. Tack four pieces of half-round molding in place to frame each entrance hole and perch.

2. Glue the dowel perches into the perch holes.

3. Nail the decorative molding to the base of the birdhouse.

4. Prime and paint the wood surfaces as desired.

B. *Assemble the rafters and fasten them to the hex frame with nails and wood glue.*

C. *Align the hex frames and attach three of the side panels to them.*

D. *Slide the baffles between the hex frames.*

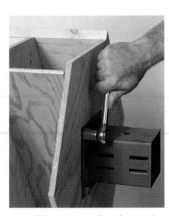

E. *Drill bolt holes, then fasten the post-mounting fixture to the base, using bolts, nuts, and washers.*

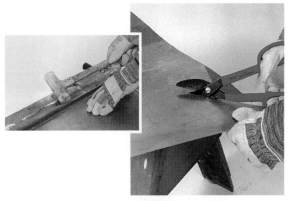

F. *Attach the remaining side panels and the hex frame/rafter assembly.*

G. *Nail the roof sheating panels to the rafter assembly.*

H. *Cut the roof flashing pieces, then use a metal straightedge and a rubber mallet to shape them.*

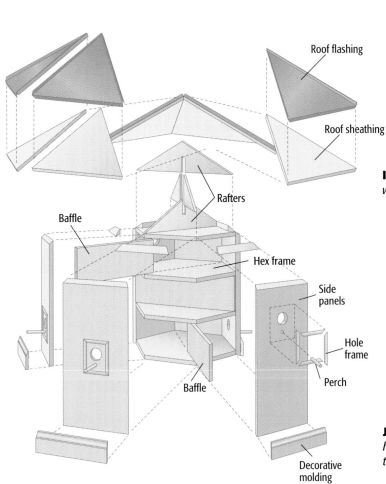

Roof flashing

Roof sheathing

Rafters

Baffle

Hex frame

Side panels

Hole frame

Perch

Baffle

Decorative molding

I. *Fasten the roof flashing to the roof sheathing, using waterproof panel adhesive.*

J. *Attach molding to the entrance holes, dowels to the perch holes, and decorative molding to the base. Prime and paint the birdhouse.*

Basic Techniques

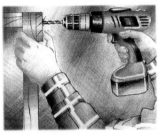

As we were designing projects and deciding how to describe construction processes, our main goal was to make sure that average people could follow the directions, master the techniques, and successfully complete any project in this book. As you look through its pages, we hope you'll see ideas that inspire you and information that gives you confidence.

Most of the projects use ordinary materials and common techniques. Still, you may need an introduction to basic skills, such as soldering or working with hypertufa. Especially if you haven't soldered before, you might want to practice with scraps before you begin a project.

If you have questions after reading through the instructions and the background for the techniques required, you have a couple of options. First, most hardware stores and home centers have staff members who are happy to answer questions. Many home centers have information desks, and some even have classes on techniques such as soldering. When you buy materials, ask for help or additional information.

If you're still having trouble, contact us. You can reach us at Creative Publishing international, 18705 Lake Drive East, Chanhassen, MN 55317 or at DIY@creativepub.com. We love to hear from people who are bringing our ideas to life, and we especially love to see pictures of your creations.

We hope you have as much fun building these projects as we've had creating them.

Cutting & Soldering Copper

A soldered pipe joint, also called a sweated joint, is made by heating a copper or brass fitting with a propane torch until the fitting is just hot enough to melt solder. The heat then draws the solder into the gap between the fitting and the copper pipe, forming a strong seal.

Using too much heat is the most common mistake made by beginners. To avoid this error, remember that the tip of the torch's inner flame produces the most heat. Direct the flame carefully—solder will flow in the direction the heat has traveled. Heat the pipe just until the flux sizzles; remove the flame and touch the solder to the pipe. The heated pipe will quickly melt the solder.

Soldering copper pipe and fittings isn't difficult, but it requires some patience and skill. It's a good idea to practice soldering pieces of scrap pipe before taking on a large project.

HOW TO CUT & SOLDER COPPER PIPE
Step A: Cut the Pipe

1. Measure and mark the pipe. Place a tubing cutter over the pipe with the cutting wheel centered over the marked line. Tighten the handle until the pipe rests on both rollers.

2. Turn the tubing cutter one rotation to score a continuous line around the pipe. Then rotate the cutter in the opposite direction. After every two rotations, tighten the handle. Rotate the cutter until the pipe separates.

Step B: Clean the Pipe & Fittings

To form a good seal with solder, the ends of all pipes and the insides of all fittings must be free of dirt and grease. Remove metal burrs from the inside edge of the cut pipe, using the reaming point on the tubing cutter or a round file. Sand the ends of pipes with emery cloth, and scour the insides of the fittings with a wire brush.

Step C: Flux & Dry-fit the Pipes

1. Apply a thin layer of water-soluble paste flux to the end of each pipe, using a flux brush. The flux should cover about 1" (2.54 cm) of the end of the pipe.

2. Insert the pipe into the fitting until the pipe is tight against the fitting socket, and twist the fitting slightly to spread the flux. If a series of pipes and fittings (a run) is involved, flux and dry-fit the entire run without soldering any of the joints. When you're sure the run is correctly assembled and everything fits, take it apart and prepare to solder the joints.

Step D: Heat the Fittings

1. Shield flammable work surfaces from the heat of the torch. Although heat-absorbent pads are available

A. *Position the tubing cutter, and score a line around the pipe. Rotate the cutter until the pipe separates.*

B. *Clean inside the fittings with a wire brush, and deburr the pipes with the reaming point on the tubing cutter.*

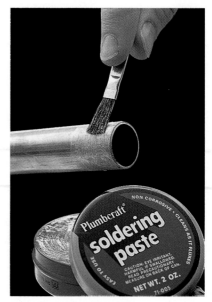

C. *Brush a thin layer of flux onto the end of each pipe. Assemble the joint, twisting the fitting to spread the flux.*

for this purpose, you can use a double layer of 26-gauge (0.55 mm) sheet metal. The reflective quality of the sheet metal helps joints heat evenly.

2. Unwind 8" (20 cm) to 10" (25 cm) of solder from the spool. To make it easier to maneuver the solder all the way around a joint, bend the first 2" (5 cm) of the wire solder to a 90° angle.

3. Open the gas valve and light the propane torch. Adjust the valve until the inner portion of the flame is 1" to 2" long.

4. Hold the tip of the flame against the middle of the fitting for 4 to 5 seconds or until the flux begins to sizzle. Heat the other side of the joint, distributing the heat evenly. Move the flame around the joint in the direction the solder should flow. Touch the solder to the pipe, just below the fitting. If it melts, the joint is hot enough.

Step E: Apply the Solder

Quickly apply solder along both seams of the fitting, allowing capillary action to draw the liquified solder into the fitting. When the joint is filled, solder begins to form droplets on the bottom. A correctly soldered joint shows a thin bead of silver-colored solder around the lip of the fitting. It typically takes about ½" (12 mm) of solder wire to fill a joint in ½" pipe.

If the solder pools around the fitting rather than filling the joint as it cools, reheat the area until the solder liquifies and is drawn in slightly.

NOTE: Always turn off the propane torch immediately after you've finished soldering; make sure the gas valve is completely closed.

Step F: Wipe Away Excess Solder & Check the Joint

1. Let the joint sit undisturbed until the solder loses its shiny color. Don't touch it before then—the copper will be quite hot.

2. When the joint is cool enough to touch, wipe away excess flux and solder, using a clean, dry rag. When the joint is completely cool, check for gaps around the edges. If you find gaps, apply more flux to the rim of the joint and resolder it.

3. If you need to take apart a soldered joint, reverse the process. First, light the torch and heat the fitting until the solder becomes shiny and begins to melt. Then use channel-type pliers to separate the pipe from the fitting. To remove the old solder, heat the ends of the pipe, and use a dry rag to carefully wipe away the melted solder. When the pipe is cool, polish the ends down to bare metal, using emery cloth. Discard the old fittings—they can't be reused.

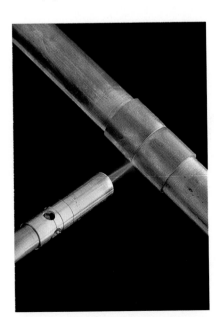

D. *Heat the fitting until the flux begins to sizzle. Concentrate the tip of the torch's flame on the middle of the fitting.*

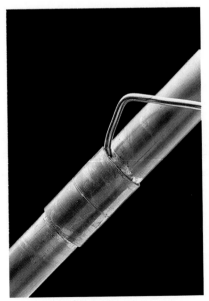

E. *Push ½" to ¾" of solder into each joint, allowing capillary action to draw liquified solder into the joint.*

F. *When the joint has cooled, wipe away excess solder with a dry rag. Be careful: The pipes will be hot.*

Working with Hypertufa

Hypertufa is wonderfully suited to building garden ornaments. There are many recipes available, and some are more reliable than others. Experience leads us to prefer these two recipes. Recipe #1, which contains fiberglass fibers, is ideal for producing lightweight, durable, medium-to-large planting containers. Recipe #2, which contains sand, is especially appropriate for smaller items and those that must hold water.

The ingredients for both recipes are widely available at home and garden centers. Use portland cement rather than a prepared cement mix that contains gravel (which contributes unnecessary weight and gives the finished container a coarse texture). In Recipe #1, perlite, a soil lightener, takes the place of the aggregate typically found in concrete. For Recipe #2, use fine-textured mason's sand—it produces a stronger container than coarser grades of sand.

Peat moss naturally includes a range of textures, some of which are too coarse for hypertufa. Sifting

HYPERTUFA RECIPES

Recipe #1

2 buckets portland cement
3 buckets sifted peat moss
3 buckets perlite
1 handful of fiberglass fibers
    powdered cement dye (optional)

Recipe #2

3 buckets portland cement
3 buckets sand
3 buckets sifted peat moss

the peat moss through hardware cloth takes care of that problem. If you plan to make several hypertufa pieces, it's most efficient to buy a large bale of peat moss, sift the entire bale, then store the sifted material for use over time.

The fiberglass fibers in Recipe #1 contribute strength to the mixture. This product is available at most building centers, but if you have trouble locating it, try a concrete or masonry supply center.

Hypertufa dries to the color of concrete. If you prefer another color, simply add a powdered concrete dye during the mixing process. Tinting products are very effective, so start with a small amount and add more if necessary. Wear gloves and a dust mask when mixing hypertufa.

HOW TO MAKE HYPERTUFA
Step A: Sift the Peat Moss & Build the Forms

1. Place the hardware cloth across a large bucket or wheelbarrow. Rub the peat moss across the hardware cloth, sifting it through the mesh. Discard any

The materials for making hypertufa are inexpensive and widely available. They include portland cement, perlite, peat moss, fiberglass fibers, mason's sand, cement dye, hardware cloth, a plastic tarp, a dust mask, and gloves.

A. Sift the peat moss through hardware cloth to remove any debris or large particles, and break up clumps.

debris or large particles.

2. Build forms (see individual projects). If the piece will be used as a planting container, be sure to provide adequate drainage holes.

Step B: Mix the Ingredients

1. Measure the cement, peat moss, and perlite or sand, and place them in a mixing trough or wheelbarrow. Using a hoe or small shovel, blend these ingredients thoroughly. If you're using Recipe #1, add the fiberglass fibers and mix again. Add cement dye, if desired, and mix until the fiberglass fibers and the dye powder are evenly distributed throughout.

2. Add water and blend thoroughly. The amount of water required varies, so add a little at a time. It's easy to add more, but very difficult to correct the situation if you add too much. The hypertufa is ready to be molded when you can squeeze a few drops of water from a handful.

Step C: Form the Hypertufa

1. Pack the hypertufa into the form and firmly tamp it down. Continue adding and tamping until hypertufa reaches the recommended depth or fills the form (see individual projects).

2. Cover the project with plastic, and let it dry for 48 hours.

3. Disassemble the forms and remove the piece.

Step D: Shape & Cure the Piece

1. Sculpt the appearance of the piece by knocking off the corners and sharp edges. Add texture to the sides of the piece by using a paint scraper or screwdriver to scrape grooves into them. Finally, brush the surface with a wire brush.

2. Wrap the piece in plastic, and put it in a cool place to cure for about a month. Remember, the longer the hypertufa cures, the stronger it will be.

3. Unwrap the piece and let it cure outside, uncovered. If you're building a planter, let it cure for several weeks, periodically rinsing it with water to remove some of the alkalinity, which could harm plants grown in the container. Adding vinegar to the rinse water speeds this process.

4. After the planter has cured outside for several weeks, move it inside, away from any sources of moisture, to cure for another week.

5. The fiberglass fibers in Recipe #1 produce a hairy fringe. Make sure pieces made with this recipe are dry, then use a propane torch to burn off the fringe. Move the torch quickly, holding it in place no more than a second or two. (If pockets of moisture remain, they may get hot enough to explode, leaving pot holes in the piece.)

6. Apply a coat of masonry sealer to basins or other pieces that must hold water.

B. *Measure the ingredients into a mixing container and blend thoroughly. Add water, a little at a time, and mix.*

C. *Pack the hypertufa into the forms, and tamp it firmly. Cover the project with plastic, and let it cure for 48 hours.*

D. *Let the piece cure. Rinse repeatedly; let it dry. Recipe 1: Use a propane torch to burn off any fiberglass fibers.*

Patterns

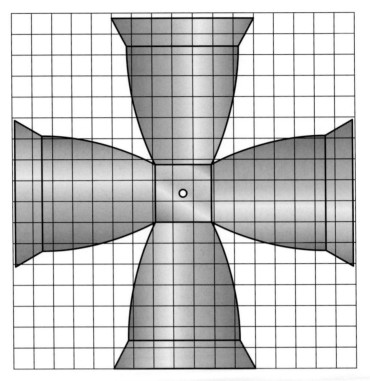

1 square = 1" (2.54 cm)

**DECORATIVE BIRDHOUSE
ROOF DETAIL**

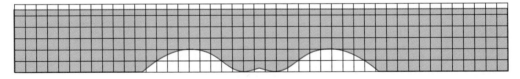

1 square = 1" (2.54 cm)

**BIRDHOUSE PLANT STAND
SKIRTING FRONT DETAIL**

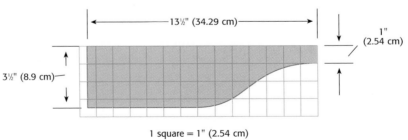

├─ 13½" (34.29 cm) ─┤

1"
(2.54 cm)

3½" (8.9 cm)

1 square = 1" (2.54 cm)

**PORCH SWING
ARM FACING DETAIL**

Photography Credits

Aquascape Designs Inc.: p. 151

Walter Chandoha: p. 16

Kyle Chesser: pp. 160, 162, 163, 164 (step E)

Robert Dolezal: pp. 32, 33, 123, 125, 127, 128 (step A), 129 (step B)

Reed Estabrook: pp. 147, 149, 158, 233, 234, 235, 237, 238, 239 (steps G,H,I)

Derek Fell: pp. 9, 142, 148

John Gregor/Coldsnap Photography: pp. 4-5, 10-11, 36, 122

Saxon Holt: pp. 8, 11, 46, 75, 91

Imagepoint: p.48

Donna Krischan: p. 150

Dennis Krukowski: p. 6

Jerry Pavia: pp. 7, 44, 78, 146

John Rickard: pp. 34, 35, 37, 38, 39, 40, 45, 47, 49, 50, 51, 96, 97, 99, 101 (step E), 102, 103, 104, 105 (steps A,B,C,E), 106, 107, 108 (steps B and D), 112, 113, 114, 115, 116, 117, 118, 119, 121, 126, 129 (steps B and C), 130, 131, 133, 134, 135, 136, 137, 138, 139, 140, 141, 143, 144, 145, 146, 152, 153, 156, 164 (step F), 165, 232, 236, 239 (step J), 240, 241, 242, 243

Charles Slay: p. 124

Index